BUILDING FINE FURNITURE from SOLID WOOD

KEN SADLER

Drawings by Kenneth Sadler, Jr.

BETTER WAY BOOKS

Cincinnati, Ohio

Disclaimer

The author and editors who compiled this book have tried to make all the contents as accurate and as correct as possible. Plans, illustrations, photographs and text have been carefully checked. All instructions, plans and projects should be carefully read, studied and understood before beginning construction. Due to the variability of local conditions, construction materials, skill levels, etc., neither the author nor Betterway Books assumes any responsibility for any accidents, injuries, damages or other losses incurred as a result of the material presented in this book.

Safety Note

To prevent accidents, keep safety in mind while you work. Use the safety guards installed on power equipment; they are for your protection. When working on power equipment, keep fingers away from saw blades, wear safety goggles to prevent injuries from flying wood chips and sawdust, wear headphones to protect your hearing, and consider installing a dust vacuum to reduce the amount of airborne sawdust in your woodshop. Don't wear loose clothing, such as neckties or shirts with loose sleeves, or jewelry, such as rings, necklaces or bracelets, when working on power equipment, and tie back long hair to prevent it from getting caught in your equipment.

Building Fine Furniture From Solid Wood. Copyright © 1994 by Kenneth B. Sadler Trust #1. All rights reserved. No part of this book may be reproduced in any form or by any electronic or mechanical means including information storage and retrieval systems without permission in writing from the publisher, except by a reviewer, who may quote brief passages in a review. Published by Betterway Books, an imprint of F&W Publications, Inc., 1507 Dana Avenue, Cincinnati, Ohio 45207. 1-800-289-0963. First edition.

Printed and bound in the United States of America.

This hardcover edition of *Building Fine Furniture From Solid Wood* features a "self-jacket" that eliminates the need for a separate dust jacket. It provides sturdy protection for your book while it saves paper, trees and energy.

Some portions of this book have previously appeared in *Popular Woodworking* magazine.

98 97 96 95 94   5 4 3 2 1

Library of Congress Cataloging-in-Publication Data

Sadler, Ken.
   Building fine furniture from solid wood/by Ken Sadler; drawings by Kenneth Sadler, Jr.
      p.   cm.
   Includes index.
   ISBN 1-55870-327-6
   1. Furniture making—Amateurs' manuals.   I. Sadler, Kenneth. II. Title.
TT195.S23 1994
684.1'042—dc20   93-29431
                                                         CIP

Edited by Perri Weinberg-Schenker
Designed by Brian Roeth

About the Author

Ken Sadler has been a woodworker for more than fifty years. He has tried his hand at every type of woodworking, from furniture making to built-in cabinetry to building houses. For most of those years, woodworking was his hobby, but during the ten years from 1974 to 1984, he turned the hobby into a successful business making handcrafted furniture. In 1982 his daughter Ellen joined him in the furniture business, and in 1983 *Sunset* magazine featured the father-daughter team among the foremost furniture makers in the Northwest.

He has had a workshop since he was a teenager, sometimes large and roomy, sometimes small and crowded, depending on the house he was living in at the time, but always there and a part of his life. "Having a workshop, building furniture, and doing my own remodeling and maintenance work have enabled me and my family to afford a better life than if we had had to pay other people to do the work for us," he says.

Ken has three sons and two daughters, all of whom have learned, in the workshop, to work with their hands. "Any one of them could," he says, "go out and, if necessary, earn a living as a woodworker."

In 1985, because of the onset of arthritis in his hands, Ken gave up the furniture business and turned to freelance writing. The result was this book and many stories on furniture building in *Popular Woodworking* magazine. He still keeps his hands on the tools, building the pieces he writes about in order to get the pictures that go with the writing.

METRIC CONVERSION CHART

TO CONVERT	TO	MULTIPLY BY
Inches	Centimeters	2.54
Centimeters	Inches	0.4
Feet	Centimeters	30.5
Centimeters	Feet	0.03
Yards	Meters	0.9
Meters	Yards	1.1
Sq. Inches	Sq. Centimeters	6.45
Sq. Centimeters	Sq. Inches	0.16
Sq. Feet	Sq. Meters	0.09
Sq. Meters	Sq. Feet	10.8
Sq. Yards	Sq. Meters	0.8
Sq. Meters	Sq. Yards	1.2
Pounds	Kilograms	0.45
Kilograms	Pounds	2.2
Ounces	Grams	28.4
Grams	Ounces	0.04

Table of Contents

  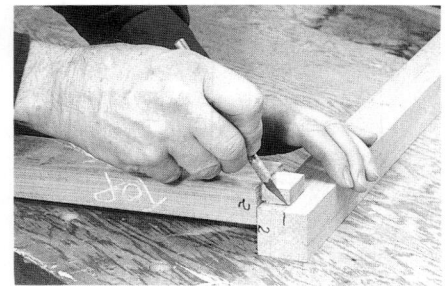

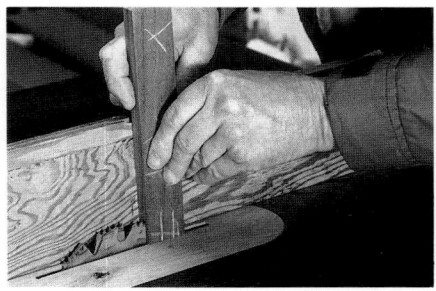

Introduction

A book introduction is usually just that, the introduction to the book. This one is different. It's also an introduction to the author. In a book like this, the author may say things that are controversial, and you, the reader, are very apt to say, "How can this guy make statements like that? How does he know this is so? What's his authority?"

My authority is fifty years as a woodworker, including ten years as a professional handcrafted furniture maker. During those years, I have done every kind of woodworking there is, from building furniture to building houses. The furniture pieces illustrated and described in this book are among the pieces that I designed and built for my clients. Some, like the chairs, I built many times over, while others were built only once. Often I would build four or six chairs at one time, for a dining room set, but every part was individually made and each chair was individually assembled and finished. My shop was in the barn on the sixty acres of woodland where I lived. It was fairly large because I needed space to build some of my pieces, but it was not elaborate. My power tools were the basic ones that you will have. My collection of hand tools, however, may have been a bit more extensive. I have been collecting them for fifty years. In this book I will try to pass on the experience, know-how and techniques I have accumulated during those years. I want to tell you of some things that work and some that don't. There are things about tools, both power and hand, that you may find helpful and surprising. Because I worked alone, it was often necessary to create helpers to make some jobs easier. I'll tell you about some of them and maybe you'll find them helpful, too. I'll tell you of simple ways to do complicated jobs—jobs that perhaps you have hesitated to try because you felt that they were beyond your skills or took too much time.

A point you may find interesting: Much of the wood I used in my work came from those sixty acres I mentioned. I had Oregon red alder and western big leaf maple trees old enough to be sixty to eighty feet tall and 30" to 36" in diameter at the base. I felled such trees, cut them into short logs, and had them hauled to a small local sawmill. There they were plain sawed to my specifications. I hauled the lumber home and stored it on sticks in the barn for at least two

years, then turned the wood into furniture. It was in this way that I was able to get the beautiful grain patterns that you will see in many of the pieces shown in this book.

In case you're not quite ready to embark on a design of your own, I have included a collection of pieces that I created for clients. I have chosen them so that, whatever your level of skill, you will find some that will challenge you. If you're rather new at furniture building, you will find projects that allow you to reach out a bit, and if you've been at it awhile, you will find some that require new techniques with which you may not be familiar.

So, with the help of this book, I hope that you will experience, either in working out your own ideas or in building on mine, the pleasure and relaxation from the stresses of everyday life that can come from working with wood.

Keys to Better Design

In this section of the book, I'm going to try to show you that you can design and build your own furniture. It's not easy. It takes thought and imagination, coupled with some ingenuity. If you are a woodworker with skills to build no more than the simplest of the pieces in this book, then you can design and build your own. Once you've done it, you'll never be satisfied with someone else's designs. You will have created something that is all yours, and that is worth whatever it takes to achieve it.

Chapter One

FURNITURE DESIGN CRITERIA

Designing your own furniture is an adventure. It stretches your imagination and challenges your ingenuity. Building your own designs creates an unmatched sense of achievement. There are two schools of thought about design. One says that the design or shape is everything and that the wood is merely a medium in which to work. These people are more sculptors than furniture makers. The other approach is to keep the lines plain and simple and let the wood provide the beauty in the piece. That I'm a firm believer in the latter is evident in my work, and this book is based on that belief. Furniture design is not easy; it's more than drawing pretty pictures. You will need some knowledge of cabinetmaking and an understanding of the following five important criteria:

- The characteristics of wood in general.
- The particular characteristics of the wood to be used.
- How wood can be joined and how it should not be.
- Tools—do you have those necessary to make what you've designed?
- Skills—can you make what you've designed?

Wood has characteristics that other materials don't have. One is that it shrinks or expands with changes in humidity. Shrinkage across the grain occurs a considerable amount; along the grain it is almost nonexistent. Consequently, two pieces rigidly fastened together with the grain running at right angles will cause trouble because one will move and one won't. The trouble? A split or a buckle. When attaching a tabletop to its base, the woodworker can't fasten it rigidly or it will shrink and split.

Woods differ in some of their characteristics. As an example, red oak is supple and can accommodate bending, while alder is brittle and can't. A case in point would be thin spindles in a chair back. They can be made from red oak because they are subjected to flexing. If alder were used, it would snap. I know because I had to remake the first chair I built. The joining of the parts is the most important consideration in any design. If a joint is weak or unsuitable for a particular application, it will fail and your piece will come apart. The simplest example of this is end grain glued to long grain. It won't hold and shouldn't be used in a vital location. If you're making a bookcase with several fixed shelves, the intermediate shelves can be simply dadoed into the sides, but the top and bottom need more strength and should be fastened with a dovetail, mortice-and-tenon or dowel joint.

When designing a piece of furniture, you must consider whether you have the tools to make the parts or the joints you're designing. Again, the chair is a case in point. There are only two ways to make those spindles—on a lathe or with a spokeshave. The latter method is difficult, long and tedious. Making dowel joints that fit properly requires a doweling jig. Butt-joining two boards to make a tabletop or panel requires a jointer or a good hand plane. Should you want to use thin panels in a door, the best way to make them is to resaw heavier stock. This can be done by hand, but it is difficult and slow. It's easier to use a band saw or a table saw. If you have an 8" table saw, then you'll be restricted to 4"-wide boards. If you're stymied in your design because you don't have the necessary tool, you have a choice—change the design or buy the tool. I usually found a way to buy the tool so that in time I had a well-equipped shop and could tackle almost anything.

The last criterion is, in my opinion, the most important because it's the one most often ignored, usually with unfortunate results. Your skills should be your foremost guide to what you design and how you design it. Each time you plan a new project, you should reach out further than on the last one. But not too far. You can't be proud of a piece you clobbered together because you ignored the limitations of your skills. On the other hand, you can be very proud of a piece that shows off the skills you have acquired.

Chapter Two

THE REASON FOR BEING

W hen you start thinking about a piece of furniture, the first thing to consider is, What do you want it to do? What is its reason for being? Next, where are you going to put it? How much space can it occupy? Remember, this is your piece: you're starting from scratch and can do anything you want (keeping in mind the five criteria). The piece will have a purpose, and it should fulfill that purpose expeditiously. For example, a chair should be comfortable to sit in when used for the purpose for which it was designed. A lounging chair is different from a dining or desk chair. It may seem silly to mention this, but if you look around (even in your own home) you'll find that many chairs are uncomfortable to sit in for any length of time. A dining table should be between 28" and 30" high; it should have a top big enough to accommodate the chosen number of people comfortably, without crowding (lay out a place setting on your present table and see how much space it occupies); the legs should be arranged so that nobody has to fight with one of them; and there should be no crossbars or stretchers that interfere with one's knees. There are similar considerations for any piece of furniture. If you'd like the standard specs for various pieces, check Ernest Joyce's *Encyclopedia of Furniture Making*, beginning on page 371.

Once purpose and size have been settled, it's time to think about lines, the shape your piece will take. The Shakers made very plain, very simple furniture. Its appeal has lasted almost two hundred years. It fits into any decor and mixes with any other style. You're designing a piece for yourself, it's true, but you want your children and your grandchildren to use it over the years—not just because you made it, but because it fits into their lives.

When I started making furniture, I favored the Shaker designs. After a while, I found that I didn't like the straight lines and sharp corners that they used. It made the piece seem harsh. Instead I turned to slightly curved lines and rounded edges and corners. For example, a tabletop, whatever size, will have a slight curve to each side—not much, just enough to

Frame large doors to hide shrinking and help prevent warping.

Smaller doors can be solid.

Designing with wood.

Distinctive grain as focal point.

be noticeable, and the upper edges will be either rounded slightly or have a small bevel. I apply the same approach to legs, whether straight or tapered. The legs of the small buffet on page 7, for example, have a slight curve from bottom to top. These are things that you will develop for yourself. What's important is to keep it simple.

Doors are usually the focal point of any piece on which they are used. They can be made in two ways, solid or framed. Large doors are better framed, as on the armoire at left (top). Smaller doors can be successfully made solid, as on the small cedar cabinet. Solid doors will shrink and expand; the wider the door, the more the movement. They also tend to warp. In a framed door, only the panel will shrink, and since it floats in the frame, the shrinkage will not be noticeable.

Then there is the wood. Earlier, I said that I believed in letting the wood provide the beauty in a piece of furniture. If you follow this tenet, the wood must play a part in your design as well as its execution. For example, the cabinet described in project one, "A Simple Cabinet," was designed around the door panel. One day I came across a piece of alder that, when cut and bookmatched, created an interesting abstract painting. To show it off, I designed the simplest cabinet I could and built it out of walnut so that the contrast would emphasize the panel. I designed the small cedar cabinet with solid doors

rather than paneled because I had that wide cedar board with such a beautiful grain pattern. I fastened the top to the sides with open dovetails because I had another cedar board that was long enough to make all three pieces. By using that joint, I could show the grain pattern flowing around the piece from one side to the other.

Another example of designing with wood is the coffee table shown above (at left). I had two boards sliced off the back side of a slightly curved walnut log. The table was designed to show off the board. The shape of the top is the natural shape of the board as it came from the mill. All I did was to clean up the rough parts of the edges. That shape dictated the design of the base. I made two tables, and they were unique. They could never be duplicated.

Finally, if you have designed a piece without having any particular wood in mind, then search for wood with grain patterns that complement the lines of your design. Think of where the use of contrasting woods may set off important elements. Also consider how an area, say a pair of cabinet doors, made from a wood with a distinctive grain pattern may act as a focal point for your piece. The small buffet shown above illustrates that. The doors were made from a single board and the handles were morticed into it and carved and sanded to blend. Get in the habit of thinking of wood from the viewpoint of how it looks instead of just what it is.

Chapter Three

DETAILS MAKE A DIFFERENCE

In the design of a piece of furniture, little things can make a big difference. If you want to make a piece look wider than it is, emphasize the horizontal lines; if you want it to look taller, emphasize the vertical lines. The small walnut TV cabinet illustrates this. Notice that the vertical members of the door frames go through the horizontal ones and are slightly thicker. Also, the figures in the door panels are vertical. On the other hand, a strong horizontal line is illustrated by the doors in the small buffet shown in the preceding chapter. Here, the strong grain pattern runs horizontally across both doors, tending to make the piece look wider and lower than it really is. If you have glass doors with wood shelves behind, use vertical mullions but not horizontal ones. If you do and the shelf positions don't match the bars, it will look terrible. This problem doesn't arise if you use glass shelves. On the low-back chair, notice the ears at the upper ends of the arms. Since the arm fits on the outside of the top rail, it can extend above it. The ear was hand carved and sanded to a pleasing shape as the mood dictated. I made a set with and a set without the ears, the latter because the client insisted on it. The difference was so striking that I never made another without them.

People don't give much thought to handles, but they're an important part of any piece. In fact, a bad handle can ruin the appearance of an otherwise fine piece. Handles can be of any shape or size. They can be attached or inlaid and carved as part of the door or drawer front, as they are on the serving table. They can be of the same wood or of a contrasting wood as the body of the piece; they can be machine made or hand carved. The important point is that they must look right for that piece. No one can make that decision but you, the one who conceived the basic design. I never did anything about handles until the design was complete, and then only if they were to be carved into doors or drawer fronts. Otherwise I left them until the piece was built. There were times when I spent a couple of days working out just what I wanted for a given project. A technique I sometimes used

Vertical lines make it look taller.

was to model my ideas in clay and then put them in place. This is particularly good when you have an idea that is hard to visualize. When I had the shape I liked, I would then make it from wood.

Another approach is to blend the handle into the door so that you don't notice it until you're right up to it, ready to use it. The small buffet mentioned in chapter two is a case in point. The chapter on handles in the next section covers this aspect of design in much more detail, and with pictures to help you with ideas. The main point to remember is: Don't rush things; take the time to make it right.

There is something called *diversity*. It's a collection of little details that, from a distance, can't be seen, but as you get ever closer to the piece, begin to be visible. Diversity adds interest to your design. Like the handles, these details have to come from your imagination. They'll be ideas that occur to you or things you see as you're working with the piece. With this sort of an adventurous approach, furniture making becomes exciting. It is your individuality, your imprint that you're putting on the work.

It will help to make a drawing of your design. Just draw the major parts; you'll work out the details as you go along. Not being an artist, I was limited to ordinary, three-view, mechanical drawings. However, I drew them to scale and thus had only to put in the major dimensions. The rest can be scaled from the drawing as you work. In many cases, you'll take the dimensions for parts like doors, back frames or shelves directly from the piece in order to compensate for small discrepancies that occur as you work. Since the drawings are only for your use, they can be in pencil and don't need to be very fancy. As long as you understand them, that's all that counts. The most important use of them, at least for me, was to make sure of the proportions. It's sometimes hard to visualize this, and putting it on paper clarifies things. Also, it's nice to have a guide and to be reminded of your ideas as you work.

Handle inlaid then carved to blend.

Chapter Four

TO STIR YOUR IMAGINATION

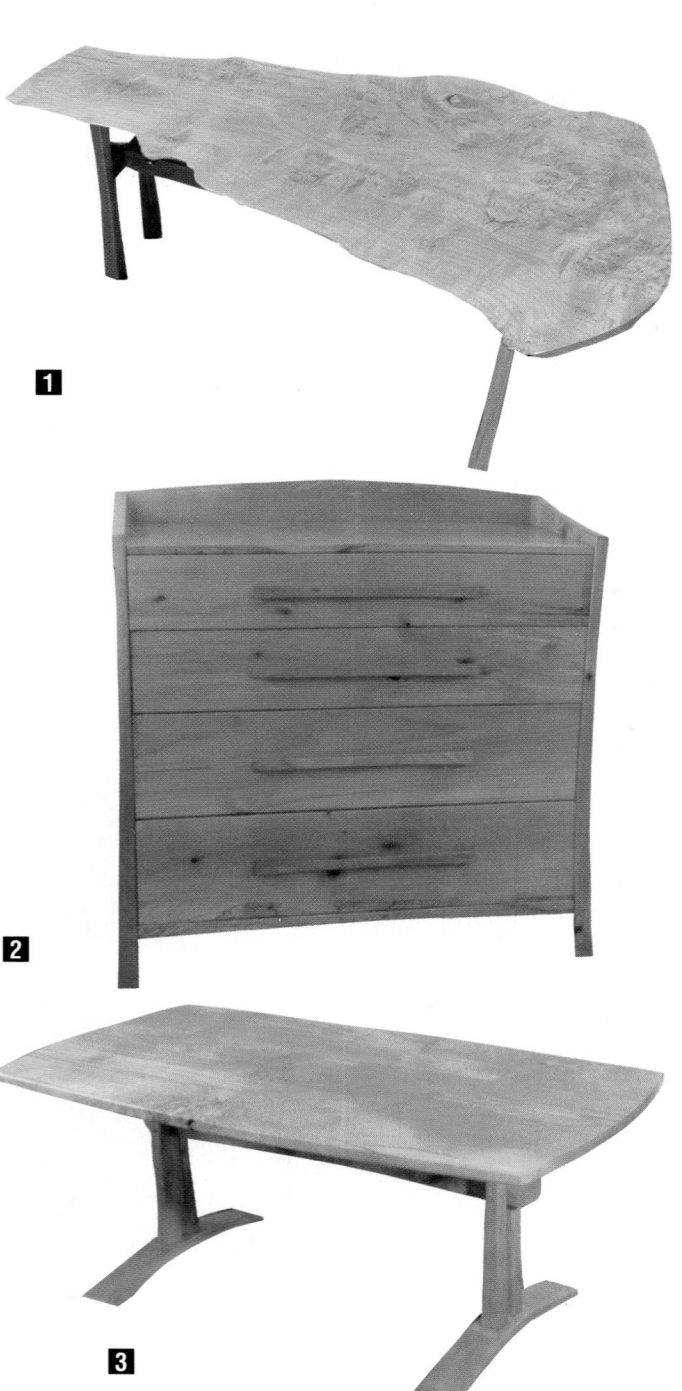

1

2

3

W hen designing a new piece, I would look through photographs of things I had already done. This stirred my imagination and focused my thinking—not to copy a previous piece, but rather to find ideas and details that I might adapt to the new one. With this in mind, I have included several pages of photographs of my work with the thought that they might do the same for you.

■ *This coffee table is what I would call a limited edition. There were only three pieces like this on the log and this was the largest. It illustrates what you can do when you find a very unusual piece of wood. The wood dictated the design; my daughter, who worked with me for several years, built it. Because of the shape and the fact that it was important to maintain the original edges, there was no way she could rip the board into narrower pieces for surfacing and then glue it back together. Therefore, she had to do the finishing with a hand plane—a time-consuming and tedious job. But, the final result was worth all the effort. The base is sturdy and simple so that the top gets all the attention. The wood is Oregon big leaf maple.*

■ *Here is a simple chest of drawers made from red alder. Notice that every edge is slightly curved. This eliminates the stark, harsh feeling that you would have if the edges were all straight and the corners sharp. The drawer fronts are made from two wide boards, which were matched as closely as possible. Each board was divided down the middle to form the drawers' fronts. This ties the entire front of the chest together as though it was made from one board.*

■ *The top of this coffee table was made from one wide board. In chapter seven, I'll tell you how I was able to get such wide boards. Of course, they couldn't be worked as one board. This one was ripped into three 8"-wide pieces, finished to the proper thickness, and then glued back together. The trick is to use a saw blade with as thin a kerf as you can find; then when you glue it back together, the missing material won't be noticed. If you make good joints, nobody will know you cut it apart. What looks like two legs are actually four arranged in two pairs, each pair being divided by the stretcher and the ends individually morticed into the foot and the top support. The stretcher is fastened in place by blind dowels. Again, all edges have a slight curve to soften the appearance.*

4 *This rocking chair was my most popular piece. Over the years, I sold about eighty-five of them. They are a great deal sturdier than they look because the arms, the rockers and the top rail are all carved from laminated blanks, which creates a much stronger part than if it was bent from a solid piece of wood. I explain how this is done in chapter eleven. Each of those eighty-five rockers was individually made. Every spindle was hand turned and the arms, rockers, top rail and seat, hand carved. Whenever I went to a show, I displayed one of these chairs. People liked the design, and when they sat in it and found how comfortable it was, I made a sale. This one is made from Oregon walnut.*

5 *One day a couple came by the shop. They said that their daughter was getting married the following year and they wondered if I could build a hope chest for her in which to accumulate her trousseau. My answer was yes, and what I had in mind was the standard style of blanket chest that you see in all the antique shops and the reproduction stores. But when I started to think about it, I decided that was too ordinary, and what I finally came up with is the one in the picture. It's made from Oregon walnut. The sides, ends and bottom are framed panels, while the top is made from a single board. The fact that wood shrinks in one direction and not in the other made the framed panel necessary if I wanted the ends to be as they are. The panels are free to move in the frames, so there is no danger of splitting or buckling. The cover is hinged at the ends with a pivot hinge similar to the one I used in the small cabinet detailed in project one, and the handle is carved from the board used to create the top.*

6 *This is a stereo cabinet of Oregon walnut. The panel across the bottom is a drawer front, and what looks like a strip of molding is the handle with which to open it. The sides are interesting because each is made from a single board 2" thick and 18" wide. To put the curve in the outer surface of the sides, I had to use a band saw, but I couldn't bandsaw a board 18" wide. I ripped it into three 6" pieces, bandsawed the shape, then glued the pieces back together. The final smoothing of the cut surface was done with a spokeshave and sandpaper. When finished, you couldn't tell that it had been cut apart. The doors on this piece are interesting, as are their handles. (See chapter twelve for an explanation and a detailed view of those handles.) I could not find matching pieces for both door panels. So, I decided to emphasize the fact that they did not match. The two strips down each door are really H-shaped dividers. The panel boards fit between the legs of the H and also into the grooves in the door frame. The frame corners are mortice and tenoned and glued together. The panel boards and H strips float in the frame. It's a simple arrangement and makes a rather striking door.*

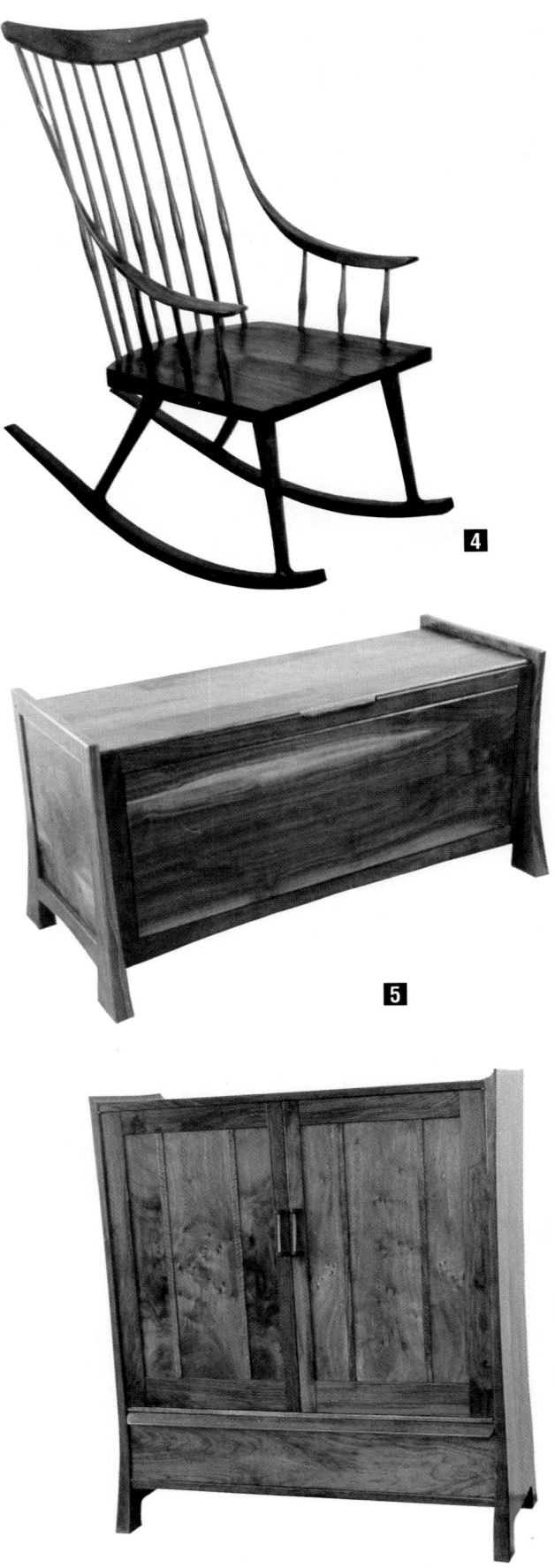

4

5

6

7

8

9

7 *Here is another stereo cabinet, quite a different design. In this piece, everything is red alder except the door panels, which are ash. Because of shrinkage and expansion and to get strength in the case, this piece is made in three sections: the top, the case and the base. Because the grain of base moldings on the sides must run at right angles to the grain of the case side, they cannot be firmly fastened together. Thus, I fastened together two sections with clips to allow relative movement of the sections with humidity changes. Since the top overhangs the sides, there is no way to join them with a really strong joint. So, the top of the case is a front-and-back rail dovetailed into the sides for strength, and the top is then fastened to these rails. To see how all this is done, look at project eleven in the last section of the book. The ash door panels all came from the same board, so there was no chance to match them. Again I chose to emphasize that they were not matched by the way I designed the door frame. The doors are mounted on L-shaped knife hinges so that they will fold back out of the way. The doors are wider than the cabinet is deep; otherwise, they would fold back against the sides.*

8 *These are two pictures of the same piece, a desk secretary. It's made from red alder that I got from a tree that was eighty feet tall and 36" in diameter at the base. As you can see, the wood is highly figured, and you can get that kind of wood only from very old trees. The three doors were designed as frames for abstract paintings in wood. The writing-surface door panel came from a single board. The panels in the lower doors again are bookmatches. An important part of this design is the long, sweeping curve of the front edge of the sides. If those edges had been straight up and down, the piece would have looked blocky and awkward. If the edge had been a straight taper from top to bottom, it would have looked much too modern and stiff. Most of the shelves, including the drawer in a box, are adjustable, resting on wood supports (see chapter thirteen). The one to which the writing-surface door is attached and the one it closes against are fixed.*

9 *This is a serving table (some call it a buffet). It is generally used in a dining room for the kind of duty its name describes. Such a table is usually 4' or more in length and 15" to 18" wide. It stands 32" to 34" high, as compared to a dining table height of 28" to 30". This is a simple design calculated to emphasize the wood from which it is made. The legs are not tapered: from a point just under the skirt to the bottom is a continuous sweeping curve. All edges of the top except the back have a slight curve to them. There are three drawers across the front, and the drawer fronts are all cut from one board so that the grain lines have a continuity from end to end. The handles, while attached rather than carved from the drawer fronts, are blended into the wood of the fronts so that they are barely noticeable. The narrow back piece completes the image of a serving table that is meant to stand against the wall.*

10 Here we have a true buffet or, as they called it in my grandfather's day, a sideboard. This piece is about 6' long; however, the center leg, which is only in the front, was not necessary for strength. It was put there to act as a visual divider to make the piece look shorter than it really is. The four outer legs are curved from top to bottom with the top smaller than the bottom but the narrowest part being about two-thirds of the way from the floor. The center leg is curved on three sides. These curves give a grace to the piece that straight, square legs would not. If you look closely, you can see that there are four doors. They were cut from the same board so that the grain pattern would flow across the entire front. The handles were roughed out of carefully chosen wood pieces and inserted into dadoes cut in the door fronts. They were then carved and sanded to blend with the doors so that they appear to have been carved from the same board. The object here was to interfere as little as possible with the flow of the pattern, yet have a handle large enough and strong enough to do the job it had to do. In this piece, the top and sides are of red gum, and the doors and legs are red alder. Behind the doors on the right are two sliding trays, and behind the left doors is an open cupboard.

11 This is a showcase, meant to show off the treasures inside. I've always felt that the showcase should be as much of a treasure as the contents. This one is made mostly from Oregon big leaf maple. The top and rear panels are English walnut, which differs from Oregon or eastern walnut in that it has a dark heartwood but a light sapwood. The back panel shows this clearly. Although you can't see it, the two sides, being cut out of a 2"-thick board, have the same pattern. If an oil-based finish had been used, it would have darkened the sapwood sufficiently to almost blend it with the heartwood, and the pattern would have been lost. To prevent this, I used nothing but paste wax as the finish. It took about eight coats, but the result, I think you will agree, was worth it. The shelves rest on wood supports and are glass so as not to interfere with the figure on the back panel. Notice the slight curve to the inner edges of the top and bottom rails as well as the contouring of the stiles. These are little details that you don't notice until you get close to the piece. It's what I meant when I spoke of diversity in chapter three. The vertical dividers between the glass panels are H-shaped as in the stereo cabinet. They are not fastened but depend on the glass being anchored in the frame to hold everything in place.

12 Here is a wall cabinet in the same vein as the one in project one. The purpose was to frame a beautiful wood panel and make it useful at the same time. The cabinet is Oregon walnut and the panel is red alder. As you can see, it's a bookmatch (described in chapter seven) of a board that I discovered while working on another piece. I designed the cabinet around the panel and built it as a spec piece. I took it to my next show at the Lawrence Gallery and it sold the first day.

13 *This is called a schoolmaster desk. It was my first piece in Oregon walnut. It is not a standup piece: the height of the front edge is scaled for sitting. The hinged top provides access to the large storage area underneath it. Aside from the overall beauty of the wood, the main feature is the two sets of small drawers. I found two pieces of walnut burl, and from each I cut the drawer fronts for one set of drawers. The picture clearly shows the result. Here again, the curve in the legs makes their appearance much more pleasing than if I had used a straight taper.*

14 *This is my other rocking-chair design. It came about when a customer asked me if I could furnish my rocker with an uphol-stered seat. I could not figure out how to do it, but the lady want-ed a rocker with an upholstered seat. I told her I would create one for her, and this was what evolved. The difficulty was designing a seat frame to which the legs could be attached and having the resulting assembly strong enough to hold an above-average adult. I designed the rear leg and back post to be one piece, which I created by laminating ¼"-thick strips in a jig. This technique is explained in chapter eleven and is used to make parts for several of the pieces described in the final section of the book. One inter-esting feature of this design was the cloth cover for the seat. I had a young lady friend who was a weaver. She wove each seat cover individually with a different design, using the colors supplied by the customer and taking into account the color of the wood in the chair. No seat cover was ever like any other.*

15 *This was one of my early pieces, created before I began to soft-en the lines with curves. This design followed the Shakers pretty closely. It was originally built as a dining table. But, at a show where I had it on display, a man came to me and said he'd like to have that as a desk if it had a couple of drawers. I said I would be glad to add them, and sold it on the spot. The entire piece is red alder, and the buyer particularly liked the knot hole I left in the middle of the top. The drawers were hung from L-shaped runners fastened to the underside of the top with screws run through slots so the there could be relative movement between the run-ners and the top when the top expanded or shrank. As in the trestle-style coffee table, the leg at each end is really two, mor-ticed into the foot and the top support with the stretcher slid between and fastened in place with dowels. This time, the dowels were not hidden.*

In addition to presenting ideas and details that you might adapt to pieces of your own, I hope I have been able to explain in pictures what it is almost impossible to convey with words: Details make a big difference in the final appearance of a piece of furniture.

Keys to Better Construction

I'd like to tell you what I believe craftsmanship to be. Craftsmanship is not now and never was machine made. Craftsmanship *means using any kind of technique or tool (power or hand) in which the quality of the finished work depends on the judgment, skill and care the maker exercises as he or she works. The essential concept is that this quality is constantly at risk during the process of making. Craftsmanship is skill with the hands, whatever tool you are using; knowledge and understanding of the material with which you are working; a feeling for what you are creating; an eye for what fits and what doesn't. In other words, craftsmanship is in the person, not in the machine or the process. Craftsmanship is not a science nor is it precise art. It's what a person puts into his or her work.*

Chapter Five

SOME THOUGHTS ABOUT TOOLS

These are thoughts about woodworking tools, both power and hand, based on what I've learned from experience over the years. That experience has shown me that a cheap tool is the most expensive tool you can buy. Cheap tools will not do the job properly, so that you often have to do it over. Cheap cutting tools will not hold an edge for very long, so that you will be constantly sharpening them or working with a dull tool. Cheap power tools are difficult if not impossible to set accurately, and they tend to drift from the settings so that you get inaccurate work. Further, a cheap tool is more cheaply built, and thus, will wear out sooner and have to be replaced. My table saw is twenty-two years old. My lathe and drill press are each forty-three years old. These tools were the best of their kind I could buy, and they still produce work of the same quality and accuracy as they did when I bought them new.

I don't intend to talk about tools in general and how they work, or compare one make against another. Woodworking magazines and other books are full of this information. I'm going to talk about the tools I consider important to have in a shop for making furniture—the essential, the not-so-essential, and those I think would be a luxury. I'm going to set out the qualities that my experience has shown me are necessary to have in these tools in order to do the work expected of a craftsman.

The Table Saw

For me, the truly essential tool is the table saw. It is so versatile and easy to use that I can't imagine being without it. Table saws for home and small industrial use are available in 8" and 10" sizes. If you resaw on this machine, and most of us do, then an 8" blade restricts you to resawing a 4"-wide board, while a 10" blade allows resawing a 6" board. This is important because in making glued up panels, it is easier and better to work with 6" boards. The machine you buy should have a solid cast-iron table, including the wings, that has been machine ground for flatness, minimum size 27"x 36". To test for flatness, take a 36"

steel scale and place it on edge across the corners, from front to back, and from side to side. If you can see light under any part of the scale, then the table is not flat. Most tables will not be absolutely flat. How much deviation you are willing to accept will have to be your judgment. The bars on which the rip fence rides should be heavy steel tubing or heavy rectangular steel bars, bolted securely to the edge of the table. They should be long enough to allow at least 24½" between the blade and the fence. The fence should lock securely at both ends with a simple lever action and have a knob to make fine adjustments. The fence itself is best made of steel; it should have two holes clear through side to side—one at the front and one at the back—to allow the attachment of an auxiliary fence. Don't worry about the measurement markings on the rail and the indicating finger on the fence. They never remain accurately set, so you should always make your fence setting using a steel scale and measuring directly between the fence and the blade.

The miter gauge must have a steel blade that fits in the table groove with little or no play, even when pulled back, so that only half the blade is in the groove. The head of the gauge should be heavy diecast metal, or preferably cast steel, but never plastic. Again, don't worry about the degree markings. They may be marked accurately on the gauge, but the pin to which you set the markings never stays put. I have a set of draftsman's triangles, and if I want an accurate angle cut, I set the miter gauge using one of them. The devices, usually present on these gauges to allow you to get quick 90° and 45° settings, are really useless and dangerous because the settings never remain as you have set them for very long. If you depend on them, you're apt to find, too late, that what you thought was a 90° cutoff, isn't. One more point about gauges. Don't depend on the gauge on the saw to set your blade angle, particularly the perpendicular position. These gauges are never accurate. I use a 6" steel try square to make the perpendicular setting and my draftsman's triangles to make the 30° and 45° settings. For other angles, I use a sliding bevel square set to its angle with a protractor.

Check to see if the yoke and trunnion assemblies that carry the blade arbor are cast iron and the mating surfaces that move relative to each other are machined. The worm-and-gear arrangements that raise and lower the blade and set the blade at an angle should have a steel worm running in cast-iron teeth machined into the trunnion and yoke. There must be no play in these parts when you try to wiggle them with your hand. The blade arbor should be mounted in ball or tapered roller bearings and be belt driven, and the motor for a 10″ unit ought to be at least 1½ HP. On a good table saw, the yoke, trunnion and motor mount are all bolted to the underside of the heavy cast-iron table. None of these parts should be attached to the base. The base needs to be of heavy steel and well braced so that it can bear the weight of the top and blade assembly, which is considerable, without any give or wiggle. It does not necessarily need to be enclosed, but if it is, there should be an easy way to clean the sawdust out of it.

Remember, this tool is at the heart of everything you do. If it isn't right, then no matter how skilled you are, you won't be able to do good work.

The Drill Press

The next tool in importance, for me, is the drill press. The size of a drill press is designated by twice the distance between the center of the spindle and the column. Thus, an 11″ machine has 5½″ between spindle and column, a 14″ has 7″, etc. They come either bench- or floor-mounted. (If you buy a bench model to save money, I'm betting in six months you'll wish you hadn't.) Drive it with a minimum ⅓ HP motor and four-speed step pulleys. You can get drive arrangements where the speed is infinitely adjustable; however, I consider this an unnecessary luxury. I have always used the four-step arrangement and never found a need for anything more. Speed in drilling wood is not terribly important. I have mine set for the slowest speed and seldom change it. Check the spindle travel: you need at least 3½″. See that it has an adjustable stop and a lock so that you can lock it in any given position. Be sure the spindle travels smoothly and has no sideways play. You will want a minimum ½″ keyed chuck. Look for an off/on switch up front where you can reach it easily and quickly with your left hand. The table should be of heavy ribbed cast iron with a machine-ground surface. It should lock tightly to the column with an easily reached lever. A raising and lowering mechanism is nice, but it's expensive and not really necessary. If it costs more to have a tilting table, don't buy it. These tables tilt side to side and not back to front. In jobs of any size, using a side tilt causes your piece to run into

the column. Instead, make an auxiliary tabletop of ¾″ plywood, and bolt it to the regular table. Mine is 14″ x 30″, and it gives good support to pieces up to six feet long. To be able to drill holes at an angle on large panels, build the angle-drilling fixture that I describe in chapter six. If you decide to build either of the two chairs described in section three, you will need this fixture, and you will understand why side-to-side tilting is not good enough.

I will not discuss drill bits here, because many different types and styles are available. You will come to know what works best for you.

The Jointer

The jointer is to many a misunderstood tool. They assume that its main purpose is to put a straight, square edge on a board, or to quickly smooth up a sawed surface. These are important uses, but they can both be done quite easily with a hand plane. The really important job for a jointer is to put a flat surface on a board. Until you have one flat surface, you can't do any accurate work on a board. Many people think that that is the job of a planer. This is not so. If you put a warped board through a planer, you will have a smooth surface, but the board will still be warped. Once you have one flat surface, however, putting it through the planer will make it a uniform thickness, and the whole board will be flat. You can't resaw a board until you have a flat surface to work from, and you can't make a square edge without a flat surface. Thus, you can see the importance of one flat surface.

Jointers used in home shops and small industrial operations are 4″, 6″ and 8″ wide. You really need a 6″ machine, and if you can afford it, get an 8″. The machine is made up of a base, two tables (infeed and outfeed), a cutter head and an adjustable fence. The base and the tables should be cast iron, and the tabletops should be machine ground for flatness. In some machines, both tables are adjustable for height; in others, only the infeed table is adjustable. If they move, the tables should run on machined ways so that they stay level and parallel regardless of their position. The movement of the tables should be easy to accomplish. This movement is usually created by turning a threaded rod in a nut fixed to the table. This mechanism is under the table, and unless protected in some way, is open to the wood dust and fine shavings from the machine. Because of this, you can only lubricate the rod and nut with graphite and without protection, the dust and shavings get into the threads and make turning hard and, after a while, often impossible. My jointer has this problem, and I constantly have to get underneath and clean out the stuff in the threads. Also, the knob that turns the rob is too small; this makes things more difficult. Different makes of jointer come with different overall table lengths. They range from 2½ feet to 8 feet. The longer the table, the easier it is to work on the machine. Unfortunately, long table machines cost big bucks. If I were strapped for money, I would rather have the wider cut than the longer table. I have an 8" jointer with 30"-long overall tables. On longer pieces, this has made doing the job somewhat more difficult; however, the capacity to accommodate wide boards, which the 8" width provides, has been more important than the added trouble with long boards.

Some machines have three blade-cutter heads and some two. I have had both and found no appreciable difference in performance. The fences on jointers are attached in two ways. One is at the outer end of the infeed table. It is attached to the table in a bracket that allows it to slide sideways and pivot from perpendicular to 45°. There are two levers to lock it in position. It moves up and down with the table. A fence of this type must be made of heavy cast iron, and so should the bracket. Since it is fastened at only one end, there is a great deal of leverage force at the other end tending to twist the fence. This type is very easy to adjust from 45° to 90°. However, if you want accuracy, don't trust the gauge. Use a sliding bevel square set from a protractor. The other type of fence attaches to a bracket fastened to the infeed table near the middle of the machine. This type does not need to be so heavily constructed. It has an entirely different mechanism for adjusting the angle—one that is the perfect devil to set accurately. You have to use squares to get the angle you want.

If you're going to take any but the lightest cut, you will need a powerful motor, especially for the wider cuts. I have a 1HP on mine, and taking a full-width cut ½" deep on hardwood, I can slow it down appreciably. Whatever your cutter size, I wouldn't have less than ¾HP. As to the stand for your jointer, you want one made from heavy steel and very solidly built. In addition, I suggest that you lag it to the floor. When you're edge jointing a 2"x 10" board 4- or 5-feet long, you don't want the machine to walk away from you. A last point: The off/on switch should be of the safety push-button type and located close to the infeed end on the working side of the machine, where it is easily and quickly accessible.

The Lathe

For me, the next most important tool in my shop is the lathe. This is probably because I like using it and have therefore leaned toward turnings in my furniture designs. I also used the lathe to create small objects like bowls, candle holders and weed bottles that I sold to keep me going while I was building my furniture business. In the project "Out of Your Imagination," you will find some ideas for doing this yourself. Lathes come in a variety of sizes. For furniture work, I would have nothing less than 12" swing and a maximum length capacity not less than 36". Anything smaller than this will, after a while, cause you dissatisfaction. I would drive it with nothing less than a ¾HP motor, better a 1HP. To do accurate work, a lathe must have a heavy, rigid, cast-iron base with carefully machined ways for the tailstock to ride on. The headstock should also be heavy cast iron and the spindle set in tapered roller bearings. The latter is very important because in turning the craftsman exerts considerable thrust force on the spindle, and a taper roller bearing is the only type that will handle this thrust. Most lathes have a four-step pulley in the headstock, although some are now made with a variable speed drive to get an infinite number of speeds. I feel that this is an unnecessary luxury and not worth the additional money it costs. I have found, over the years, that most of my work was done at one of two speeds and even when I needed the other two, it was no trouble to switch the belt from one step to another on the pulleys. The spindle should have a #2 morse taper bore and an exterior 1"-11' NC thread at each end. The thread must be right hand on the inside end and left hand on the outside. This allows a variety of chucks to be inserted in the spindle and faceplates to be screwed onto it. The tailstock should also be heavy cast iron carefully machined to slide on the bed ways and to be easy to lock firmly in place. It should also have a #2 morse taper bore. The tailstock spindle must have a crank handle to move it in and out and should be calibrated so you can tell how far you have moved it. There must also be a lever lock to lock the spindle where you have positioned it. A good, solid toolrest holder as well as an easy way to lock it in place are required. You need two tool rests, a short one, about 4" long, and the other 12" long. These can be cast steel or welded steel—just so they are of heavy cross section so that they will be strong enough to stand up to the work you'll be doing on them. I would also be sure to get a good steadyrest, because if you're going to make some of the pieces in the back of this book, you'll need it.

The Band Saw

Band saws are available in numerous sizes and configurations. The size of the machine is determined by the distance between the blade and the frame. Usually these figures are nominal rather than accurate. My 14" saw actually has 13" clearance between blade and frame. The frame should be cast iron with a heavy cross section for rigidity. Look for a cast-iron table with a machine-ground surface and mounted in front and back trunnions that can be locked in position with simple handles. Check the table for flatness in the same way as the table saw. Most important are the blade guides. You want the upper one mounted on a heavy steel bar that is arranged so that it raises and lowers true and can't be twisted from side to side. The assembly that holds the actual guide blocks must be attached to the bar in a way that it can't move from side to side once you have it locked in position. It should be easy to adjust the guide blocks. If you expect to do any accurate resawing on your band saw, then the points I just mentioned are critical. The lower guide is usually mounted in a way so that twisting is not a problem; however, adjusting the guide blocks often is. Be sure to check this out. Both guide-block holders must allow independent forward-and-back movement of the guide-block holder and the blade back-up wheel to accommodate different width blades.

On a two-wheel saw, the upper wheel should be adjustable up and down to accommodate blades of slightly different lengths and to apply the proper tension to the blade. You should be able to tilt it slightly back and forth vertically to make the blade track properly. You ought to be able to remove and replace blade wheel covers quickly and easily. As to the stand, for the machines that need one, I prefer a heavy steel frame, open all around. The enclosed ones are made of sheet metal, and while they are generally sturdy enough, the sheet metal vibrates when the saw is running, and the noise can drive you crazy. As in the case of the other tools I've talked about, be sure that the *off/on* switch is a push-button safety type located where the operator can easily reach it while working on the machine. Power depends on what you want to do. On mine, I have a ¾HP motor, and I resaw 8"-wide boards easily.

One last point: Just because a saw is 20" and stands on the floor does not necessarily mean that it is of better quality than a 14" on a metal stand; it means only that it's more expensive. I have a 14" on a metal stand that has served me very well for fifteen years and has done some quite heavy work.

Hand-Power Tools

In this category, I'll talk about four tools that I have found very handy to have around the shop. The first is a hand-held power circular saw. I have a good quality, medium-priced unit with a 7" blade. I use it almost entirely for rough cutting, particularly cutting long, wide, rough planks, up to 2" thick, into shorter lengths that I can handle on the table saw and jointer. The second is a hand-held power drill. Mine is a standard pistol grip, variable speed with reverse, with a ⅜" key chuck, and again it's medium priced. I use it whenever I can't get the piece into the drill press.

Some craftsmen get a ½" unit, but I think that's too big, heavy and unwieldy for furniture work. The hand-held jigsaw is a tool I don't use very often, but on certain work it's very nice to have around—for example, when you have to rough cut a 42"-diameter tabletop. (See project nine.) To do the job by yourself on a band saw is very difficult, and since you're holding the panel at a point quite a distance from the blade, it's easy to cut on the wrong side of the line. The work becomes easy when you do it with the hand-held jigsaw.

The fourth hand power tool in my shop is the router. I'm not a router fan, and frankly, my greatest use of the tool is as a shaper mounted in a table that I made. I use it as a router primarily for cutting dadoes or rabbets I can't do on the table saw; for cutting long dovetail slots; and for molding the edges of pieces that are too big to handle on the shaper table. I've found that cutters with ball-bearing guides are worth their added cost. One thing I never do with a router is cut joints, particularly dovetail joints. A dovetail joint cut with a router is so obviously machine made that it loses the individuality that a craftsman can put into a hand-cut joint. Many craftsmen swear by a router for many jobs. My position is: Do what feels right for you. That's the value of building your own furniture: It's your work, so do it your way. But remember, the result is yours, too.

Hand Tools

To write my thoughts about hand tools would take a book by itself. Here I'll only make a few comments. Later on in some of the construction chapters and projects, I'll mention specific tools that are very nice to have and suggest that you ought to get them so as to build a particular piece more easily.

It is the same with hand tools as with power ones: The cheap tool is the most expensive tool you can buy. Unfortunately, the American tool companies have dropped out of the quality hand-tool market. In the past ten to fifteen years, the only quality hand tools I have been able to find are made in England, Germany or Japan. They are expensive but worth it. When you are looking for a new tool (the used market for quality hand tools is almost nonexistent), look for a specialty store. If you can't find one, turn to the catalog houses, many of which are listed in the woodworking magazines. For me, the best one over the years has been *Woodcraft Supply.*

Chapter Six

JIGS AND FIXTURES

Jigs and fixtures are devices that you create to make work easier or to make certain jobs possible. An example of the latter is the angle drilling fixture I'm about to explain.

Drilling Angles on a Drill Press

Drilling wood at a precise angle can be difficult no matter how you do it. When done on a drill press, it's always a problem because many drill press tables don't tilt; when they do, it's usually in the wrong direction for drilling large parts. (The column gets in the way.) The fixture described here solves the problem simply and easily. It's also simple to make.

You'll want two pieces of either ¾" A-B grade plywood or high-density chipboard. Although it's heavier, I prefer the chipboard because it will stay flat. The top piece is 16" x 22", and the bottom piece is 16" x 18". As for hardware, you will want 18" of 1½" continuous hinge and two heavy-duty locking lid supports. These supports should have rods at least 10" long. You may have a little trouble finding them. Different stores call them by different names. Take the picture along to show the clerk what you want. One place you are not apt to find them is in one of the more modern hardware stores where everything is put up in plastic packages and hung on hooks. Go to one of the more old-fashioned stores, if you can find one, or look in some of the catalogs. I found some in Woodworker's Supply of New Mexico. Be sure you get the heavy-duty kind, because they must be as rigid as possible. Thin, flat bars have a tendency to flex.

The 16" dimension is the depth (front to back) of the fixture. Take the bottom piece and draw a centerline front to back. Starting at the back edge, measure along this line a distance equal to the distance from the drill press column to the center of the table. Drill a ½" hole through the bottom at this point. Draw a centerline front to back on the top piece. (Carry the centerline on both pieces over the front edge.) Center the top over the bottom, clamp them securely together, and screw the piano hinge to the front edge as shown in the picture. Be sure you have installed the hinge so that when

Drilling fixture in place on the drill press.

The hardware.

Installing the hinge.

Lid supports in place.

Setting the angle.

Figure 6-1

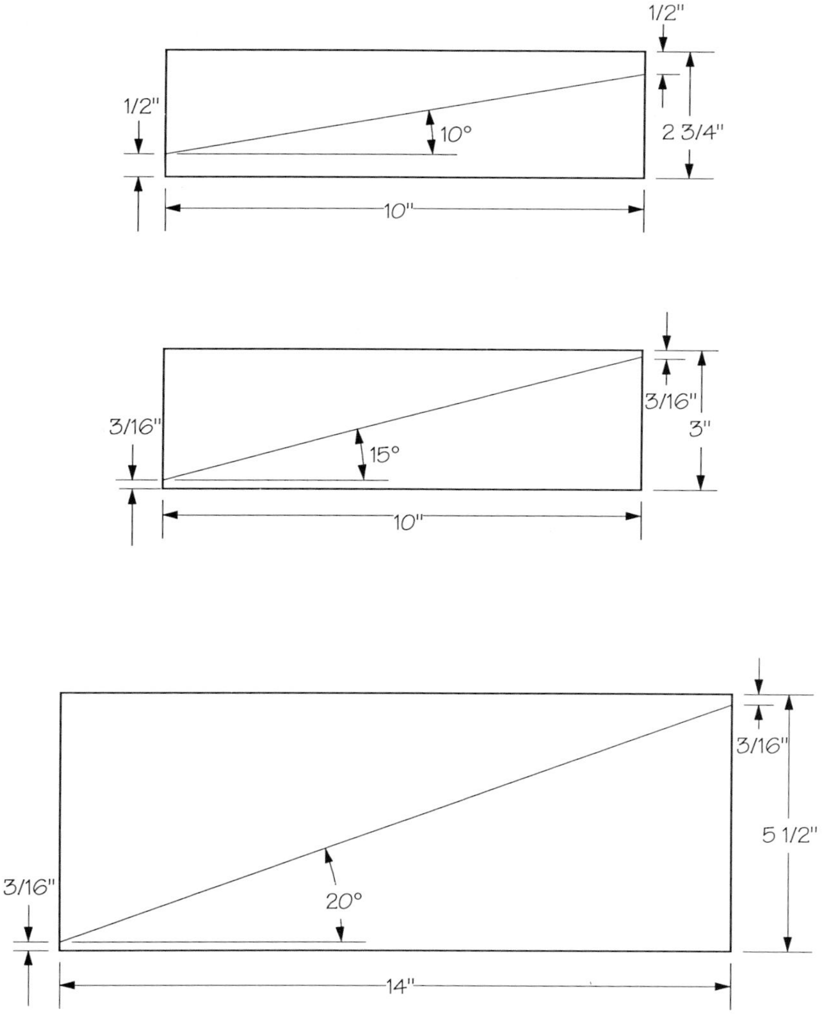

1/2"

1/2"   10°   2 3/4"

10"

3/16"   15°   3/16" 3"

10"

3/16"   20°   3/16" 5 1/2"

14"

Marking the center.

Finished jig.

A finished tool rest.

it is closed the two pieces will lie flat, next to each other. Put some masking tape on each leaf at the center so the centerline can be clearly marked.

The next step is to install the two locking lid supports. The attachment fitting for the rod goes on the underside of the top, centered 3″ from the back edge, and the lock fitting goes on the side edge of the bottom as close to the back edge as you can get it.

The fixture itself is now complete. Attach it to the drill press table by a ⅜″ bolt through the hole drilled in the bottom. Use large, flat washers under the head and the nut. The reason for the ½″ hole and the ⅜″ bolt is to allow room for a small adjustment in positioning the fixture. The centerline should be exactly under the center of a drill bit placed in the chuck, and the back end of the centerline should match the center of the drill press column. Using a square, carry the centerline down across the hinge. Do this with a narrow marker pen so that you can see it clearly. The reason for this will become clear when you use the fixture to drill the seats for the chair projects in the last section of the book.

Now that you have a fixture that will allow you to drill a large part (such as a chair seat), there remains the problem of setting the fixture at the proper angle. It's not difficult and you may already know the procedure, but I'll describe it anyway. First set your sliding bevel square to the angle you want. For accuracy, it's best to do it with a protractor. Cut a straight piece of ½″ dowel about 8″ long and mount it in the drill-press chuck. (Don't grip it too tightly—you'll throw it out of line.) Drop the drill-press table until you have clearance to raise the top of the fixture to the approximate angle you want and tighten one of the locks just enough to hold it in place. Now, place the square on the top and slide it up to the dowel rod, ease the table either up or down until the square blade and the dowel rod touch along their entire length. You now have your angle: tighten both locks as tightly as you can.

For angles that you'll use frequently or when you're drilling a large hole that takes considerable pressure on the drill, a better way is to make angle blocks. When drilling the chair seats, you will need settings of 10°, 15° and 20°. Cut a piece 1½″ x 2¾″x 10″ long for the 10°, 1½″ x 3″ x 10″ long for the 15°, and 1½″ x 5½″ x 14″ long for the 20°. Lay out the degree line on each piece and cut along it. (See Figure 6-1.) The two pieces should match when put side by side on the bench. If they don't, take light cuts on the jointer off the bottom

An angle block in position.

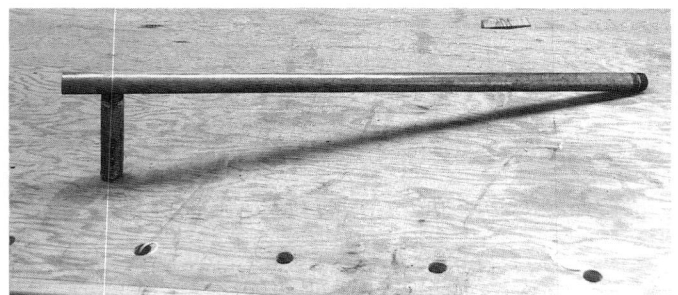

A finished tool rest.

edge of the larger one until they do. On angles where you don't use a block, be sure and tighten the lock on the supports as tightly as you can. You don't want any movement while you're drilling the hole. When in use, these blocks should be placed at the outer edges of the bottom in such a way that both bottom and top fit flat on the block surfaces.

Finally, when the fixture is in place on the drill press and the proper angle set, the centerline should be exactly under the center of any drill bit that's in the chuck, and the back end of the centerline should match the center of the drill-press column. This is very important when drilling compound angles, as you will see on the chair projects. Tighten the attachment bolt as tightly as you can so that there is no chance for the fixture to shift while you're using it. (You can make doubly sure by adding a C-clamp between the fixture base and the table.) This fixture will make building the chairs easier. However, you'll be surprised how many times you'll use it for other projects that you haven't even thought of yet.

Lathe Accessories—Headstock Jigs and Special Tool Rests

These jigs and fixtures are also necessary for the chair projects, but you'll find them very handy to have around for other turning work. (You never can tell—you might wind up making more than one chair.) To

The long rest installed on the lathe.

A variety of saw table inserts.

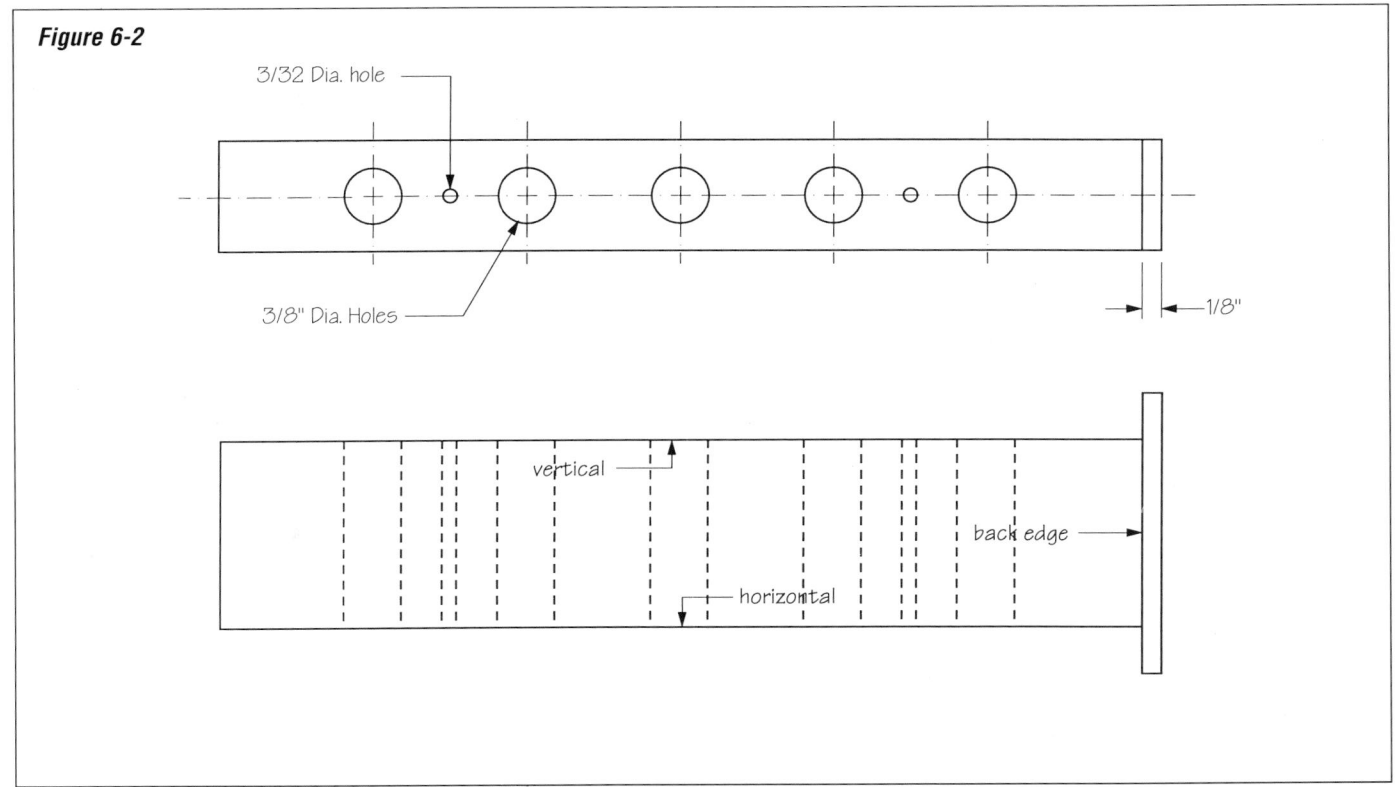

Figure 6-2

3/32 Dia. hole

3/8" Dia. Holes

1/8"

vertical

horizontal

back edge

Crosscutting a large heavy board.

Squaring a large panel.

save a lot of time and energy, particularly in repetitive turning, you need to make four small jigs and rig up two special tool rests. The jigs go on your 3" faceplate. They automatically center and drive the turning blanks. Make one each for 1", 1¼", 1½" and 1¾" square blanks. They're all made the same way, so I'll just describe the 1" jig.

Start with a piece of wood 1½" thick by 3" square (cut it from a 2x4). Center it on the 3" faceplate and attach it. Mount the faceplate on the lathe headstock. While turning the headstock spindle slowly by hand, bring the tailstock up and make a mark on the wood with the point. Remove the faceplate and draw a 1" square around the center point just marked. Using the square as an outline, cut a ½"-deep recess. Put the faceplate back on the lathe and turn the block to the diameter of the faceplate. With a marking pen, clearly mark one corner of the square recess. The 1" jig is now complete, and you can make the other three the same way. All four jigs should be interchangeable on the same faceplate.

For the two special tool rests, get three pieces of ½" galvanized pipe, 32", 24" and 3½" long. Also get a ⁵⁄₁₆" x 4" NC hex head bolt and a ⁵⁄₁₆" flat washer. On one end of the 3½" piece, file a curve so that it will fit, at 90°, snugly against either of the other pieces. At a point 2" from one end of each of the two longer pieces drill and tap a ⁵⁄₁₆" NC hole. Assemble the tool rest by passing the bolt through the washer and then through the 3½" piece and screwing it into the hole in either of the long pieces. The longer rest is for spindles, and the shorter one, for legs. To install either of these rests, put the short leg in the tool rest holder and clamp it so that the top edge of the rest is just a little below the centerline of the headstock spindle. Set the rest holder so that the end of the rest almost touches the face of the jig. Move the tailstock back so as to allow easy insertion of the turning blank into the square recess in

the jig, and lock it there. Push the outer end of the rest against the tailstock, place a small block of wood under it to bring the top edge level, then clamp the rest to the tailstock with a C-clamp. If you're using the right rest for the job, the outer end will not interfere with the feed handle of the tailstock. You'll find these jigs and tool rests a very useful addition to your shop. This type of rest is so much easier to use because it allows you to turn anywhere on the piece without resetting. I've made at least six different lengths for my own shop. As to the faceplate jigs, they are indispensable when doing multiple turnings, and they provide a surer drive than the standard headstock center. They also allow you to remove and replace a partly turned piece and still have it perfectly centered.

Dowel Drilling Jig—to Accurately Drill Dowel Joints

This jig will make it easy to accurately create the dowel joints that join the top and bottom to the sides of both the cabinet in project one and the showcase in project five. Once you have made it, I'm sure you will find many other projects where you can use this type of joint. I have three of them, each one for a different size joint. Figure 6-2 shows how to make it. Be sure to mark the jig as shown so that you won't get confused when using it. To find out how the jig is used, refer to projects one and five.

Special Inserts for Table Saws

Table saws generally come with one all-purpose table insert. It takes care of most blades but does not accommodate dado heads or molding cutters. The insert is usually made from pot metal or tin, and after a while it gets pretty beat up, making it hard to do small work on the saw. I'm sure you have also found that in ripping thin pieces or cutting an open-end mortice, the slot is so much wider than the blade that you don't get proper support for the work. I solved this dilemma by making a number of special inserts to take care of various situations that often arise. The ones in the picture are mine, and as you can see, they have had heavy use. An extra advantage of making them yourself is that when one gets too beat up, you just make a new one.

To make one, cut a piece of maple or oak just wide enough to fit the insert opening in your table. Measure the distance from the tabletop to the insert supports, and resaw the board to that thickness. Now place the present insert on the board and draw the rounded ends. Cut these on the band saw or jigsaw. Clean up the cut edges, and see that the blank fits snugly in the insert recess.

If you look at the insert that came with your saw, you will usually find a small projection in the center of the front edge. This fits into a groove in the side of the recess and prevents the front of the insert from kicking up in your face should anything get caught. To create a similar projection when making an insert, drive a small brad partway into the edge in the same location as the projection on the old insert.

The idea is to have an insert that fits closely around each of your blades, which have a different kerf width. A general use carbide blade will have a wider kerf than a planer blade. I have found it worthwhile to have two inserts for my dado head—one that takes the two outside blades of the head, cutting a ¼" wide dado, and one that takes the full width of the head. I use the ¼" dado head to cut open mortices when making cabinet door and back frames (see chapter eight). When you're cutting a ¼" mortice in a ⅝"-thick rail or stile, you need support close to the blade.

To cut the proper opening in the insert is quite simple. Put the blade or dado head with which you are going to use the insert on the saw arbor. Lower the arbor until the blade clears the bottom surface of the insert when it is in position. Put the insert blank in place and start the saw. Holding the back edge of the blank down with a stick, slowly raise the blade through the blank to whatever height you normally use it. This is particularly true with dado head inserts. If you don't normally cut dadoes more that ¾" deep, then you don't want to have the gap in the front and rear that you would have if the slot accommodated a blade height of 1½". Once you've started on this, you'll find yourself making a special insert to fit each new situation you run into.

Sliding Cutoff Cradle

Some jobs are very difficult to do on any table saw, for example, trimming the end of a long board, cutting a long board in two, or squaring up a wide panel. Even

The auxiliary rip fence.

with an extension fence on the miter gauge, these operations are hard to accomplish accurately. The fixture I'm about to describe will make those jobs easy. It is a sliding cutoff cradle. To make this fixture, you must have a carpenter's square, and it must be accurate within 1/32" in the 24" length of the blade. To determine if this is so, set the rip fence of your table saw at the right edge of the table, and then tape a piece of paper to the table so that it is about the middle of the fence and stretches clear across the table. Now place the square on the paper with the short leg against the fence pointing left, and draw a fine line on the paper. Flip the square so that the short leg points right and the bottom of the long leg is exactly on the pencil line. Draw another line. If the two lines coincide, the square is accurate. If the lines are no more than 1/16" apart at the outer end, the square is within the allowable tolerance. If it is not within the tolerance, the cradle, if you make it, will not cut accurately.

Making the cradle is easy and inexpensive. Start with a piece of ½" A-B grade plywood or high-density chipboard that is 28" x 48", two 48" lengths of 2x4, and two 28" long sticks whose width and thickness match the miter gauge slots in your saw table. See that the sticks fit snugly in the miter gauge slots and that they are flush with the top of the table. Make sure that they slide easily in the slots. Lower your saw blade until it is below the tabletop, and place the panel on the table with the 48" edge lined up with the back of the table and centered over the blade. Clamp it in this position. Slide the sticks into the miter gauge slots so that they are entirely under the panel, and using 1" brads, tack them in place through the panel. Do not drive the brads in fully because you will be pulling them out shortly. Remove the clamps, turn the panel over, and fasten the strips firmly to it using at least five ⅝" brads per strip. This time drive them in and set them. Turn the panel back over, fit the guides in the slots, and see that the panel slides back and forth easily and that there is no sideways play. Remove the brads used to tack the strips in place.

Take one piece of 2x4, and joint two adjacent surfaces square and flat. Now, with the panel in place on the table and the back edge slightly behind the rip fence rail, turn on the saw and slowly raise the blade until it's at its highest position, then turn the saw off. Place the 2x4 on the panel with the jointed narrow surface down and the jointed wide surface facing toward the blade, then line up the back of the 2x4 with the back edge of the panel and clamp one end. The clamp should be loose enough that you can move the other end. Using the carpenter's square, with the short leg against the 2x4, square it with the blade and clamp the other end. (Be sure to avoid the set in the blade teeth.) Now both clamps should be quite tight. Lower the blade and carefully turn the assembly over. Screw the assembly together with #8 x 1¼" flat head wood screws. Use six screws, three on either side of the centerline. Be sure to stay clear of the centerline so the saw blade won't hit a screw. Fasten the other 2x4 to the front edge of the panel in the same manner. It does not have to be square with the saw blade—just be sure it lines up with the front edge of the panel. Mark this 2x4 on its top edge in large, heavy letters "FRONT" so that you won't, by accident, use the fixture backwards.

For the final step, place the fixture in its proper position, start the saw, and raise the blade to just under its full height. Feed the fixture forward slowly until you have moved the blade through the back 2x4, then, going around the saw, push it slowly until you have moved the blade through the front 2x4. The fixture is now complete and ready for use. (I drilled a ¾" hole through the panel at one end so that I could hang it on the wall out of the way when not in use.)

Once you've made this sliding cradle, I predict that you will use it more than you anticipate. It makes cut-off of almost any board or panel so easy, and you

don't have to check its squareness beforehand as you do with the miter gauge, which might have gotten bumped out of square. When you have multiple cut-offs of a given length to make, it is simple to clamp a stop on the back fence. If you want to do this for lengths longer than 24", just clamp an extension stick to the upper part of the back fence and clamp the stop to the extension stick.

Auxiliary Rip Fence

Here is an attachment for your table saw that you may already have. In case you don't, I'll just take a minute and tell you about it. This is a fence that you bolt to the inside face of your regular rip fence. It is, as you can see from the picture, quite a bit higher than the regular fence, and that is one of the reasons for having it. The high fence gives better support when resawing a wide board and when making shallow rabbets on panels. The higher support is helpful when cutting tenons and open-end mortises. Notice also the small cutout at the point of the blade. This is to allow a dado head to be set slightly under the fence in order to cut a rabbet.

The fence is made from ¾" A-B grade plywood. It is slightly longer than your regular fence and is 5" high. Slightly round the top corners. My rip fence has two ¼" holes through it from side to side, one front and one rear. I bolted my auxiliary fence through those holes, using ¼" bolts of sufficient length, and counter-boring so the heads would be just under the inside surface of the fence. I used wing nuts on the bolts so that it's easy to put on and take off. To size the cutout, put one of the outside blades of your dado head on the saw. Raise it to a height of ¾". With the auxiliary fence in place, move the rip fence against the blade and mark the blade's outline on the fence. Now remove the auxiliary fence and bandsaw the cutout. You'll find that you'll have a lot more uses for this attachment than you think. That's mine in the picture—the same one I've been using for twenty years.

Chapter Seven

CHOOSING THE WOOD

As I said earlier, let the wood provide the beauty in the piece. In order to do this, you must choose it very carefully. In some cases, I spent almost as much time picking out the wood as I did building the piece. Go to a hardwood lumberyard, ask to be shown their stock of whatever kind of wood you're after, and then have them leave you there alone. You should have brought with you a cutting list of the rough sizes of all the parts in the piece, a measuring tape, a stick of chalk and a sharp block plane. Why the block plane? Most hardwood is stocked in the rough. It is often hard to see the details of the grain pattern unless you shave off a little of the rough surface. Hence the block plane. What are you looking for? For boards with unusual and interesting grain patterns that you can use in the major portions of your piece. If you're building a table, you'll want to find boards for the top that will match so that they'll look like they belong together. You may want to find a grain pattern that will follow, at least to some degree, the contour of your cabinet side or tabletop. You'll look for a board from which you can create a striking panel for a cabinet door. You discover these things by pulling the boards out of the stack and studying them. (I've had them spread all over the lumber shed.) When you find a board you want, outline the part or parts in chalk and check it off your cutting list. When you've found everything you need, put the stack back the way you found it. (If your present lumberyard won't let you do this, find one that will.) You can easily spend most of a Saturday morning doing this. But, believe me, the final result will justify whatever time and effort you spend.

As a particularly fine example of what I am talking about, study the walnut armoire in the accompanying photo. This is another of my designs that my daughter built. Notice first the matching of the grain on all the drawer fronts. Then study the door panels. This is what is known as *book-matching*. It is done by taking a

A beautiful example of book-matching in the door panels.

thick piece, resawing it down the middle and laying it open like a book. In this case, because of the width of the panel, two boards were matched, then both were resawed, finished to proper thickness, and glued together to form the panels. You can also do this for a tabletop by starting with 2"-thick material. If you find the right piece, you can create a beautiful, one-of-a-kind design. You may have a problem in that some yards are now stocking hardwood lumber with sanded surfaces, down to ¹⁵⁄₁₆" thickness. This does not assure flatness, and it leaves less material to make a twisted or warped piece flat and still finish with ¾" thickness. However, it is easier to see the grain pattern. Take care to get a piece without much twist or warp, especially if you're going to cut long pieces from it.

There are other ways of getting the wood you need. If you live in an area where good hardwood grows, you might reconnoiter the country within a 50-mile radius of your home, looking for a small sawmill that mills local hardwoods. These small mills are around, but you have to really search for them. It's time-consuming, but if you find one, the result could be well worth the effort. Many years ago, when I lived in northeastern Ohio, I found such a mill and got some very beautiful cherry lumber. If you find one, then you can take logs to it. In cities, people are always cutting down old trees because they have died or are in the way or to make room for new development. Some of these almost certainly will be maple, cherry, oak or, if you're lucky, walnut. Very often, the people are happy to have you take them away so they don't have to worry about disposing of them. If you happen to live on some acreage in the country that has some hardwood on it, then you might do as I did in Oregon in the 1970s. I went into the woods and cut my own trees. The Oregon alder, maple, and walnut that was available in the hardwood lumberyards was from young trees. I found that the wood from young trees does not have the character that you find in old trees. The reason for this is that when they have been around long enough to become sixty or more feet high, they have weathered many storms and have cracks in the bark and in the body itself that let the elements in. These elements have minerals in them that impart colors to the wood. The older the tree, the more things have happened to it—things that cause twisting and warping, which develop strange and different grain patterns.

By felling my own trees and having them custom milled under my supervision, I could get the best out of the logs, including some boards almost 30" wide. Then I would keep the boards together in the order in which they were cut from the log. Stack them on sticks in a sheltered location, under cover but not necessarily inside, and let them air dry. The reason for keeping them in order is so that you will have matching grain patterns when you go looking for special wood for a special place, like the sides of a cabinet or the panels of mating doors. I always did this and it paid off handsomely in some beautiful and unusual pieces of furniture that no one else could equal because they didn't have the matching boards. I had the logs hauled to a small sawmill about twenty miles from my home, and I was always present when the milling was done to make the decisions on the cutting. This was a regular sawmill, not a chainsaw mill. My logs ranged from 8"-diameter-by 6'-long English walnut that I got when a neighbor tore out an old walnut orchard, to 30"-diameter-by-10' alder and maple logs cut off my land. They were cut into 1" and 2" planks, what I call full, that is, the 1" roughed out at around 1⅛" and the 2" at 2⅛". Rough boards tend to warp some when air drying. With wide boards, this can be particularly troublesome. Unless you mill them full, you often have trouble getting a finished ¾" on 1" boards, especially the longer ones. The same is true with the 2". About moisture content, I wasn't very scientific. I didn't have time to be. I just let it dry for at least two years and then used it. When I was going to build a piece, I rough cut all the parts and stacked them on sticks in the shop for a week or so to adjust the wood to shop conditions before I finished it to size.

There you have three ways to get beautiful wood to build your fine furniture. To be honest about it, the last two are more satisfying and in the long run produce more beautiful wood, if you're lucky enough to be able to follow one of them. If not, the lumberyards are not devoid of beautiful wood. You just have to take the time to look for it.

Chapter Eight

JOINTS—WHICH TO USE WHERE

There are literally hundreds of joints you can make with wood. Ernest Joyce, in his *Encyclopedia of Furniture Making*, devotes forty pages to them. In this book, I'm going to talk about five basic ones that I have used in most of my work and are used in the projects described in the last section. If you are imaginative and like to try new things, you might get Mr. Joyce's book and take a shot at some different ones, but these five will serve for 90 percent of situations that arise in furniture making. I'm also going to explain some simple and easy ways I've worked out to make these joints.

Butt Joints

These are also called *edge joints*, which is perhaps a more descriptive term. They are used to combine boards into panels, cabinet tops and tabletops. The most common versions of this joint are plain, tongue and groove, and dowel. For me, the plain butt joint has been the best. Many people think this is a poor joint, that a dowel or a tongue and groove is stronger. I've found that this is not so, providing the joint is properly made. The dowel and the tongue and groove are difficult and time-consuming to make, and they often wind up out of line, which requires a lot of hand planing to smooth up the panel. The proper way to make the plain butt joint is to plane the mating edges slightly hollow by about ½". Put the boards on supports, place a clamp across the middle and pull it up. If, with your fingers, you can move the ends of the boards relative to each other, you don't have a good joint. If the ends are tight but you can't bring the center together, you have too much hollow. If the panel is not too large, you can hold it up to a bright light, and if you can see light anywhere along the joint, it's not good enough. When you have made this joint properly, you'll break the surrounding wood before you'll break the joint. The advantage of the hollow is that the ends of the boards are put in compression and will not open if there is any later shrinkage. When you are satisfied that you have a properly made joint, apply the glue to both mating edges of each joint, and

Gluing up a thin panel.

making sure your ends are lined up, apply the clamp or clamps in the center and pull them up until you squeeze the glue from the entire length of the joint. Be sure to put strips of wax paper between the boards and the supports to keep them from sticking together. Don't try to wipe up the excess glue at this time; just set the panel on the floor with the joints vertical so that if the glue runs, it will run down the joint. When it has dried, then remove the excess with a plane.

When making thin panels, ¼" to ½" thick, you use the same procedure but add an extra element. Prepare a pair of sticks ¾" x 1" x an inch or so longer than the panel is wide. Place one on each side of the panel, and clamp them together at the ends with C-clamps. Don't tighten the C-clamps too tight—just enough to keep the panel flat; do this before tightening the bar clamps. Don't forget the wax paper strips under each stick. If it's a long panel, you may want two pairs of sticks, or even three, to be sure that the panel stays flat overall.

The Open-End Mortice-and-Tenon Joint

I have used this joint extensively in making door and back frames, in fact, frames of any kind. It's simple and easy to make and is very strong because of the relatively large areas of gluing surface. Here's an easy

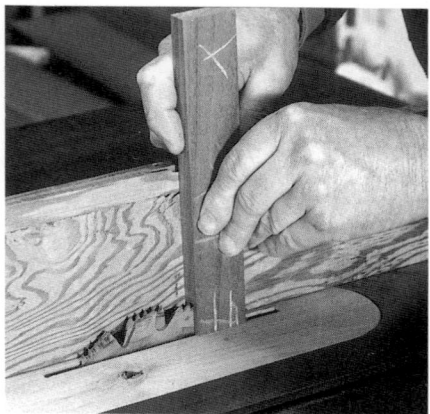
Cutting the open-end mortice.

Making the horizontal tenon cuts.

Making the vertical tenon cuts.

way to make it on a table saw. First be sure that your blade is absolutely perpendicular to the table. Don't trust the gauge: check it with an all-metal try square. If it's the least bit out, you will not be able to cut the joint properly. At the same time you're doing this, check that the miter gauge is exactly square with the blade. Don't depend on the setting on the gauge: check it with the try square.

Assume you're dealing with rails and stiles that have a ¾" x 1½" cross section. You will use a ¼" x 1½" tenon. However, in making this joint, it is best to cut the mortice first. Attach the high auxiliary fence to your rip fence, then put the two outer blades of your dado head on the arbor to get a ¼" cut. Now set the fence so that the dado head will cut in the exact center of the ¾" dimension of the piece in which you want the mortice. Set the blade height at 1½" and cut the mortice as shown in the picture.

You make the tenon with a regular combination blade; the procedure requires two cuts. First, set the fence at 1½" to the outside of the blade and the blade

height at ¼". Using the miter gauge to keep the piece square, make the cuts across the 1½" faces of the piece. Reset the fence at ½" to the inside of the blade and the blade height to just under 1½". Make the vertical or face cut on both sides of the piece. Notice, in making this cut, that the waste is on the outside of the blade, so that it falls away from the blade. If you have been careful with your measurements, the joint should fit together easily. You don't want a tight fit, because that will tend to force the outer ends of the mortice apart and spoil the joint. Nor do you want a sloppy fit; just a nice, easy hand-pressure fit. If the fit is too tight, make the adjustment on the tenon, not the mortice. Use a paring chisel and shave the face of the tenon until you get the right fit. Work first one side and then the other to keep the tenon in the center.

The reason for using the fence as a guide is to make sure that all the joints you're cutting come out the same. Therefore, once you have set up to cut the mortice, cut them all. Handle the two tenon cuts the same way.

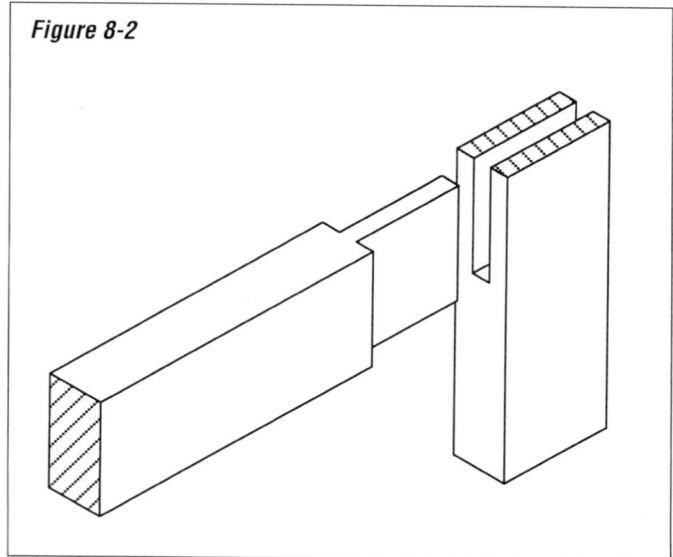
Figure 8-2

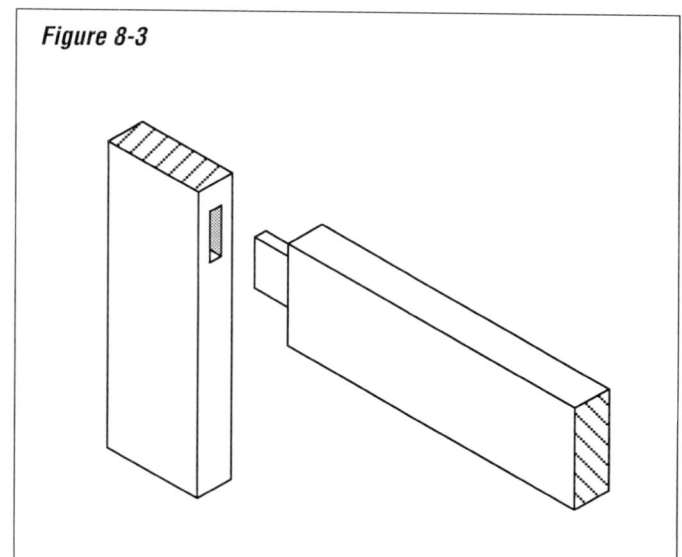
Figure 8-3

Extension fence supports the edge cut.

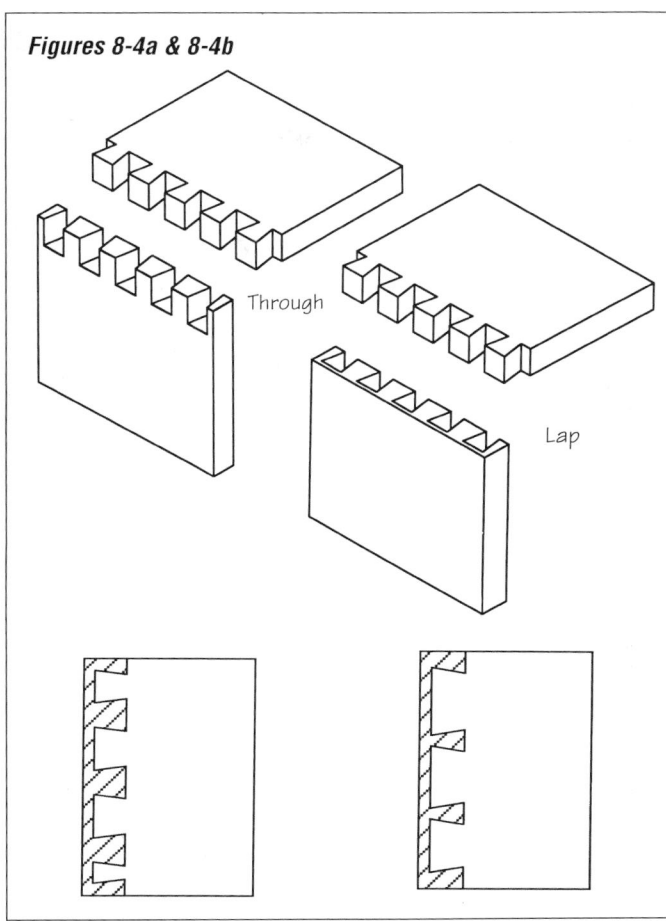

Through

Lap

The Blind Mortice-and-Tenon Joint

I generally use this joint for mating legs with stretchers, skirts, rails and other such parts. I always cut the tenon first because it is easier to make the mortice fit the tenon than the other way around. In this case, the tenon is cut the same as the open tenon except that here, end cuts are necessary. Again assume that the tenon is going on the end of a ¾" x 1½" stretcher. In this case, the tenon is to be ½" x 1" in cross section and ¾" long. Notice that the tenon shoulders are ⅛" on the sides and ¼" on the edges. The greater edge shoulder is to provide resistance to racking, while the side shoulder is just to cover the edges of the mortice. That's so that if you mess up the mortice edges, it won't show. With the auxiliary fence in place, set the fence ¾" from the outside of the blade with a blade height of ⅛", and using the miter gauge for squareness, make the horizontal face cuts. Raise the blade height to ¼", and make the horizontal edge cuts. Reset the fence to ⅝" to the inside of the blade and the blade to just under ¾" high. Make the vertical face cuts. Leaving the blade height the same, set the fence to 1¼" to the inside of the blade and make the vertical edge cuts. To make this cut easier and more accurate, I clamp an extension fence to the miter gauge extending over almost to the fence. This supports the rail and holds it square while making the cut. The blade will cut into the extension fence, but that doesn't matter, since it's a piece of scrap anyway. To ensure a good fit, lay out the mortice from the tenon, never from the drawing. My way of cutting a blind mortice is to drill out the major waste, as close to the lines as possible and to the correct depth. That depth should be slightly more than the length of the tenon. Do this on a drill press. I finish and shave to the lines with a butt chisel. I use a depth gauge to check the depth

and the squareness of the sides. Mortice-and-tenon joints should be made with a snug fit, preferably one you can push home by hand. If the fit is too tight, you'll have two problems. The application of the glue may swell the wood so that you won't get the joint together at all. If that doesn't occur, the tight fit will wipe most of the glue to the bottom of the mortice, and thus, weaken the joint. I found good practice to be ensuring a snug fit and having the mortice about ¹⁄₁₆" deeper than the length of the tenon. This lets the shoulder seat firmly. If you make the joint too loose, you can still save it by using a glue with filling properties; however, it will be a weak joint at best.

The Dovetail Joint

This is one of the best joints that a furniture maker can use. It is also one that takes considerable practice. For my money, the only way to make it is by hand. Dovetail joints made with a router must be made in a jig, which creates a joint that looks machine made. If you make them by hand or with a slight assist from the table saw, you can design them any way you want. When you look through the projects in the last section, you will understand the individuality dove-

Cutting the tails on a table saw.

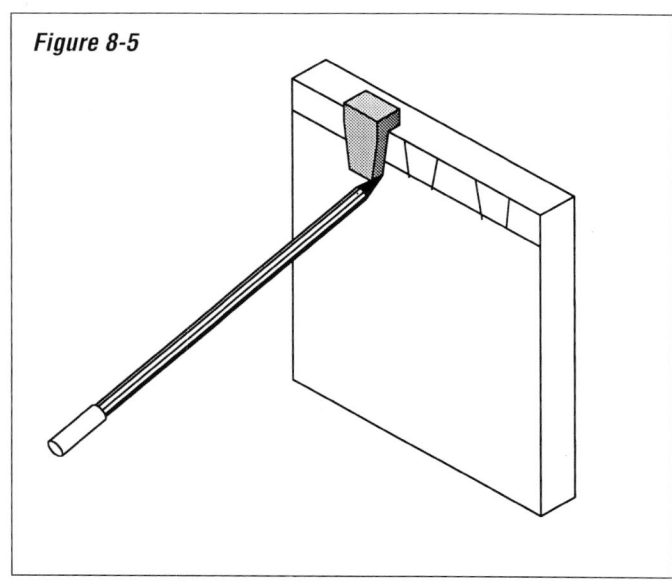

Figure 8-5

tail joints impart to a piece of furniture. The accompanying drawing shows the two major forms of the joint and illustrates a couple of ways they can be designed.

The two parts to this joint are called the *tails* and the *pins*. In the drawing, the tails are on the horizontal pieces, and the pins, on the vertical. It is important to understand where the two parts generally go. It depends on where the load will be applied to the joint. As you can see in the illustration, the strength of those joints is in the horizontal direction. In a drawer, for example, the tails are put on the sides, and the pins, on the front and back. In a cabinet, the tails go on the horizontal members, while the pins go in the vertical ones in order to provide resistance to spreading and racking. One more important point: Always lay out the tails first and cut them, then lay out the pins from the tails. You will find this a much easier way to do it, and you will invariably get a better fit.

When laying out a dovetail joint, it is handy to have a marking gauge. Figure 8-5 shows what one looks like and how it is used. It saves a lot of time and fussing around. I made mine with a 15° angle and a lip on only one side. I devised a quick, easy way of cutting the tails on drawer sides. This method necessitates a very thin kerf saw blade for your table saw. Mine is an 8" planer blade with a ⅟₁₆" kerf. It's been sharpened many times so that it's somewhat less than 8" in diameter, but it works very well on a 10" saw. You're seldom going to cut more than ¾" deep.

Start by laying out the tails on the outside face of one drawer side, both ends. Put the other side against the first so that the inside faces are touching and the edges all line up. Now, using masking tape, tape the sides tightly together. The tape should be at least three inches from each end. Using a square, carry the lines of the tails you have already drawn across the ends of the sides and then draw the tails on the second side. Clearly mark the areas between the tails that will be

waste. Put the blade on the saw and set it at 15°. Stand the sides on end, and raise the blade until its top edge is just below the bottom line of the tails. Now lock the trunnion so it can't move. Clamp a 2¾" high extension fence on your miter gauge (having first checked that it is square with the blade) so that it extends well beyond the blade. Use a piece of scrap because it's going to get cut up a bit. Turn on the saw, place the pair of sides on end against the fence, and holding them there, make a cut in the waste very close to every line that angles in the same direction as the blade. Turn the sides around and repeat the operation. You have now outlined the sides of the waste areas with saw cuts. Holding the sides in position as before and moving them sideways by the thickness of the saw kerf, remove the waste by repetitive cuts. You will have to reverse them to get the final bit of waste in each area. Because you will be laying out the pins from these tails, the angle doesn't have to be exact, nor do you have to be perfect when cutting to the lines. However, the depth must be exact. Before taking the sides apart, be sure to mark the top, front and outside of each. This is important because if, once they're apart, you get the ends mixed up, they won't match. Also, when you lay out the pins, mark which side goes where relative to the front and back, for the same reason. I always number the parts of any joint, 1-2, 3-4, etc.

To finish the joint, lay out the pins on the front and back of the drawer by placing the sides in position and tracing the tails with a sharp knife. Use a sharp X-Acto knife with a #11 blade, and cut as deeply as you can. Now comes the ticklish part—making the saw cuts that delineate the pins. By far the best saw for this purpose is a fine cut Japanese dovetail saw. This saw has a very thin kerf and fine teeth, and since it cuts on the pull stroke rather than the push, it is easier

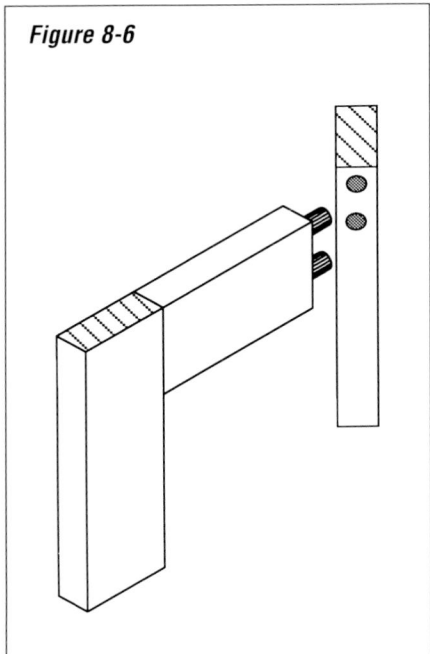

Figure 8-6

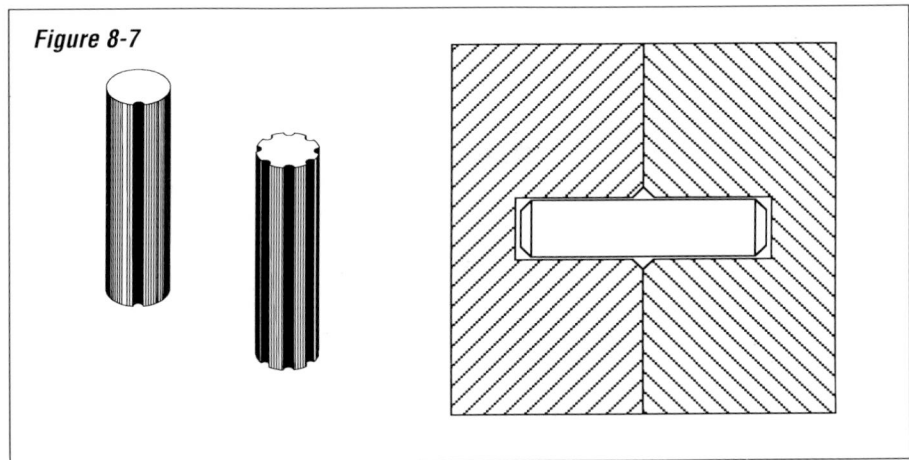

Figure 8-7

to control. If you've marked the way I suggested, the saw will fit into the mark you've made and be accurately positioned to start the cut. Once you have made all the saw cuts, finish removing the waste with a chisel. The fit for a dovetail joint should be no tighter than a slight tap with a mallet and no looser than a firm push with the hand.

Dowel Joints

In my opinion, this is not a very good joint, but there are times when it's handy to have around. The reason it's not a very good joint is that it tends to be weak. Invariably, half of the joint matches long grain with short grain, which is a weak combination when glued up. The trick when using it is to design the piece so that the joint carries a minimum of stress. It is difficult to construct because of the problem of locating the dowel holes in the mating parts so that they match. In the projects where I use this joint, I have solved the hole-locating problem by constructing a drill jig.

In the two wall-cabinet projects in this book (projects one and five), I have used this joint because I wanted the top and bottom to overhang the sides and there was no other reasonable way to accomplish that. However, I designed them so that they are hung from the sides or back and not the top, thus keeping stress off the joints.

The dowel joint is sometimes used in making frames as illustrated in Figure 8-6. Here again it is not

as good as the open-end mortice-and-tenon joint. The positioning problem is helped if you use a drill jig. In this case, it's one you buy rather than make. I have a Stanley that I've had for forty years. Several others are available—just look in one of the woodworking tool catalogs.

In making this joint, you need to remember several things, all of which have to do with the fact that you're going into a blind hole. If the dowel is too tight, you'll trap air and glue at the bottom of the hole, and the dowel won't go in far enough. If that happens, the part protruding will be too long for the matching hole, and the joint won't go together. You solve this by first sizing the dowel so that it can be pushed or tapped into the hole, not driven. Then be sure there are grooves in the sides of the dowel to let the air and the excess glue out; and finally, slightly taper each end of the dowel. This allows it to enter the hole more easily besides providing some room in case you have a little too much glue in the joint. A precaution I've learned to take: After putting dowels in one side of the joint, measure the protruding length of each dowel against the depth of the hole it's to go into. If one is too long, you can trim it, but if you put the joint together not knowing, you could have lots of trouble.

You can buy ready-made dowels in the configurations shown in the drawing; however, it has been my experience that I never had one the length I wanted. So, I took to making my own from dowel rods I bought at the lumber yard. A word of caution about this. I have never yet bought a rod that wasn't oversize. The answer is to buy yourself a dowel sizer. This handy little tool will size your dowel for a proper fit, and in some tools, also score the breathing grooves in the sides. The Woodcraft catalog shows a dandy.

Chapter Nine

PUT IT TOGETHER SO IT STAYS

Glue two pieces of wood together and they'll stay that way forever. Not necessarily. Use the wrong glue and they'll come apart. Have the wrong relationship between grain directions and the joint will fail. Use too little glue and they won't hold, too much and they won't go together right. Apply the glue improperly and you'll have a mess to clean up. All these are very simple and common sense points, but they're frequently overlooked—until too late.

As a professional furniture maker, fitting and gluing joints was very important for me. If the joints came apart, I got the piece back and had a blot on my reputation, neither of which I could afford. I found experience to be the best teacher, not only in finding the right glue but also in learning how to use it properly. I'll try to pass on some of what I've learned.

Types of Glues

The right glue is the first consideration. Many products are available today; my Woodcraft catalog lists at least seven, all distinctly different. The range of types is wide, from old-fashioned hide glue to the latest plastic concoction. How do you know which one is right for the particular job you're doing? The best way to make the initial choice is to look closely at the properties of each particular type.

Hide Glue: This has been around since the beginning of time and is available in either liquid or powder form. The liquid form is simply squeezed from a bottle, while the powder form must be melted in a glue pot and used hot. Hide glue holds very well, but it has two drawbacks: it has very poor moisture resistance, and it becomes brittle in time. If you've had a piece of antique furniture come apart in a damp atmosphere, you'll know what I mean. Also, if you get it where you don't want it, it's next to impossible to remove because it tends to penetrate the pores of the wood deeply, particularly the hot type. It's very slow setting, and that may be good or bad, depending on you.

White Glue: Another that holds well but has little or no moisture resistance. It keeps well and is always ready to use, but the low resistance to dampness rules

it out for furniture work. I once had a very lovely small table just fall apart at the end of a rainy summer. White glue is fast setting, but it softens under the heat of sanding and turns dark.

Yellow Glues: These are made from aliphatic resins and have high moisture resistance, although they are not waterproof. They're strong, fast setting (thirty minutes to one hour for handling), set at low temperatures, keep well and are easily applied. They don't gum up or turn color from sanding, but they're hard, and if you're not careful, you'll sand the surrounding wood faster than the glue and get an uneven surface. Another important advantage of these glues is their ability to fill space. If you've made a sloppy joint, this glue, generously applied, will save it. I've used this type of glue since it came on the market and swear by it. I buy it in gallon jugs from a professional supply house and transfer it for use to a clean peanut butter jar. This saves me five to six dollars over the price at the local hardware or lumberyard. Just look in the yellow pages for such an outfit.

Plastic Resin Glue: There are several brands of this type on the market, all equally good. It comes in powder form and is mixed with water for use. Herein lies one of its major disadvantages: It's wasteful because you always mix more than you use, and it doesn't keep once mixed. On the plus side, it's completely waterproof (in the marine grade), very strong and durable, and easily applied; further, it keeps well in powdered form. The other big disadvantage, at least for me, is that it won't set up at low temperatures. In the early days of my furniture business, there was no heat in my shop at night. I'd glue up a piece before I quit for the day and in the morning find that it hadn't set up and that the glue had crystallized so that it would never set up. So I had to scrape it all off and start over. That's when I changed to yellow glue.

Pheno-Resorcinol Glue: Here is another product that requires mixing, only this time it is two chemicals rather than a powder and water. This consists of a liquid resin and a powder hardener. Again you'll have the same problem with waste; if you mix too much, it

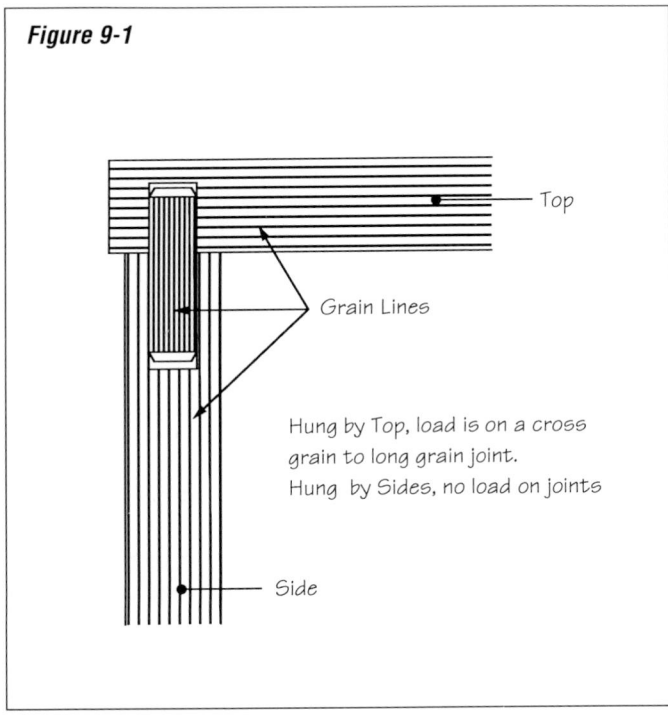

Figure 9-1

Top

Grain Lines

Hung by Top, load is on a cross grain to long grain joint.
Hung by Sides, no load on joints

Side

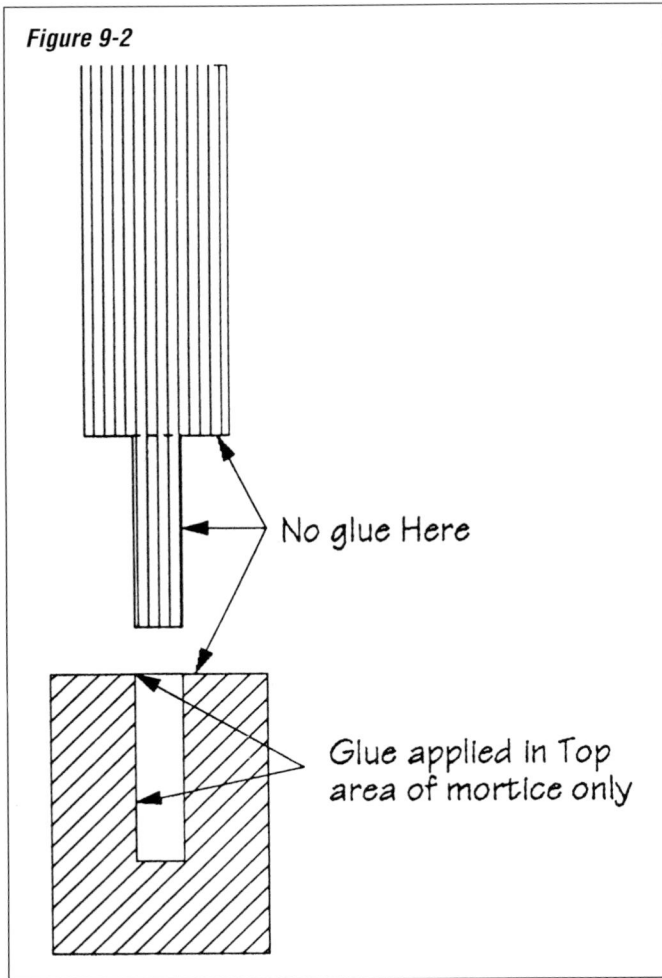

Figure 9-2

No glue Here

Glue applied in Top area of mortice only

The job clamped up—a dry run.

won't keep. Pros: it's strong, durable and completely waterproof. Cons: it's messy to use, wasteful, leaves a dark glue line and is quite expensive compared to other glues.

Epoxy Glue: This was never really intended for use in woodworking—an occasional small job perhaps, but not furniture or similar work. Epoxy always comes in two parts and must be mixed—a messy job at best, particularly in the amounts needed for ordinary woodworking jobs. It is hard to apply, difficult to clean up and very expensive. I do not recommend its use in the kind of woodworking I'm talking about in this book.

Cyanoacrylates: These are the so-called instant or super glues. Here too is a product that was not designed to be used on wood. It will work, but only in certain applications. It works much too fast for ordinary glue jobs, and its cost is out of all proportion to its usefulness. If you look in the stores and catalogs, you may find other glues. They may or may not be suitable for the kind of work you're doing. Read the labels and look at the properties. If all the information you want isn't on the label, don't buy the stuff. If you want to experiment, do it on a small job that you don't care too much about. As for me, I think that the yellow glue is by far the best for the kind of projects you'll find in this book. My next choice is plastic resin, certainly if it must be waterproof.

Gluing Joints

Now that I've covered the types of glue, it's time to talk about the joints on which you're going to use them. Not all joints make good glue joints. The first things to remember are that long grain to long grain holds very well; cross grain to cross grain will not hold at all; and cross grain to long grain is marginal, depending on the amount of surface being glued. On this basis, a mortice-and-tenon joint with a large flat area on the tenon is a good joint and will hold well, while a round tenon is marginal and needs as much length as you can give it. Probably the best joint from this point of view is the dovetail. It starts with a mechanical lock and then has a considerable amount of long-grain-to-long-grain area to get the best holding power. If you will notice, most well-made cabinet cases are held together top and bottom with dovetail joints. That's because the dadoed shelf joint is entirely cross grain to long grain with small areas involved, and thus, quite weak. If the top and bottom joints were of this type, any racking or twisting of the case would break it apart. The value of the dowel joint depends on how you use it. In a wall cabinet, for example, if you dowel the top and bottom to the sides and then hang it by the top, the joint is a poor one. However, if you hang the cabinet by the sides, the joint becomes a good one. Figure 9-1 shows why this is so.

Now I want to talk about something that many woodworkers don't think about when putting a project together. I call it the dry run, and I consider it one of the most important parts of building anything from wood. When you are ready to do a glue job, big or small, several parts or just two, first get together all the tools and equipment you will need to do the job— all the clamps, pads, supports, protectors, glue applicator and glue. Lay them out on the bench, or wherever you're going to do the job, in position around the pieces to be glued. Now put the job together without glue. Make sure that everything fits, that you've got the right size clamps and pads, and that everything works the way it should. Having made sure, take it apart, put the glue in place and reclamp. There is nothing as frustrating as finding, after having applied the glue, that the joint won't go home or that you haven't enough pads or that the clamps don't fit or that they won't work smoothly, or any one of a dozen things that can go wrong. A very good example of this is in gluing the butt joint I spoke of earlier. Put the boards on supports, place a clamp across the middle and pull it up. If, with your fingers, you can move the ends of the boards relative to each other, you don't have a good joint. If the ends are tight but you can't bring the center together, you have too much hollow. Once the glue has been applied, these little flaws can't be easily corrected.

And finally there is the question of how and where to apply glue to a joint. What do you mean how and where? You just spread it on the parts of the joint and put them together. If you do, you're very apt to wind up with a joint that doesn't fit right or glue all over the

place to clean up later. To apply glue to surfaces, use brushes of different widths, depending on the size of the area to be covered; for joints where one part fits into another, use a small stick. (I use the handle of a 00 artist's brush.) I've found that with a small stick, you can pick up just the amount you want and put it exactly where you want it with considerable precision. The latter is particularly important when working with small joints, such as spindles in a chair seat or mortice-and-tenon joints in the frame of a cabinet door. In such joints, the placing of the glue is very important. I'll use a blind mortice-and-tenon joint as an example. Place a moderate amount of glue around the upper part of the mortice. When you put the joint together, the tenon will wipe this glue down over the entire face of the mortice. If you put too much on, then the surplus will wind up at the bottom. That's another reason you want to have the mortice 1/16" deeper than the tenon. It allows room for the surplus glue. Without it you'll create a pressure pocket and the joint won't go home. Of course, with a great deal too much, even the extra space won't save you. Then either the joint won't go home or you will force glue out the top. Never put any glue on the tenon or the tenon shoulder. If you do, it will wipe upward, and when the joint goes home, squirt out all over everything.

When applying glue to a butt joint, spread it on both faces; be sure that all the surface is covered. Pull the joint together with clamps until the glue squeezes out all along the joint. Don't try to wipe up this excess; just let it dry there on the surface. Wiping pushes it into the pores of the wood, where it's almost impossible to get out. When it dries on the surface, you can remove it quickly and easily with a plane or sharp chisel. Doing this will dull the cutting edge, so I keep a separate block plane and chisel just for this purpose. A point to remember in gluing up framed panels: glue the frame together, but never put any glue between the frame and the panel. It must float in order to adjust to the changes in humidity.

There are a lot of other examples I could cite, but I'm sure you see what I'm driving at. Gluing up a project seems like a simple operation, and it usually is, but it can also be a trap that can cause a great deal of woe. I've tried to point out some of the problems that arise and a few ways to avoid them.

Chapter Ten

TURNING—SPINDLES AND LEGS

If you're a woodworker to whom time is important, there is only one way to make long, thin spindles—turn them on a lathe. Any other way takes too long. If you're a professional, working for a living, you can't afford it; and if you're a hobbyist, it gets boring and the fun goes out of it.

Perhaps I'd better explain what I mean by long, thin spindles. Figure 10-1 depicts the ones used in the chair projects (six and eight). They are double-tapered spindles of ¾" maximum diameter, ½" at the bottom, ⅜" at the top, and they run 18"-28" long.

I'm also going to talk about turning chair legs. I've developed a technique that's somewhat different from most; it makes them not only easier to turn but also easier to fit to the chair seat. For turning the spindles, there is one more piece of equipment necessary. It's a steadyrest and should be among the accessories you got with your lathe. They come in different forms. Mine supports the piece at three points, but some are only two pointers. The steadyrest is clamped to the lathe bed at the point of the largest diameter of the spindle. In this case, the center of the supports should be 10" from the face of the jig. Now you can see the need for the special tool rest. It allows you to work on the entire spindle without moving the tool rest. Nor is it necessary to move either rest to get a finished spindle out and a new blank into the lathe. This saves much time and frustration.

The last things to be discussed before actually turning the spindles are the turning and measuring tools you'll use. For turning, you'll want a ¾" deep flute

The steadyrest in place for turning a long, thin spindle.

roughing gouge, a 1½" straight chisel, a ¾"-wide, square-face scraping tool and a parting tool. The parting tool won't be used for parting, only for sizing specific locations on the spindle or leg. At this point, I want to talk briefly about the 1½" chisel. In most cases, this tool, when you receive it from the store or catalog house, has its cutting edge improperly ground. The angle is much too abrupt, and it won't cut properly. Figure 10-2 illustrates the way they usually come (left) and the way they should be ground (right). Notice I have shown the proper grinding to be slightly hollow. They can be ground flat, but the edge will last longer if they're ground hollow. If the surface comes out convex, they won't cut at all. The sharpness of this tool is important, so it's a good idea to hone it frequently while you're using it. There is an easy way to do this if you have a fair-sized flat stone.

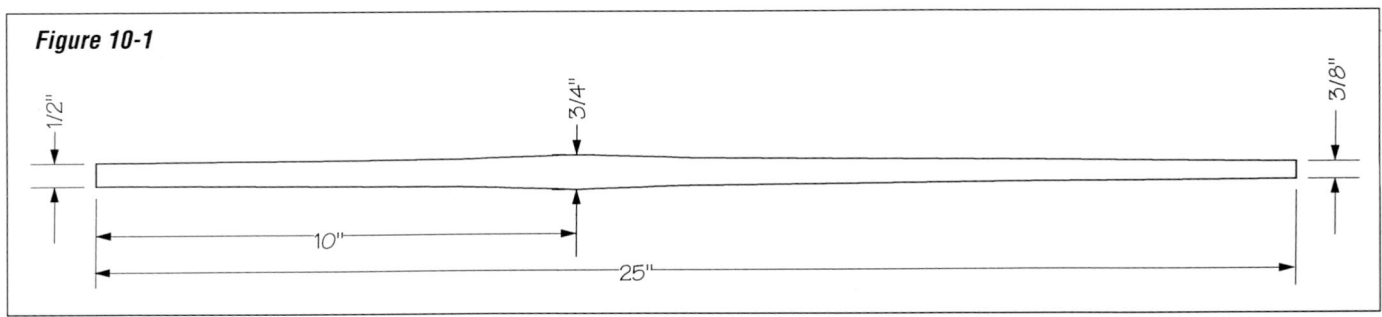

Figure 10-1

½"   ¾"   ⅜"

10"

25"

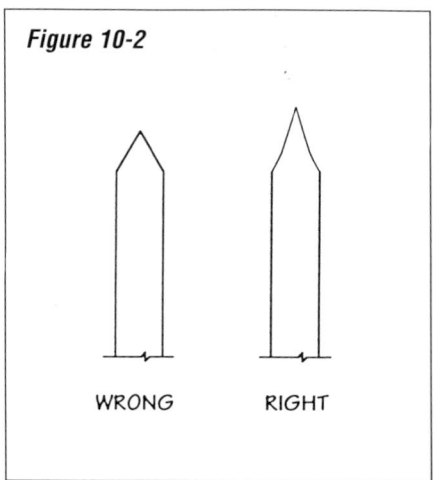

Figure 10-2

WRONG   RIGHT

The easy way to hone the chisel.

The measuring tools.

A spindle blank ready for turning.

Roughing out the center.

It's hard to explain, so I'll just show you a picture of myself doing it. As you can see, you're moving the stone and not the chisel. Stroke it sidewise, across the edge, not up and down.

To do your measuring without constantly resetting calipers, you'll need three ordinary calipers and two vernier calipers. You'll see why as I explain the turning process.

Turning Long, Thin Spindles

As a trial piece, make the spindle shown in Figure 10-1. Use any hardwood you have that will make a blank 1" square by 27" long. This should be straight—not even a slight bow in it. On whichever end you decide will be the top, mark a center point. Put the bottom end into the square mortice in the jig, then bring the tailstock centerpoint up and press it slightly into the mark on the top end. Turn on the lathe and continue to advance the tailstock until it's firmly seated. This

action will also press the blank firmly into the jig. Lock the tailstock so it can't back off. The speed that you run the lathe is important. I've found that running too fast is dangerous, and too slow makes turning difficult and produces a lousy job. My lathe is equipped with a standard four-step pulley set. I've found that the next-to-fastest speed produces the fastest and best job. (Over a period of ten years, I made about 150 spindle-back chairs, each one taking a minimum of ten spindles of varying length. When I first started turning them, it took about thirty to thirty-five minutes per spindle; after I got the hang of it, I cut that down to twenty minutes.) Set the calipers. Of the regular type, set one to ½₂" over ¾"—that's the maximum diameter. Then set one to about ½₂" over ½" and one to ½₂" over ⅜". Of the vernier calipers, set one to exactly ½" and the other to exactly ⅜". These last two dimensions are important because the spindle ends are going into drilled holes. If they're too big,

The handles in the collection shown here are all of the applied type. They are simple in design because my work in general is that way. The three long ones and the short, rectangular one were done on the shaper. The round ones were obviously done on a lathe, and the big square one, which has a round base, was also done on a lathe. The square blank was mounted on a single screw faceplate and the base turned to size. The little square ones were made by ripping a square stick and cutting the pieces to length from it. Decide which is to be the bottom end and drill a ¼" dowel hole about ⅜" deep. Then taper the sides with a paring chisel. Do this by placing the piece on end and holding it firmly with the left thumb, then carefully taper each side the required amount with the paring chisel, making a downward cut. Finish by sanding all edges, except the bottom ones, round. Perhaps I should mention that I almost always use dowels and/or glue to attach applied-type handles.

The little flat handle with the notches at each end has an interesting application. It is clearly shown in the picture. These are drawers in a stereo cabinet. The cabinet doors had to close over them; therefore, the handles could protrude only a little, yet they had to provide a firm grip. The answer was to cut a 2" diameter hole in the drawer front (with a hole saw), then cut the handle to fit as shown. It protrudes barely ¾6" beyond the front of the drawer but has ⅜" of gripping surface to get hold of. Notice that the front edge and both faces of the handle are made slightly concave. This takes the stiffness out of the shape.

There are two other applied-type handles shown in the pictures. Both of these are a bit tricky to make work. As you can see, the one at the top of this page is made up of three parts: the top and bottom posts and the connecting piece that forms the actual handle. None of these pieces is round, neither are they square with one another, although the posts are parallel. The best way to make this is to lay it out full size on paper. This way you can accurately determine the size of the various pieces and the angles involved. The tricky piece is the connecting section, a rectangle with round tenons cut on each end. You must cut each tenon at the same angle but in opposite directions, so that they will go into holes drilled perpendicular to the face of each post. The only way I found to cut those tenons was with a knife. The posts are fastened to the door face with dowels. Use the largest dowel that you can get into the base of the post, and set it into the post about ⅜" to ½". It should go into the door about ½". This will make the handle strong enough to withstand the sideways forces to which it is apt to be subjected.

The handle in the picture at right (center) is quite different. It is made from one piece of wood, the starting block being big enough to encompass the entire

A tricky three-part handle.

A one-piece wood carving.

Simple handles that take careful planning.

An interesting variation of the carved handle.

Handles carved directly into the part.

weak, and without being reinforced, they could snap off with a sideways twist. The answer to this is to mount it with long screws. I used a #8 flat-head wood screw long enough to go through the door and into the handle almost its entire thickness. Drill two body holes in the door and body holes in the posts for half the length of the post; then drill pilot holes to within ⅛" of the face. Apply glue to the base of the posts when you make the installation. (Don't use too much or it will squeeze out the edges and make a mess to clean up.) With this installation technique, you will have a strong handle. The last step in making it comes when the glue has dried. Using sandpaper, feather the flared posts into the door face. Be careful that you don't create a depression in the door face while doing this.

The type of handle that is added on but made to look as if it had been carved from the piece is not difficult to make, but it takes some careful planning. The most important consideration is to have the color and grain pattern of the handle match those of the drawer front or door. The picture shows clearly what I'm talking about. In this piece, the drawers are of different widths, and so are the handles. Also, the handles must line up exactly. The simplest way to do this is to make the drawer fronts from a single board and keep it that way until the handles have been finished. The thickness of the board should be at least ¾"; the width should be whatever is correct for the depth of the drawer; and the length should be longer than the width of the two drawers combined by the about ½₂" plus the kerf of the saw blade you're going to use to cut the fronts apart. Having chosen the face you want to be seen, draw a line across the board at the point where it will be divided, and then cut a groove ¾" wide and ⅜" deep the entire length. Its position in the width is up to you. From the wood you have chosen for the handle, cut a piece slightly longer than the drawer fronts, the width you want the handle to be, and finish the thickness to make a snug fit in the groove. This fit is very important, because when you are through, you don't want the joint to show. Place the piece in the groove, and draw a line on each side at the surface of the drawer fronts and one at the dividing point of the two fronts. Remove the piece and sketch your handle shape on one face. Be sure that each handle is centered in the drawer front to which it belongs. Now, cut out the shape, leaving about ⅟₁₆" above the line in the areas where the handle will be flush with the drawer front. Put the piece in the groove and check to see that the handle placements are correct and that you haven't cut too much away at any point. Glue the piece in the groove. Be careful that you don't use too much glue, and put it mostly in the bottom of the groove.

handle. Draw the shape on the side of the block, and rough saw it out on the band saw or scroll saw. From there, it's just a matter of using a knife, carver's rasps, files and sandpaper to bring it to finished condition. Notice that the posts are narrower than the handle proper, made oval, and flared at the base. The face is concave, and the sides of the handle are convex. The mounting of this one is different also. Because the grain in the posts is parallel to the face, the posts are

From here on it's a matter of careful carving, filing and sanding to get your finished handles. In the areas that will be flush, the easiest way is to use a paring chisel to bring it down flush and then use sandpaper to finish. In the areas of the handles proper, I made the top and bottom surfaces slightly concave (to give a better feel to the handle), then feathered them into the drawer front. The tools I used to do this job were a couple of carver's rasps, for rough shaping; a small, fine-cut, half-round file; a fine-cut, full-round file; and 50, 80 and 150 grit sandpaper. When you have everything finished to your satisfaction, you can then cut the drawer fronts apart and proceed with making the drawers.

An interesting variation of the carved handle is shown at left (top). Here, a handle has been carved from a strip of contrasting wood and then glued to the inner door stiles. Notice that the strip does not extend through the rails. This is important because the rails were designed to be a continuous line across the top and bottom of the doors, thus making the piece look longer and lower.

The last of the three types of handles is the kind that is actually carved into the part itself. The drawers in the breakfront are a good example. For this type, there isn't much explanation to give. You work out your idea and then go ahead and carve it into the wood. As before, the three drawers were made from one board, and the carvings were completed before the piece was cut apart. A word of caution: Be sure your piece is thick enough to let you do what you have in mind. The lower door handles were made by cutting the inner door stiles extra thick, cutting the mortices in the ends, and then carving the thickness to create the handles.

As I said in the beginning, handles can make or break your design. Creating your own will exercise your imagination and expand your skills. Plus, they're a lot of fun to do.

Chapter Thirteen

SMALL PARTS YOU CAN MAKE

W hen building furniture, you always have small parts that are common to many different pieces. Most of these you can buy from hardware stores, craft shops or woodworking catalogs. If you do, you will get a mass-produced item—often in metal—that will detract from the handcrafted impression your work creates.

In this chapter, I'm going to tell you about three small parts that, if you build many of the projects in this book, you will need in considerable number. So, when you make them, don't just make one set. Make several sets and put them aside for the future. You don't have to go out and buy the wood for these; just use small, leftover pieces that you have lying around the shop. If you're like me, you have more of this than you know what to do with but can't bear to throw it away.

The Shelf Support

The first of these is a shelf support. Among the projects are four different cabinets that require this part in varying numbers. Figure 13-1 shows you what one looks like. They are easy to make: a stick ¼" x ¾" x 9" finished on all four sides will make four pairs. Most furniture is made from either dark or light woods; therefore, when making more sets than you need for a given project, make some from each type. In general, I favor having the supports blend with the rest of the cabinet and not stand out. In some instances, however, a sharp contrast can be effective. It's one of those things you decide when you're building the piece.

Start the process by putting your dado head on the table saw set for a ¾" cut. Next, set the height to ½", and clamp an extension fence to your miter gauge extending well beyond the dado head. Stand the stick on edge against the fence, and make a cut ¾" from one end. Move over 1½" and make another cut; again move 1½" and make a cut; and do this a third time. You will now have four notches in your stick, the outside ones ¾" in from the ends and the other two at 1½" intervals. From light cardboard, make a template of the side view of the support. Place the template on the

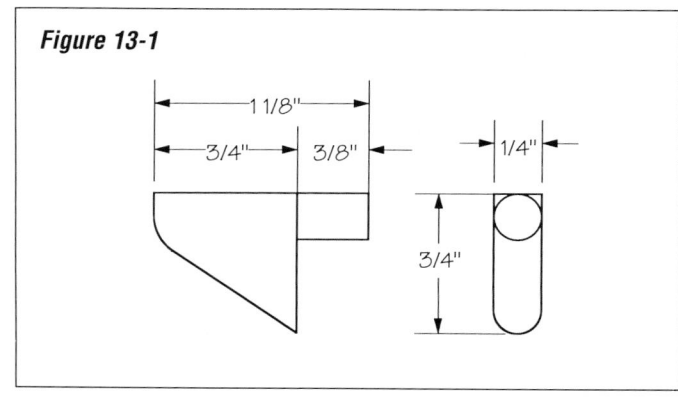

Figure 13-1

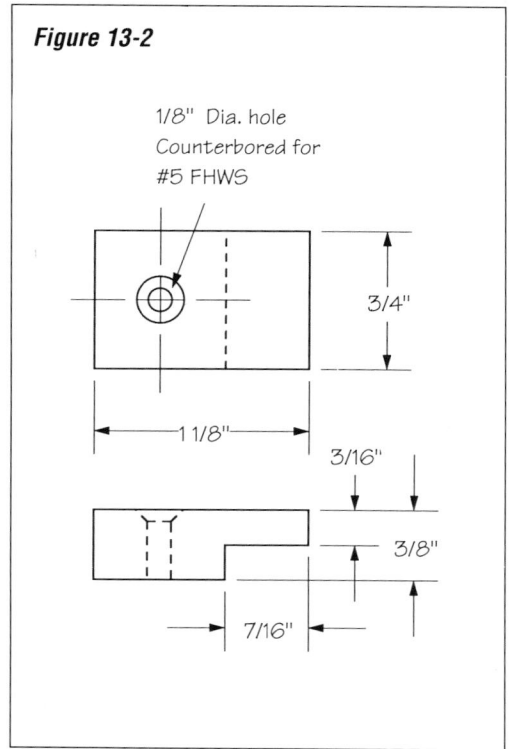

Figure 13-2

1/8" Dia. hole Counterbored for #5 FHWS

flat of the stick at one end and trace it, then flip it over and trace it again. Keep this up until you reach the other end. With a band saw or jigsaw, make the V-cut that outlines the shape of the supports. Cut the pairs apart, not the individual supports—it's easier to work on the body when in pairs than to do each one separately. Using fine files and sandpaper, finish the bodies. Now cut each pair apart; use a very thin-kerf hand saw for this. The last operation is to size the peg section. The most accurate way to do this is to tap it into a ¼" dowel sizer as far as you can, then pull it out and clean off the attached shavings with a sharp knife. Test the peg in a ¼" hole. It should be a snug hand fit and should go in so that the body bears fully on the surrounding surface. Rounding and fitting the peg can be done freehand with a knife, but it's a tedious job, so if you don't have a dowel sizer, now is the time to get one.

The Hold-Down Clip

The second small part, not as glamorous but equally important, is the hold-down clip. This part is used to hold tops on tables and cabinets, and bases on cabinets, as well as to fasten any other place where you have a problem of expansion and contraction between two parts. Because these clips need to be strong and are not generally seen, I make mine from oak, but any strong hardwood would do just as well. Start this one with a stick ⅜" x ¾" x 9" long. Put a ¾" dado head on the saw and set the height at ³⁄₁₆". Use the extension fence, and with the ¾" face down, make the first cut ¾" from one end. Proceed with the subsequent cuts 1½" apart, and you will have four pairs, or eight clips. (Hold-down clips are not necessarily used in pairs.) Mark, drill and counterbore the screw holes as shown in the drawing, then cut the clips apart with that thin-kerf hand saw you used before. Because hold-down clips are used so frequently and seldom less than six on a project, I usually make about three dozen at a time. They keep quite well.

The Wedge

The last of the small parts I'm going to describe is the wedge. For the most part, I have used them to strengthen the bond between chair legs and seats. You will need some if you make either of the two chair projects in the book. It may seem silly to spend time describing how to make such a simple thing as a wedge, but they're tricky to make without a lot of waste. It took me a while to figure out how to do it, so I thought I'd just pass along this know-how. Make some sticks ³⁄₁₆" x 1¼" and cut pieces 1½" long from them. (The surfaces of the sticks can be rough-sawn.) Clamp a block of wood to your workbench tightly enough so that you can drive against it with a mallet without moving it. Place the piece from which you are making the wedge against the block; the 1½" dimension should be perpendicular to the block. Using a 1¼" or wider chisel and the mallet, start about ⅛" from the outer end, and taper the piece into a wedge with the bottom edge about ¹⁄₁₆" to ³⁄₃₂" thick. It should take two or three cuts to do this. In making wedges for the chairs, I often use a contrasting wood for the effect it creates; for example, walnut wedges in maple legs. However, I don't use maple wedges in walnut legs. This looks terrible.

I have described here a rather large wedge, but the same technique can be followed to make smaller ones used for strength and effect through wedged tenons. Page 188 in Ernest Joyce's *Encyclopedia of Furniture Making* has some good drawings of this type of tenon.

Chapter Fourteen

FINISHES—TO EACH HIS OWN

This is a controversial subject and a writer can get into all kinds of trouble because most woodworkers have their own idea of what is the best finish for a piece of furniture. So, I will tell you what I do and why, and describe the road by which I got there.

There is one cardinal principle to which I hold religiously. I never, under any circumstances, use stain. Because different areas of a board have different densities, they will adsorb different amounts of stain, and more stain creates a darker hue than less stain. Also, these areas of different densities do not necessarily follow the grain patterns of the wood. For this reason, stain will muddy the grain patterns, sometimes beyond recognition.

When you talk about a natural finish, you have to know what is meant by the word *natural*. If you apply any clear liquid to a piece of wood, it will come out darker than before. For example, when I want to see what a piece will look like after it has been varnished with a clear varnish, I paint it with clear water. The only difference is that when the water dries, the color returns to that of the raw wood. The only way I have found to keep the color of the raw wood is to finish with nothing but paste wax. The showcase in chapter four was finished in that manner in order to maintain the contrast between heartwood and sapwood that would have been lost if a clear liquid finish had been applied. These are the two types of natural finish, and their use depends on how you wish your piece to look.

I'm sure you know that any liquid finish will raise the grain of the wood— some more, some less, depending on the wood. Therefore, a certain amount of sanding is necessary between coats of all of the finishes I'm about to describe except the straight wax finish. For this one, you need to have a very smooth sanded surface before the first coat is applied.

I have never used a brush-on varnish for finishing. This is not because I have anything against a brushed-on varnish finish. It's because I'm a lousy painter. For this reason, early on I gravitated to the brush-on-and-rub-out type of finish. When I began building furni-

ture professionally, I used Watco's Danish Oil Clear Finish. You brush this on with a generous brush and let it soak for thirty minutes or so and wipe off the excess; then let it dry for twenty-four hours and apply the next coat. It's a good finish even if it does take several days for the smell to dissipate to the point where you can move the piece into a house. The main problem I found with it was that it took a great many coats before I could get even a low-gloss finish. In fact, it required too many coats for the amount of time I could afford.

My next finish was given to me by a fellow furniture maker. This one consisted of a half gallon of boiled linseed oil and a half gallon of turpentine heated together just enough to melt a half pound of beeswax in it. This was allowed to cool before applying. It was a very good finish and provided the amount of sheen I wanted with less than half the coats. It did have, at least for me, one serious drawback. It would water-spot, and alcohol dissolved it, usually leaving a white mark. This drawback was not appreciated by many of my clients.

My third venture in finishes turned out to be the best I ever used. It was DuPont's penetrating varnish. I would be using it today except that the manufacturer quit making it.

That brought me to what I use today, a tung-oil finish that is applied the same as the penetrating varnish and works the same way. However, it doesn't give you the same amount of gloss per coat. This takes six or seven coats, depending on the density of the wood, to get the required sheen. I have found a shortcut, however; a generous first coat of tung-oil finish with extra soaking time, followed by a lighter coat wiped sooner, and that followed by two coats of a good paste wax. I use clear Trewax, recommended to me by a man who specializes in refinishing high-quality, very valuable antiques. But remember, if you want to hold the colors in the raw wood with no darkening, use just the paste wax. A cautionary word: Don't use this on a tabletop where you might have alcohol spills.

Build Fine Furniture

This collection of pieces was chosen so that, whatever your level of crafts-manship, you would find some that would challenge your skill. Your skills should be your guide to the project you choose. Each time you try a new pro-ject, reach out further than on the last one. But not too far. You can't be proud of a piece you clobbered together because you ignored the limitations of your skills. On the other hand, you can be very proud of a piece that shows off the skills you have acquired. If you are an experienced woodworker, you can, of course, build a less challenging piece simply because you like it. You should get satisfaction and pleasure from what you build. After all, that is why you have a hobby in the first place.

GALLERY OF PROJECTS

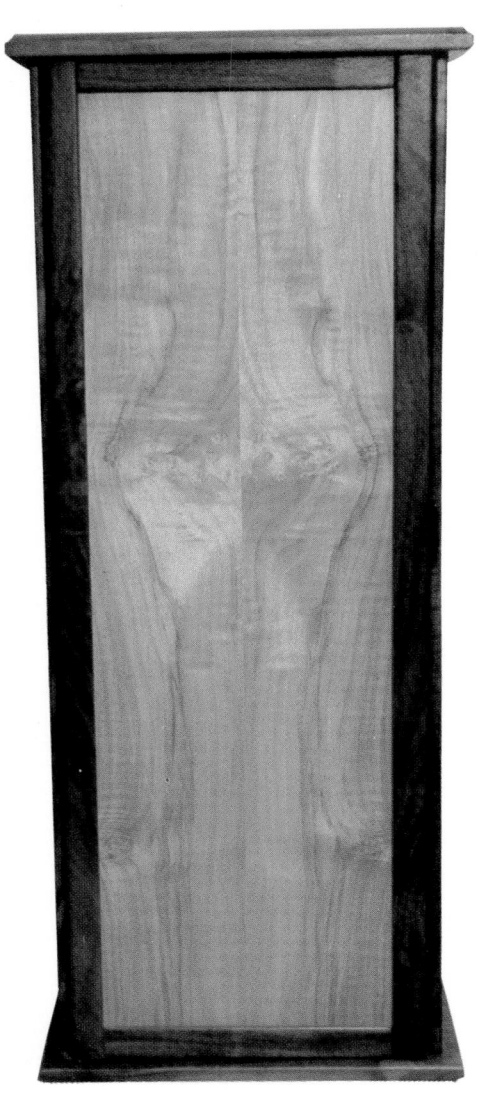

Project One
A SIMPLE CABINET

Project Two
A LITTLE TABLE

Project Three
OUT OF YOUR
IMAGINATION

Project Four
A HANDSOME CABINET

Project Five

SHOW OFF YOUR TREASURES

Project Six

HAVE A SEAT

Project Seven

WRITE A LETTER

Project Eight

AN INTERESTING
COFFEE TABLE

Project Nine

ABOUT A
DINING TABLE

Project Ten

A CHAIR FOR
ALL REASONS

Project Eleven

THAT'S
ENTERTAINMENT

A SIMPLE CABINET

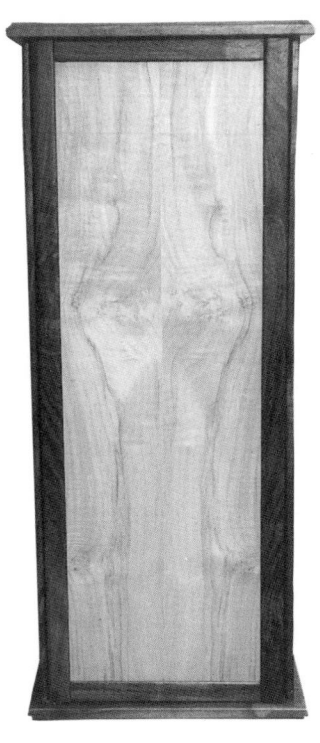

This cabinet was created to display the beauty of wood. As I have said many times, wood has great beauty in and of itself. If you are careful in choosing the wood for this piece, you can create a work of art as beautiful as anything done by a sculptor or painter. The centerpiece of the cabinet is the door panel. After discovering the wood in the course of some other work, I designed the cabinet around it. See page 149 for a cutting list for this project.

You can do the same. The dimensions in the drawings are not fixed; they can be altered to accommodate whatever you find for your panel. Find the wood, determine its size, and then adjust all the other dimensions to match. Some of the most interesting pictures can be created by the book-matching technique. That is how my panel was created. The wood you choose for the rest of the cabinet should be in sharp contrast to that of the panel. The two sides should have as interesting a grain pattern as you can find. One way to do this is to find the pattern you want in a 2"-thick piece and resaw it to make the two ¾" sides. Then both sides will have approximately the same pattern.

The most difficult part of this project will be finding the right wood. After that it's pretty straightforward cabinetry. There are, however, a couple of interesting departures from the ordinary: the door hinge, and the arrangement for opening the door. Before going farther it would be a good idea to study the exploded assembly drawing. It will give you a better understanding of how the various parts I'm going to talk about fit into the completed cabinet. Just follow the circled letters.

Drawing 1-1. Exploded view.

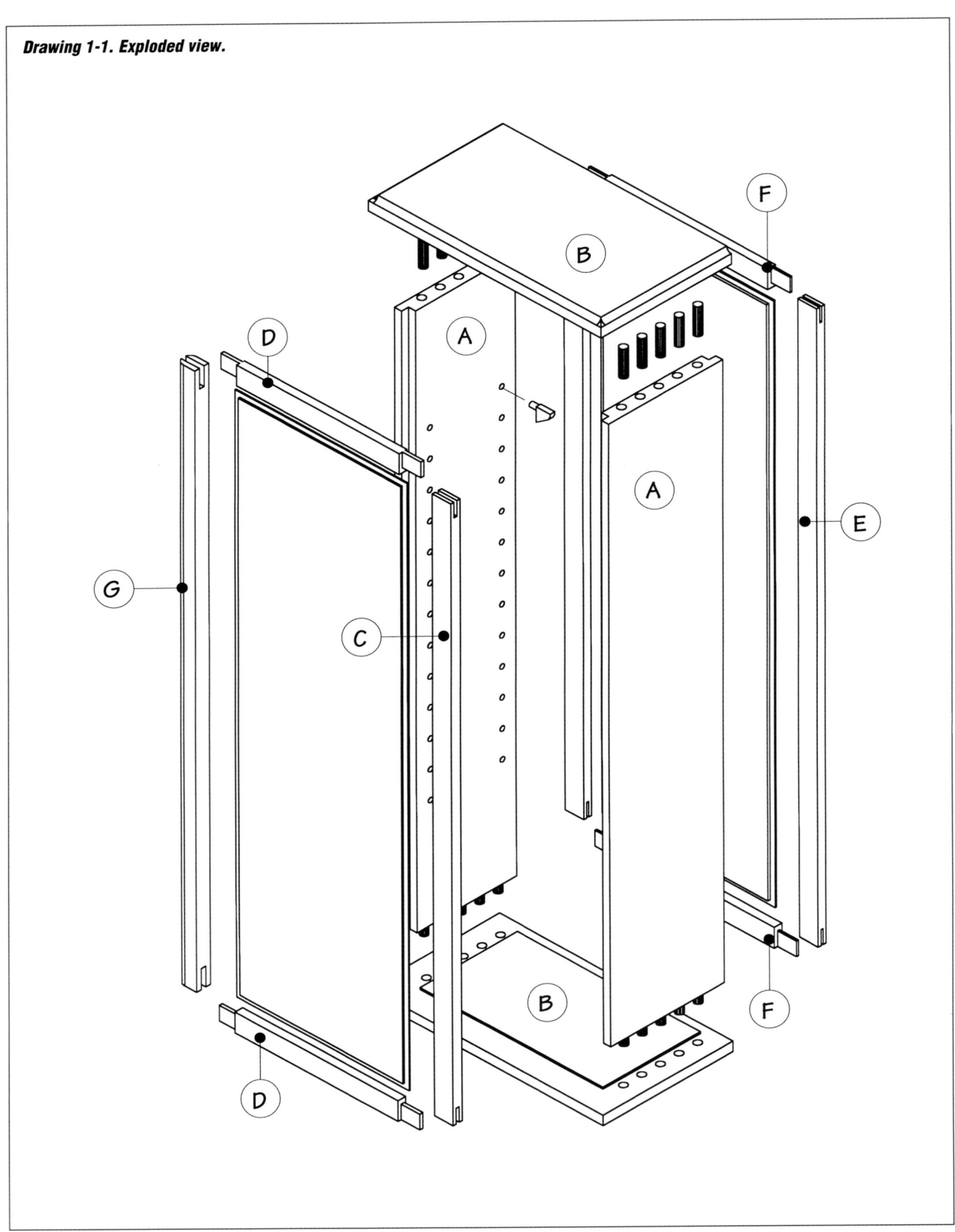

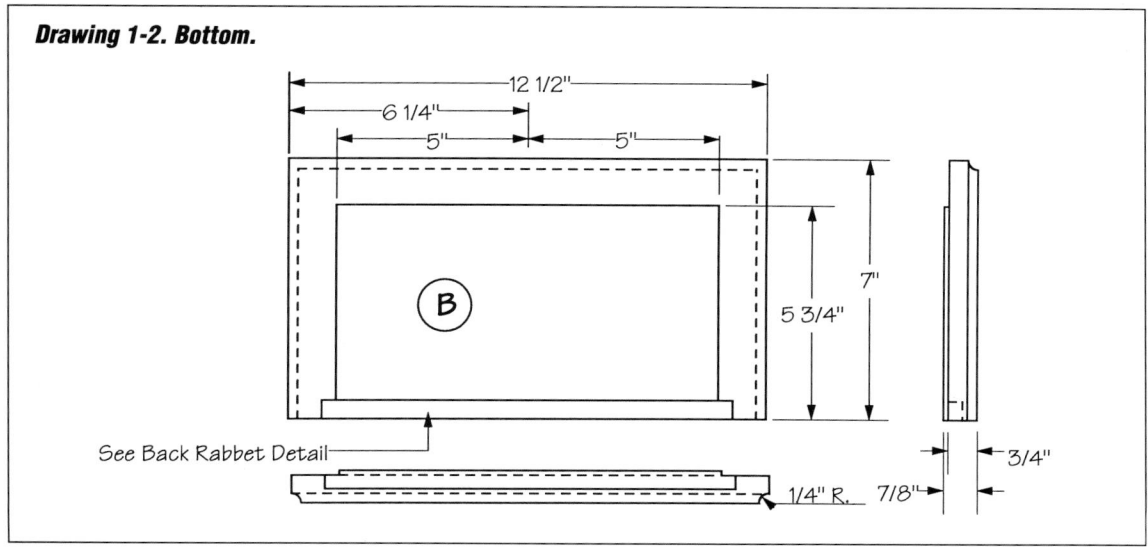

Drawing 1-2. Bottom.

12 1/2"
6 1/4"
5"
5"
B
7"
5 3/4"
See Back Rabbet Detail
3/4"
1/4" R. 7/8"

The Case

The two most important parts of this cabinet are the top and the bottom. If they're not done correctly you will never be able to square up the case. The key here is the dimensions of the area left after the rabbets have been cut. They must be exactly the same on both parts because the shoulder of the side rabbets positions the sides and the shoulder of the front rabbets positions the door. (See Drawing 1-2.)

Cut the parts to their overall sizes and joint the top and bottom faces smooth. The rabbets are best cut on the table saw. Use a high-auxiliary fence and a planer blade. Set the fence at ¾" from the inside of the blade and the blade height at 1¼". Test the setup with a piece of scrap. Run the side rabbets first and then the front. If you've been careful to cut both top and bottom to the same overall dimensions, the result will be right. Check it to be sure, and if there is a discrepancy, correct it now. Cut the molded edges on both pieces. Use a ¼"-cove router bit. One having a ball-bearing guide is better than one with a pin guide because, in my experience, the pin guide will invariably leave marks that you have to sand out later.

After you've made your test run, cut the sides to size and mark which will be the inside faces as well as the front and top edges. This is important, because the front and rear rabbets are different, and if you get them mixed up, you'll be in trouble. Cut the rabbets and then lay out and drill the shelf support hole pattern as shown. (See Drawing 1-3.) The case is held together with dowel joints. (See Drawing 1-4.) To get the necessary accuracy and proper positioning of the parts for this joint, it is best to use the dowel-drilling jig described in chapter six. Be sure it is marked as shown on page 62 so that you won't get confused when using it. The positioning of the jig on the pieces

is very important. Again mark the sides with chalk to indicate the inside face and the top, bottom and back edges. Place the jig on the top edge of one side with the gauging piece at the back and the side of the jig flush with the inside face of the side. Push two #6 finishing nails through the small holes, and tap them into the side far enough to hold the jig firmly in place.

Using a hand electric drill and a ⅜"-brad-point drill bit, drill all five holes ¾" deep. Remove the jig, pull the nails completely out, and push them in from the other side. Position the jig on the matching face of the top, with the gauging piece at the back, and with the same face as was to the inside of the side tight against the shoulder of the rabbet. Tap the nails home to hold the jig in place, and with your ⅜" drill bit in the drill press, drill all the holes ½" deep. Now do the other three joints the same way. It is very important that you follow this positioning procedure carefully; otherwise the holes in the top or bottom and the sides won't match.

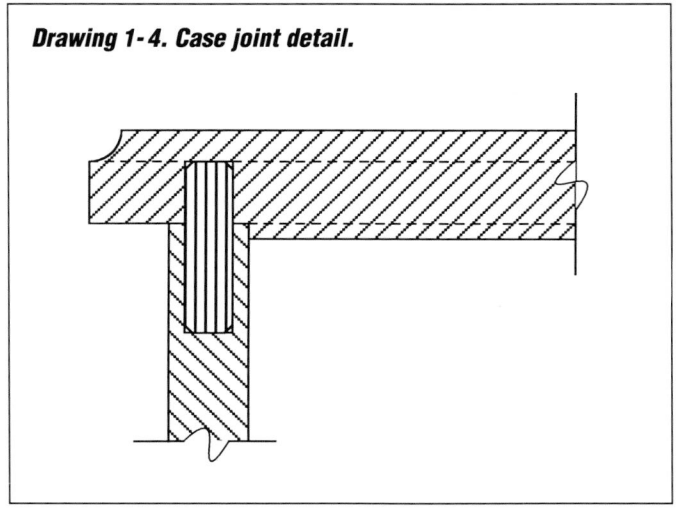

Drawing 1-4. Case joint detail.

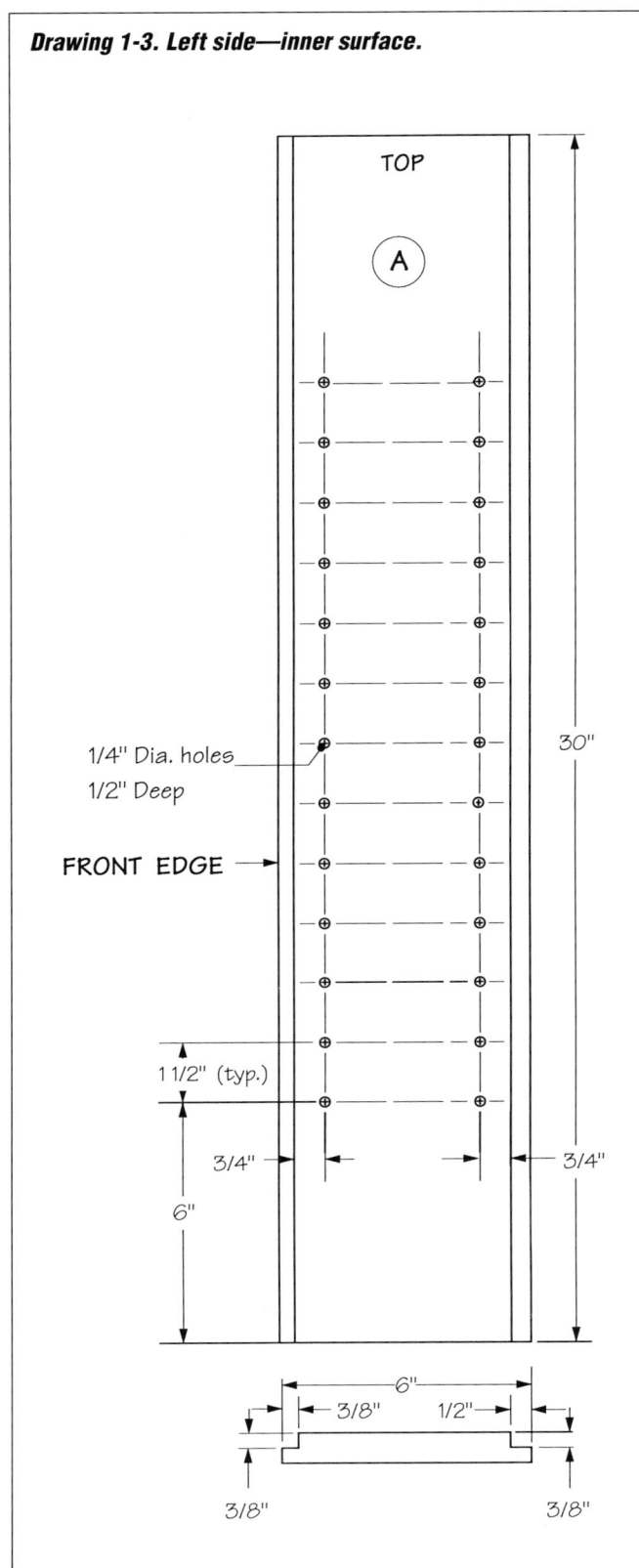

Drawing 1-3. Left side—inner surface.

TOP

(A)

1/4" Dia. holes
1/2" Deep

FRONT EDGE →

30"

1 1/2" (typ.)

3/4"

3/4"

6"

6"

3/8"   1/2"

3/8"   3/8"

Using the jig to drill the dowel holes in the sides with a hand drill.

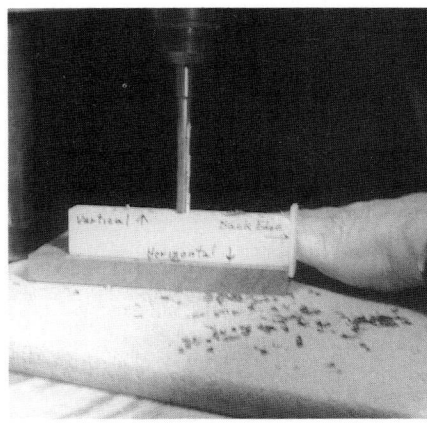

Jig used with the drill press to drill dowel holes in top and bottom.

It is also important to finish drilling each joint before going on to the next one. In other words, don't drill all the holes in the sides and then go back and do the top and bottom. You're very apt to get confused, and then the holes won't match.

Cut twenty dowels 1⅜₆" long. Slightly taper each end, and be sure to put one or two air-escape grooves down the sides of each. They should be a firm, hand-push fit into their holes. Now make a dry (no-glue) assembly of the case, putting the dowels first into the top and bottom. Push them in until they bottom. Using a depth gauge, check the amount of each dowel protruding against the depth of the hole it is to go into. If one is too long, trim the dowel. Assemble the sides to the top first and then to the bottom. Be sure everything fits properly and the two parts of each joint go together completely. Square the case (if you can't do this, make adjustments until you can), and turning to the back, mark the limits of the rabbet in the top and bottom that match the ones in the sides. The dimensions of this rabbet are ½" by ½". (See Drawing 1-5.)

At this point, it is necessary to discuss the hinge system used in the cabinet. The top part is simple, a ⅛"-diameter steel pin pressed into a hole drilled in the top edge of the door, as shown in the hinge detail. The

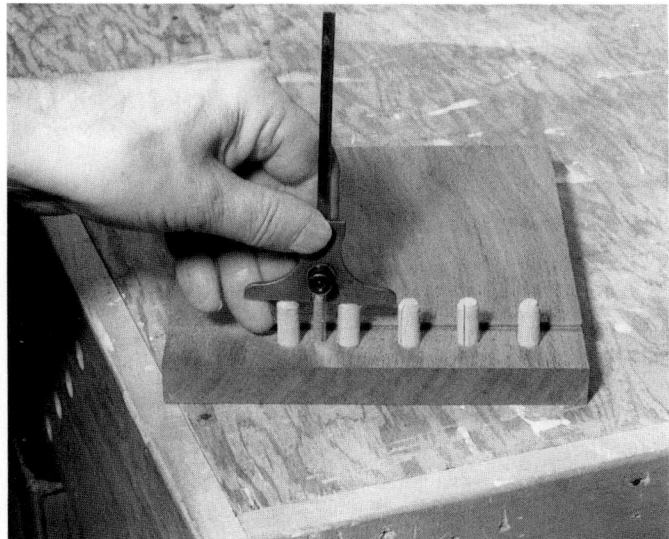

Checking dowel length against hole depth.

Locating the rear rabbet in the bottom.

Drawing 1-5. Top and bottom back rabbet.

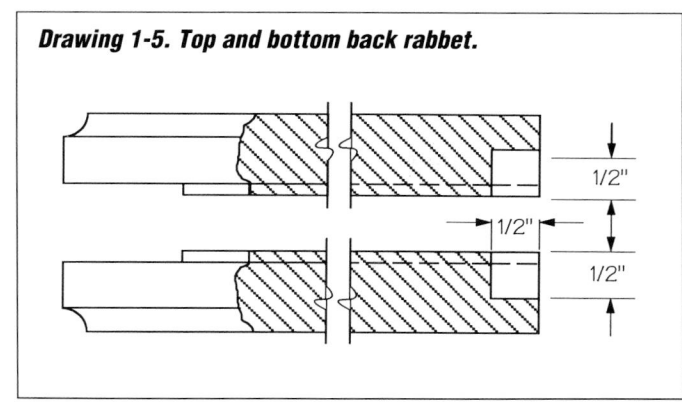

1/2"

1/2"

1/2"

Drawing 1-6. Hinge detail.

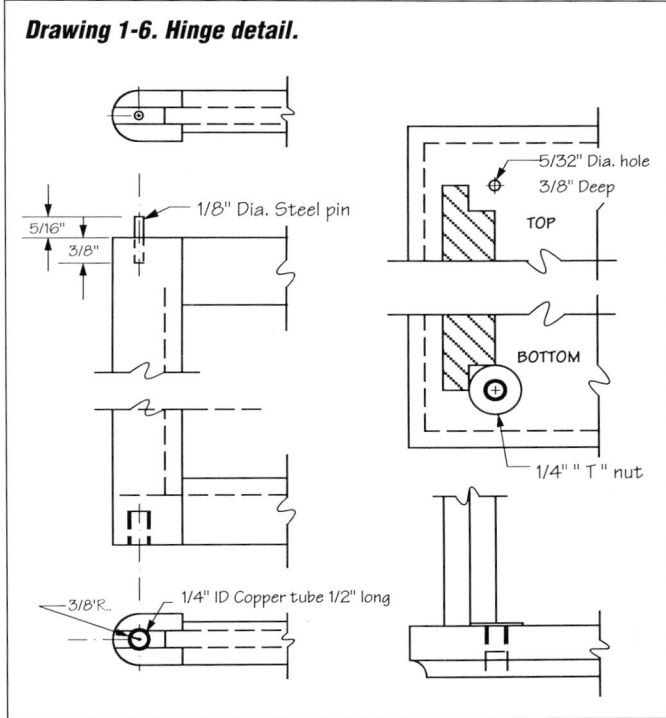

5/32" Dia. hole
3/8" Deep

TOP

BOTTOM

1/4" "T" nut

1/8" Dia. Steel pin

5/16"

3/8"

3/8'R

1/4" ID Copper tube 1/2" long

bottom is the interesting part. It consists of three pieces: a ¼" T-nut, a short piece of ¼" ID copper tubing, and a 1" x ¼" 20-steel bolt with the head cut off. After removing the head of the bolt with a hacksaw, file a sharp point on one end (be sure the point is centered), and cut a slot big enough to take the blade of a small screw driver, in the other. Screw the bolt, pointed end first, into the T-nut from the bottom. Hold the T-nut, face down, in position, as shown in the hinge detail, and carefully screw the bolt into the nut until the point makes a distinct mark on the case bottom. Do the same on the top. (See Drawing 1-6.)

Take the case apart and cut the top and bottom rabbets with a router, then square the corners with a chisel. Drill the hinge holes just marked, ⁵⁄₁₆" in the bottom and ⁵⁄₃₂" in the top. Notice that the top hole does not go through, while the bottom hole does. Use a brad-point

drill for the larger one so that it won't wander from the mark. Do your finish sanding of these four parts now. It's much easier than after you've glued them together, which you can do after sanding. Do it as you did dry, putting the dowels in the top and bottom first and making sure they bottom. Put glue only in the top third of the holes. Do not put any glue on the faces of the joints. When you have the dowels in the top and bottom and before you put glue in the side holes, again check length against hole depth on each one, and trim any dowel that's too long. Then finish the assembly. Square the case, clamp it that way if necessary, and set it aside to dry. When it is dry, install the T-nut. It goes in from the top so that the flat head will act as a bearing on which the door can swing. Be careful doing this: take it easy, but be sure that it goes in all the way.

Parts for the bottom hinge.

Use T-nut and bolt to mark hinge hole locations.

T-nut in place.

Drawing 1-7. Door.

Finger Recess

29 15/16"

1"

1"

1"

10 3/4"

3/4"

5/8"

Bottom view

The Door

The door is simple to construct, but there are a couple of details that require attention. The first is that the stiles extend past the rails, and the rails are thinner than the stiles. However, they are not cut thinner until the mortice-and-tenon joints have been cut and the door fitted together. The second detail is the installation of the hinge system. I'll take that up after I give instructions for the door.

The first thing to do is to measure the door opening in the case. Do not build the door to the overall measurements on the drawings. The door must fit snugly into the front rabbets on the sides and should be ¹⁄₁₆" shorter than the top-to-bottom opening. Using ¾" x 1" stock, cut the pieces accordingly. (Also cut a piece about 10" long for test cuts.) Mark what is to be the outside edge of each piece, and then cut a ¼" x ¼" groove in the exact center of the inside edges. Do this on the table saw using a dado blade and the high auxiliary fence on the rip fence. Measure the distance from the bottom of the groove to the outside edge, and raise the dado head that distance above the table. Now cut through the mortices in the ends of the stiles. The tenons should be cut on the rails in the manner described in chapter eight.

Put the frame together and see that it fits the opening. Measure the panel opening to the bottom of the grooves, and then set the frame aside for the moment. (See Drawing 1-7.)

We come now to the door panel. As I said in the beginning, this is the centerpiece of the cabinet. I hope you chose the wood for it and designed your cabinet around it when you began the project. It will finish ¼" thick, and the glued-up dimensions should be slightly larger than the measurements you took from the door frame. Cut it and glue it up now, and while it's drying, there are a couple of things you can do. First, number the joints in the door frame and mark what will be the inner face of each part. Then rip the rails to ¹⁄₃₂" over ⅝"

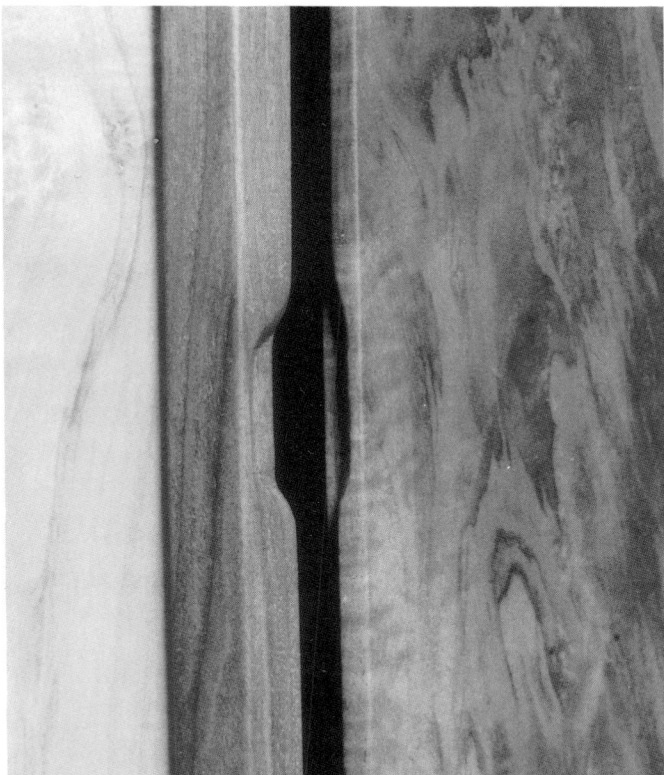

The door-opening recess carved half in the door and half in the side.

thick, taking the cut off the outside face. Lightly joint this cut face. Slightly round (¹⁄₁₆″ R) the inside edges of the outer faces of both rails and stiles. Put the frame back together, and again fit it to the opening.

The panel should be dry now, so cut it to size. Make it ¹⁄₁₆″ shorter and ³⁄₃₂″ to ⅛″ narrower than the opening. It should slide easily in the grooves. If it's too tight, take some off the panel rather than trying to widen the grooves. Having done this, assemble the entire door dry and see that everything fits, that the joints go home tightly, and that the assembly is square. Again fit it to the opening. When you are satisfied that all is well, glue it together. Remember, in gluing an open-end mortice-and-tenon joint, put the tenon in the mortice from the top down, and always put the glue in the mortice, never on the tenon. Use the glue sparingly, and put it in the first third of the opening so that the tenon will wipe it down over the rest of the joint when you put it together. This way, you won't have a lot of excess glue to clean up. If some glue does squeeze out of the joint, don't try to wipe it up at this time. Wait until it dries and then clean it up with a sharp chisel. Do not put any glue between the panel and the frame. The panel must float free in the frame, or you will run into trouble with expansion and contraction. Finally, be sure everything is tight and square. If it takes clamps to hold it that way, use them.

Drawing 1-8. Back panel.

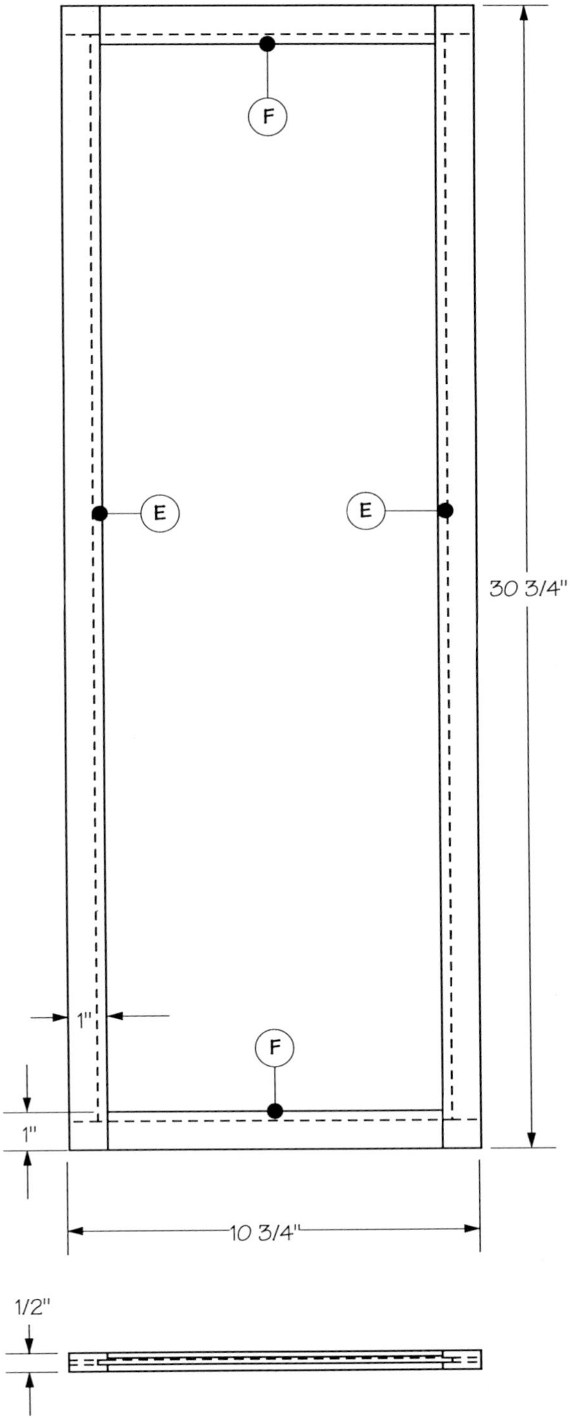

30 3/4"

1"

1"

10 3/4"

1/2"

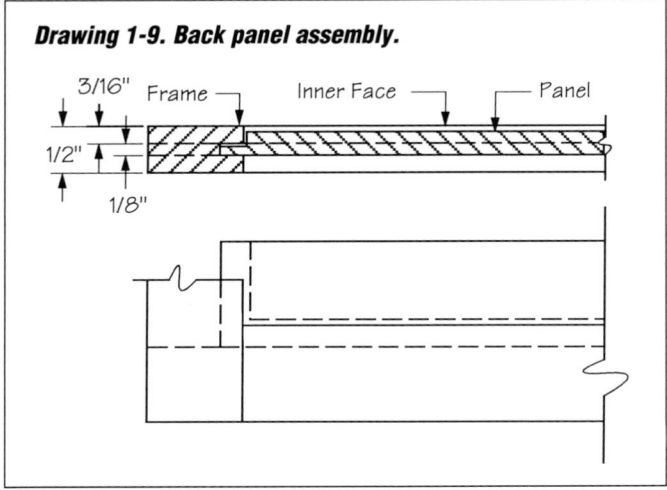

Drawing 1-9. Back panel assembly.

3/16" — Frame — Inner Face — Panel
1/2"
1/8"

The holes for the hinge parts must be absolutely parallel to the vertical surfaces of the stile. The diameter of the hole in the bottom edge should be such that the short length of copper tubing fits with a hand push or a gentle hammer tap. The diameter of the top hole is shown in the hinge detail. (Refer again to Drawing 1-6.) The location of these holes must match exactly if the door is to sit and swing properly. The best way to make sure of this is to locate the centers with a marking gauge. With the hinge holes drilled, you can round off the back edge. A ⅜" round-over-router bit does this just fine. Finally, push or tap the copper tube and the steel pin in place. Thread the bolt into the T-nut from the bottom; then install the door by sliding the pin into its hole at a slight angle (that's why the hole is a bit oversize). When the bottom is moved into position, screw the bolt into the copper tubing. Try the door to see that it opens and closes smoothly. If it doesn't, trim it where necessary until it does. The door can be easily removed by simply unscrewing the bolt until the bottom will slide out. Install a ¼" bullet catch under the door. Mount it in the center of the frame about ½" from the outer edge.

The door is opened by a hidden-finger recess, half of which is cut in the edge of the door and half in the side of the cabinet. The picture shows this better than I can explain it. (See Drawing 1-7.) Take the door off to make the recess. I've found that the best tool for this work is a small wood-carver's gouge followed by #50 sandpaper for final shaping and finer sandpaper for finishing.

The Back

The back of this cabinet is a complete, framed panel. (See Drawing 1-8.) The reason for this is that this cabinet is going to hang from the back panel, and thus more strength is needed in that area. It is made in the same manner as the door with a couple of exceptions. Since the frame thickness is ½" instead of ¾", the groove in it for the panel is ⅛" wide x ¼" deep. Because of this, the tenons are ⅛" thick instead of ¼". Both stiles and rails are finished to ½" thickness. Other than this, the back frame is made in the same manner as the door frame. As in making the door, get your overall frame size from the cabinet and not from the drawing.

The panel can be glued up from wood similar to that used in the case. Since it will not be seen except when someone opens the cabinet, the grain pattern is not important. Glue up the panel using ¼"-thick material, and size it as you did the door panel. Rabbet the edges to make an easily sliding fit in the ⅛"-wide groove. The rabbeted face should be inside the cabinet. (See Drawing 1-9.) The assembly should be fastened in place with #6 x 1" flat-head brass wood screws. Use two each on top and bottom, and four on each side. If this seems excessive, remember that the entire cabinet is going to hang from this panel assembly. To provide for this, drill two ³⁄₁₆" diameter holes in the top rail, 1½" from the ends and ½" from the top edge. If you are going to hang it with #8 x 1½" flat-head wood screws into plastic expansion shields, counterbore the holes. If you are going to hang it with Molly anchors, skip the counterbore.

The Shelves and Shelf Supports

The number of shelves you have depends on you and what you plan to store. They should be made from the same wood as the case, ¼" thick and ¹⁄₁₆" shorter and narrower than the free dimensions inside the cabinet. As for the shelf supports, use the wood ones that I described in chapter thirteen. If you happen to be a pipe smoker, you can fit out the inside to hold your pipes.

And now it's ready for finishing. If you have your own finishing system, use it. If not, you can pick one of the schedules I described in chapter fourteen. Above all, don't use any stain. If you have taken my suggestions in choosing the wood for this cabinet, you will have a lovely piece of art. Hang it in a prominent place and accept the accolades of friends and guests who will see it.

A LITTLE TABLE

Some years ago, while I was still making furniture, a young lady came to me and asked me to make her a pair of small tables. She wanted them to be simple, with a delicate air, like a ballet dancer. This is the table I designed and made for her. The pair graces her living room, at either end of the couch, and elicit admiring comments from her friends. This piece can do the same for you. To capture the right feeling, it should be made from a light-colored wood: use western maple or perhaps alder if you live in the West; maple or birch finished natural if you're an Easterner. The top should have an interesting and distinct grain pattern. A dark wood will look heavy and spoil the delicate air. See page 149 for a cutting list for this project.

This really is an easy piece to make. One look at the drawings will tell you that. It consists of four legs, two side rails, two end rails and a top. The legs start as 1½"

square x 23¾" long. Joint two adjacent faces. All faces must be square with each other. The side rails start as ¹³⁄₁₆" x 2¼" x 22⅝" long. (See Drawing 2-2.) Joint the two ¹³⁄₁₆" faces and one 2¼" face. Again, make sure all faces are square with each other. The end rails start as ¹³⁄₁₆" x 2¼" x 11¾" long. (See Drawing 2-3.) Joint these the same as the side rails. All these faces must be square with each other, too. Do not, at this time, lay out or cut the shapes of any of the parts.

Establish, by marking with chalk, that the jointed 2¼" face of all the rails will be the inside face. Now measuring from this face, lay out and cut the tenons on all the rails as shown in the drawings. Do not now cut the 45° angle. The tenons must not exceed ¹³⁄₁₆" in length, but they can be a bit shorter. The distance between the tenons does not have to match the drawing exactly, but it must be exactly the same for each pair. Matching the

Drawing 2-1. The assembled table.

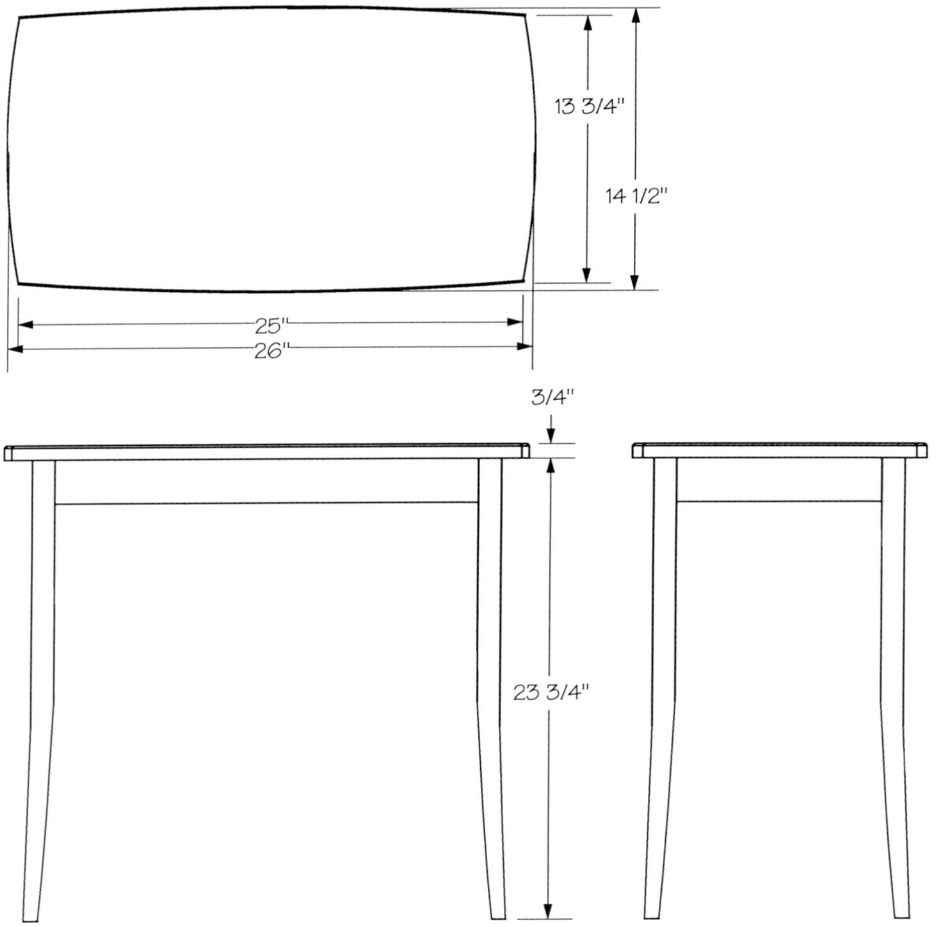
13 3/4"
14 1/2"
25"
26"
3/4"
23 3/4"

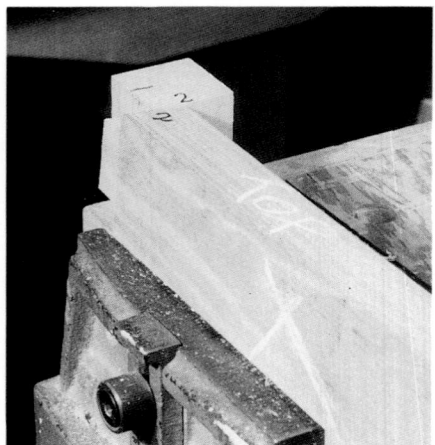

Matching and marking legs and rails.

two pairs back to back, establish which edge is to be the top, and mark it. Set the rails aside.

On the leg pieces, the corner common to the two jointed faces will be the inside corner. Assemble the legs in square based on this. On the end that is to be the top, mark the mating faces in a clockwise direction from one to eight. Now decide where the rails are to go and mark, on the top face at each end, the number of the leg face that it will mate with. The mortices go in the jointed faces. Mark, with a sharp knife, the top and bottom lines of each mortice by placing the tenon on the leg with the top of the rail and the top of the leg flush with each other. Measuring from the inside corner, locate, according to the drawing, the inner vertical line of the mortice, and after measuring the thickness of your tenon, locate the outer vertical line. Notice that you do not locate the horizontal lines or the outer ver-

Drawing 2-2. The side rails.

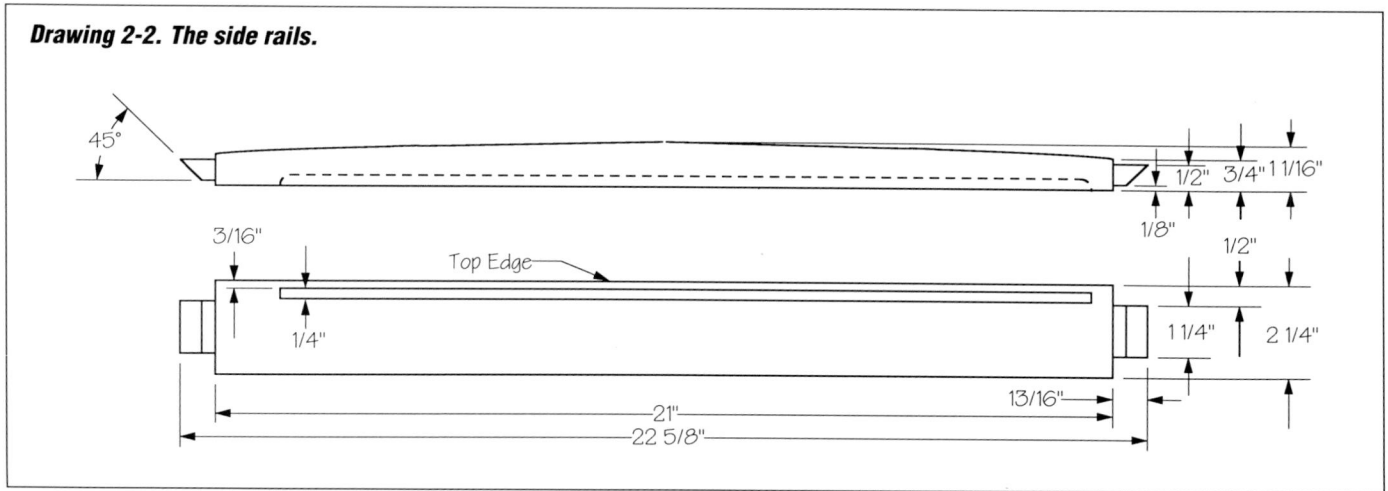

tical line of the mortice from the drawing, but from your tenon. This is very important for a good fit. (See Drawing 2-4 for detail.)

When you have laid out all eight mortices, cut them. If you look at the detail drawing of the mortices, you will see that it is very important that they do not exceed ⅞" in depth. I've found that the easiest way to cut a mortice is to drill out the main waste and then clean up the sides to the lines with a chisel. If you use a spur bit in a drill press with a depth gauge, you can be sure that you won't exceed the ⅞" depth. Set your gauge so that the cutting edge of the bit, not the point of the spur, gives you your depth. It is also important that the sides of the mortice be perpendicular with the

face. I use a depth gauge as a square to accomplish this.

As you fit each tenon to its mortice, draw a line with a sharp pencil on the face of the tenon that shows through the opposing mortice. This is the line to which you cut the 45° angle on the tenon. Be sure, when you make this mark, that you have the tenon in the right way, because if you cut the angle backwards, you'll have to throw the rail away and start over. When the mortice and tenon have been properly fitted (be sure both tenons in each leg go home together), there will be ¹⁄₁₆" between the bottom of the tenon and the bottom of the mortice. (I will explain it when we do the final gluing.)

Now is a good time to route the groove shown on

Drawing 2-3. The end rails.

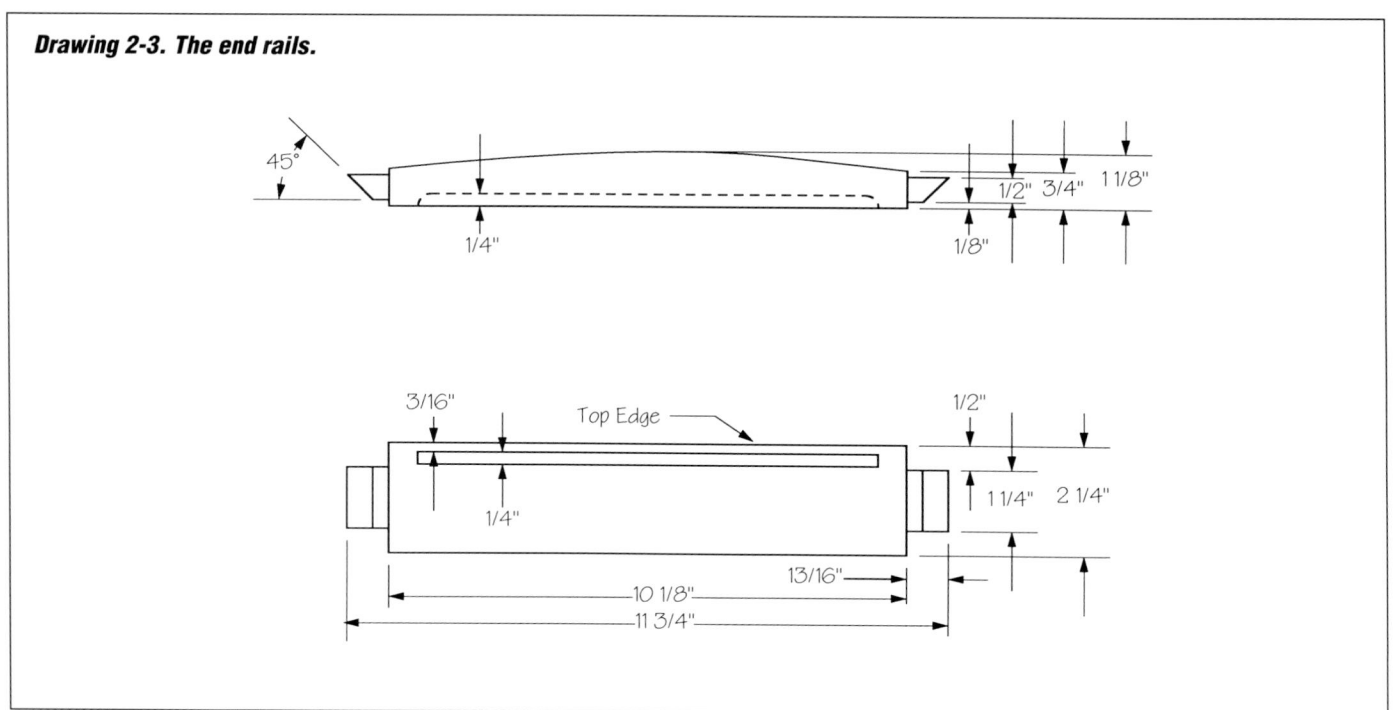

Mark the outlines of the mortice from the tenon.

The depth gauge is an easy way to square up the side of the mortice.

Marking for the 45°-angle cut on the tenons.

the inside face of the rails. The purpose of this groove is to receive the hold-down clips that will hold the top in place. Before going any further, it's a good idea to assemble all the pieces and check that they fit together tightly and that the assembled structure is square in all directions. Putting the parts together in this manner is the only way you can check for interference between the tenon ends in the right-angle mortices. This is your last chance to make adjustments easily, because the next step is to shape the pieces, and once that is done, some of the surfaces will no longer be square or flat.

The easiest way to mark the shapes on the pieces is from templates. (See Drawing 2-5.) Even though you may never use them again, templates are better than making the layout on the piece because you're work-

ing on a flat piece of cardboard. Also, with a template, the pieces on which they are used will all be the same shape. For best results, the cardboard should be about the thickness of the back of a scratch pad. The curve of the leg is away from the inside corner, so place the template on the leg with the template's back edge against the inside corner and its top flush with the top of the leg. Now draw the shape. Bandsaw to this shape. Do this for all four legs. Now place the template on the fully sawn face, being careful to get the curve in the right direction, and draw the lines. Take great care with these markings. It's easy to get confused, and if you do, the best that will happen is that the leg will curve inward, and the worst is that you will cross the curve cuts and destroy the leg entirely.

Place the rail templates on the top edge of the rails as indicated in the drawings. When bandsawing this shape, I found that it's best to do it in two cuts, from the center in opposite directions. At the ends, the cut is at an angle to and very close to the tenon. Starting the cut at this point, you might encounter interference with the tenon.

Clean up and smooth all the sawn faces with a spokeshave followed by sanding, beginning with 80 grit paper. In fact, if your spokeshave is sharp and you're careful with it, you can bypass the 80 grit and go right to 150. When sanding the legs, go very lightly around the mortices so as not to alter the flatness of the surfaces. On the rails, leave the top corner sharp, but put a small radius (⅛" would be fine) on the bottom corner. On the legs, put a ⅛" radius on all vertical corners. Put a ¹⁄₁₆" bevel on all four horizontal edges at the foot. This gives a nice finished look to them. Leave the top edges sharp.

Now you're ready to assemble the parts for a final check before gluing. Be sure everything fits as it should. See that the rails fit tightly and squarely against the legs when all the parts are assembled. This

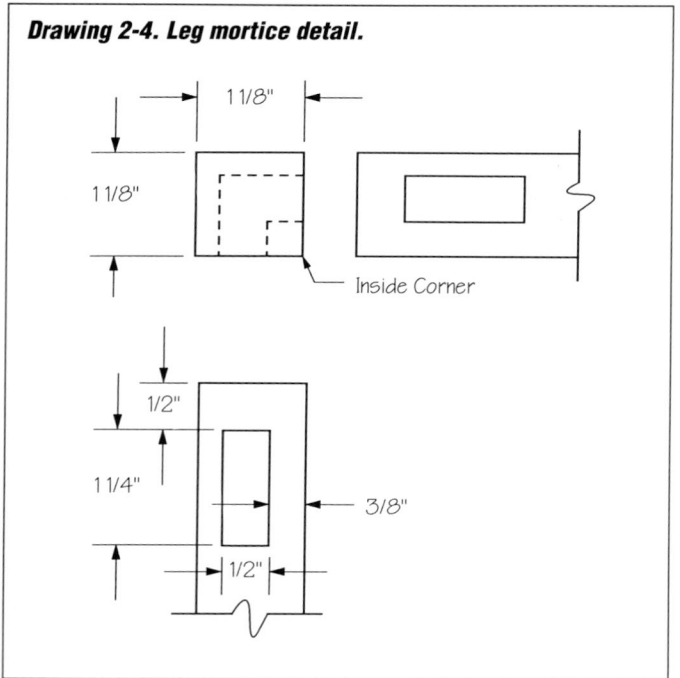

Drawing 2-4. Leg mortice detail.

1 1/8"

1 1/8"

Inside Corner

1/2"

1 1/4"

3/8"

1/2"

is your last chance to check for interference in the joints. When you are satisfied that all is well, glue the legs to the end rails first. Put the pieces together, and use a bar clamp to hold them. See that the legs are square with the rail. Look in the side rail mortice and make sure that there isn't any excess glue where it will interfere with the side rail going home. To avoid this, follow the gluing practice I outlined in chapter nine. If you've put in way too much on the first joint, it will have to be cleaned out. Too much in the second joint will either squirt out or form a block and not allow the joint to go home. If it squirts out, don't wipe it up; let it dry and then clean it up with a sharp chisel. Wiping it will just drive it into the pores of the wood and you'll never get it out. When the end assemblies have dried, assemble them to the side rails in the same manner, and the base will be done.

While you're waiting for those end assemblies to dry, you can glue up the top. Depending on your equipment, you can make it with two, three or four boards. As I said at the beginning, the appearance of the top is important, so try to find wood with an interesting grain pattern. If you could find a 2"-thick board 8" wide with a pattern that would make an interesting book-match, rip it down the middle into two 4" pieces, resaw these, and then lay them open like a book and glue the four pieces together. Make the glued-up panel slightly larger than the finished top. Since all the sides will have a slight curve, the best way to lay it out is to draw end-to-end and side-to-side centerlines and work from them. Here's an easy way to draw those curved edge lines. Cut a stick about ⅛" x ⅝" and about 6" longer than the length of the top. Clamp small blocks so that a corner is positioned at a corner of the top. Now place the stick on edge and against the blocks, and with your finger on the centerline, pull the stick into position at the center. Holding it there, draw your line. When the layout is complete, bandsaw the shape, then clean up and smooth the edges. When you have as slight a curve as these are, I've found that a smooth plane works better than a spokeshave. You can get a smoother curve with it.

Put a slight radius on the bottom edge and about ⅛" bevel on the top edge. Both of these operations should be done with a spokeshave. On the ends, you're cutting across the grain, so be sure that your spokeshave is sharp; otherwise you'll get tearing that will be hard to get rid of.

You will need eight hold-down clips. (You made them in chapter thirteen.) Place the top, upside down, on the bench (be sure to protect it with padding), and center the base on it. Mark all four corners with a pencil. Place three clips on each side and one at each end, put the screws in them (#5 x ⅝" flat head brass), and tap them to make marks. Remove the clips and the

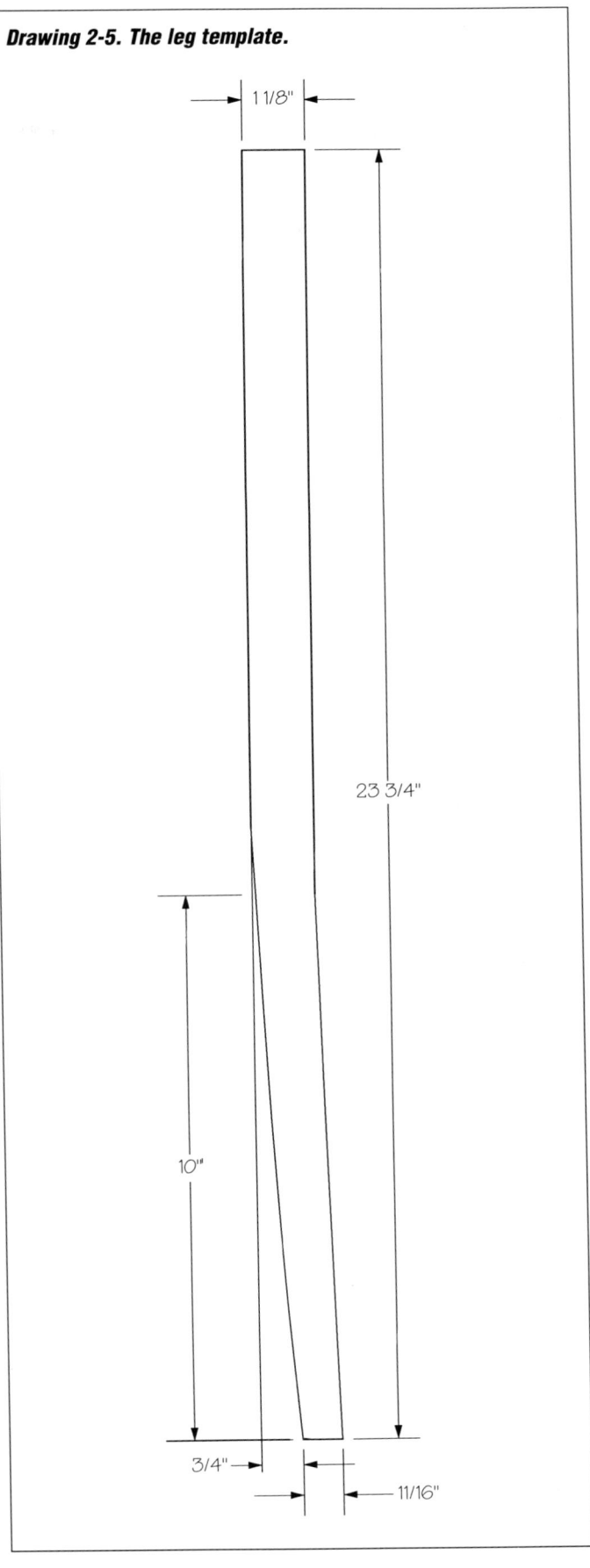

Drawing 2-5. The leg template.

1 1/8"

23 3/4"

10"

3/4"

11/16"

Place the template on the leg with its back edge against the inside corner, and draw the shape.

Place the template on the fully sawn face. Be careful to get the curve in the right direction. Draw the lines.

An easy way to draw the curved edges on the top.

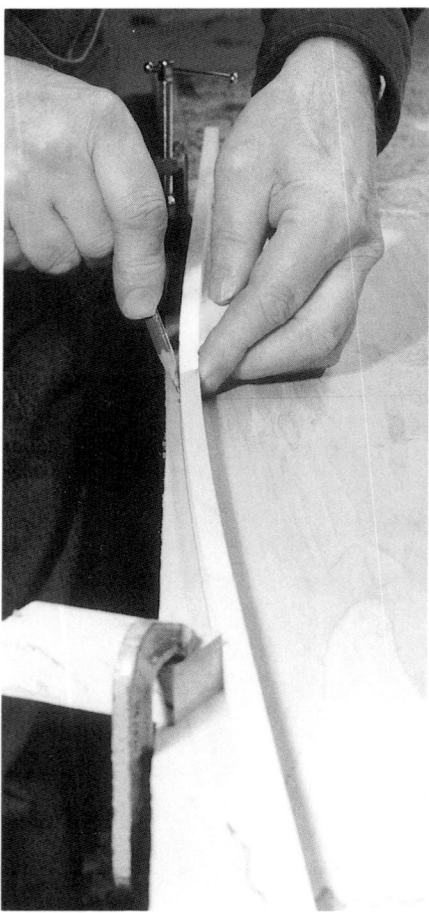

Fastening the top in place with hold-down clips.

base, and drill pilot holes at the marks. To do this, I use a ⁵⁄₆₄" drill bit with masking tape wrapped around it ½" from the point, in a hand drill. (Use a hand drill, not a power hand drill.) This is the best way to be certain that you don't accidentally drill through the top. Now put the base back on the marks and the clips in place, and drive the screws. Pick it up, set it on the floor, and stand back and admire it. It's ready for finishing.

So there you have my little table. I made quite a few after those first two. People like them because they can be used in many different ways. Look around your house—you may find a place for another one. One would make a fine gift for someone close to you for whom you want to do something special.

OUT OF YOUR IMAGINATION

Ideas to spur your imagination.

In woodworking, so often we just follow someone's drawing or go along with what has been made before. There comes a time, however, when the artist in us just has to come out, when our imagination seeks expression. If you ever have those feelings, here's an answer. Out of your imagination you can create unique and exciting items on your lathe. Weed bottles, candle holders, small boxes and bowls all can be turned from pieces of tree branches, parts of small tree trunks, or chunks like burls, cut from larger trees. Take a walk in the woods or visit your wood pile, and you'll find all kinds of interesting pieces to start with. Just put one in your lathe and go where your imagination takes you.

The pictures above will give you some ideas, but they are meant to be only a springboard for your creativity. You decide what each piece is going to be and how it's going to come out; develop it according to what you uncover as you progress in your turning. As you can see, you can leave most of the bark on, cut it all off, mount the piece off center and get strange patterns, take advantage of contrasting colors between sapwood and heartwood—here is where you apply imagination and an artist's eye. Starting with the kind of wood I've talked about, you never know what's under the surface until you cut into it. A branch that has died and fallen off a small tree, leaves a grain pattern inside the trunk. When you begin to cut into it, that pattern comes out in a variety of ways depending on how you cut it. There are so many variables: how you mount it, whether it's straight or slightly curved, whether the bottom is square with the axis or at a slight angle, whether there are knots or rotted spots, and on and on. The possibilities are infinite.

Here is a group of pieces of wood that I collected for this project. It's a motley assortment, but that's what I was after. The more motley, the better. Many of the best pieces you find will be green. Don't worry about it. You may get a little checking, but in pieces like bottles and candle holders that will only enhance the appearance. In bowls, you may lose one now and then, but if it's a particularly decorative bowl, the cracks won't matter. You can consider it an art piece and display it rather than use it to hold anything.

This is where you begin.

The essential accessories.

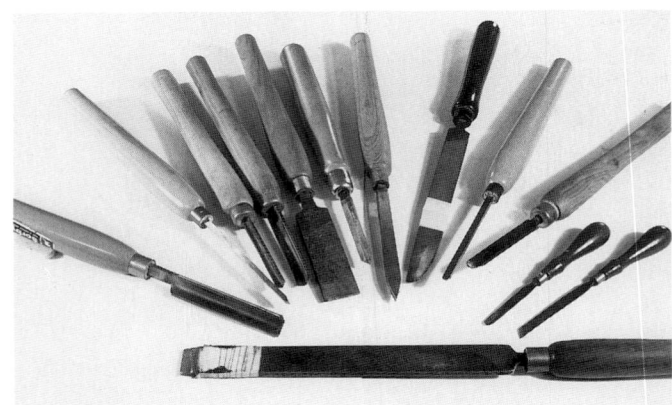

A collection of tools that I use for this kind of work.

These are essentially faceplate turnings, and you will need certain accessories to do the work. First will be a small screw-center faceplate with a morse taper shank to fit in your headstock spindle. You'll then need a 3"-diameter faceplate that threads onto your headstock spindle. The third important accessory is a ½" or ⅝" key chuck mounted on a morse taper shank to fit your tailstock. As to turning tools, you will, in the end, use almost every one you have, both cutting and scraping. I'd like to recommend, if you don't have one, that you get a ¾"-deep flute roughing gouge. This gouge is ground square rather than like a thumbnail. It can cut with the bottom or either side of the *U* and it is, for my money, the best tool for roughing any job on a lathe. They've become quite expensive, but over the long pull, you'll find it worth the expense. If you can't find one locally, look in the Woodcraft catalog.

As your imagination begins to generate new ideas, you may want to create some scraping tools to your own design. A quick and inexpensive way to do this is to go to the nearest machine shop and ask them for a few of their worn-out metal files. Take them home, grind them to the shape you want, put a handle on them and you're in business. A tip here: rather than grind the teeth off, just wrap the part that rides on the tool rest with masking tape; it's much easier.

Mounting the wood on the faceplate is important. If you can stand a 3"-diameter base, use the 3" faceplate. This is particularly true if you're off center or have some knobs to knock off before you get to the main body. The 3" gives you better holding power for the roughing operation. The screw plate is good for the smaller pieces and those that are more symmetrical. With the screw plate, it's a good idea to support the outer end with the tailstock during roughing. A suggestion to strengthen the mounting on this plate: Drill a ⅛" hole near the outer edge of the plate. When you have mounted your blank on the main screw, put a

A blank mounted on the screw faceplate.

smaller screw through this hole into the bottom of the blank. This prevents the blank from twisting on the main screw and working loose. A piece on either faceplate must be securely fastened, but it does not necessarily have to be exactly centered. In fact, you will usually get a more interesting result if it isn't. Nor does the bottom of the blank have to be square with the ver-

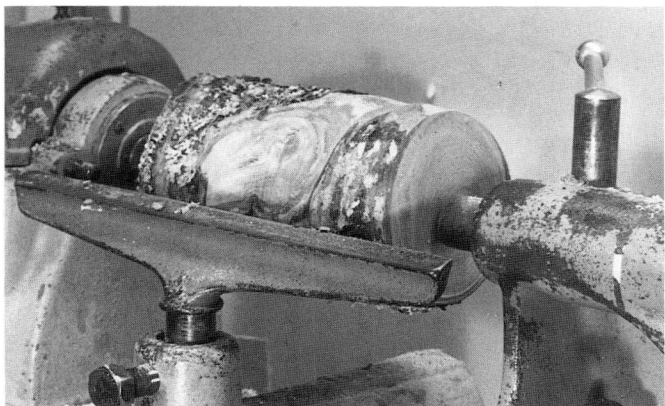

The roughing out just begun. The tailstock supports the outer end.

A partially turned candle holder.

Drilling the hole for the candle with the drill and chuck mounted in the tailstock.

The drill remaining in the hole supports the outer end during final finishing of a weed bottle.

tical axis. Such situations often create beautiful patterns that you can't otherwise achieve. Don't worry if you get some vibration because it's off balance. Unless it's excessive, you can work with it. However, be careful as you start your turning. Use the slowest speed and advance your tool slowly and hold it firmly, taking just little bites until you can see where you're going. Moving too quickly can result in too deep a cut and might tear the piece from the faceplate. If the piece is irregular or somewhat long, or there's quite a bit of vibration, run the tailstock up to support the outer end during the initial roughing. When you get to detailing the outer end, pull it back out of the way. If the piece is unusually long, keep it in place until the very last, light, finishing cuts.

Weed bottles and candle holders need holes. This, of course, is why you need the chuck that mounts in the tailstock. If you're doing a bottle with a long, thin neck, drill the hole right after you've roughed out the neck area, then leave the drill in the hole as support while you finish the neck. You can get some really nice, delicate work this way—even putting a lovely, flared lip on the neck opening. If the drill starts to squeal, just give it a few drops of light oil. When you make the hole in a candle holder, be sure to put a slight taper on the sides to fit the candle you'll be using; otherwise the

candle will wobble all over the place. I also use a large drill (1½") to make the initial hollow in a small bowl. It gives a better start and makes it easier to define the inside surface of the bottom.

This seems a good place to pass on a tip I have in mind. If you want to see what you develop as you progress, just paint the piece with water. This will bring out the natural colors of the wood and then dry quickly. You can continue turning even before it's dry.

All the pieces we've been talking about up to now have been fastened to the faceplates with screws, necessarily about ½" long. This requires solid pieces, or if bowls or boxes, bottoms at least ½" thick. I've made many a piece with thick bottoms, and they look and work fine. There are times, however, when you want a thin bottom or thin cross sections throughout. To achieve this requires a different faceplate mounting. The one I'm going to describe may sound strange, but it works very well. I've used it for forty years. Mount a ¾"-thick piece of pine or fir on your 3" faceplate, and turn it to the diameter of the faceplate. Put a very small brad point in the center of this while it's mounted on the lathe. (The point should barely protrude from the face.) Remove the faceplate from the lathe, and on the surface that is to be the bottom of your bowl, find the center, as close as you can, and put the faceplate brad point on this center. Trace the outline of the faceplate on the other surface. Separate the two, and spread yellow glue generously on each of the mating surfaces, keeping within the scribed circle. Place two or three layers of newspaper on the faceplate so that the brad point sticks through, and fit the faceplate back in its position on the piece to be turned. Press them firmly together, and let the glue dry for about twenty-four hours. If you're turning a chunk of burl or something similar, rough cut it round on the band saw before mounting. This type of mounting won't stand the jolts of turning from a square. You can now turn the piece, and when finished, gently separate it from the faceplate using a long-bladed, sharp knife or a thin chisel. Using this mounting, I have turned plates and bowls with bottoms as thin as ⅟₁₆″.

The brad point is hard to see, but it's there, and that's as it should be.

When it comes to finishing the pieces, again there is much leeway. Almost anything you put on them (except stain) will bring out the natural colors in the wood and bark as well as anything else that might be there. There are a couple of words of caution: don't use anything that will result in a glossy finish. The pieces you are going to create will not look right with a glossy finish. They will, in fact, look like something you bought at a souvenir counter somewhere. The other word is also a don't. On any piece that will contain food don't use Watco or anything similar that will impart a taste to the food. I used Watco, which is a very good finish (but not for this purpose), when I first started making bowls. I had to throw them away. No matter how much time passed after the finish was applied, the popcorn still tasted of it. I have found that mineral oil (not mineral spirits), hand-rubbed in, does a very nice job on the inside of a bowl; outside you can use clear shellac and then a good paste wax on the bare wood (use just the shellac on the bark). When you've left the bark on, entirely or just in places, be careful how much finish you use on it. Too much may cause it to curl and start to peel, then dry in that position. You may want that to happen. I'm telling you about it in case you don't. I think you'll find imaginative turning a lark. If you're a hobbyist, the pieces make wonderfully unique gifts that will be highly appreciated. If you operate a small shop and sell your output at craft shows and fairs, they make an unusual product that will attract considerable attention and bring a good price. Early on in the furniture business, when I didn't have enough furniture orders to keep me busy, I made many such pieces. They sold so well—at prices of $10 to $50 each—that I couldn't keep up with the demand. These were pretty good prices in

The faceplate, the paper, and the blank, with glue spread and ready to assemble.

the middle 1970s. The bottom line is that this is a uniquely different project that will stimulate your imagination, and the results you get will more than repay the time and effort expended. You may also learn some things about turning that aren't in the books.

A HANDSOME CABINET

This cabinet has several attributes: It will challenge your skill (it's not quite as simple as it looks at first glance); it will be a handsome addition to any room in any style home; and it can hide a 13" television, house your stereo components, or just store items like big books that don't fit on ordinary bookshelves.

Building the cabinet starts with choosing the wood. Use any wood that suits your fancy, but to fulfill the idea behind the design, you should choose one in which the grain has a distinct character and pattern. The one in the picture is Western maple, and the drawers are walnut. There are four important panels in the piece, and the sides and top are readily seen, but the

doors create the real visual impact.

All of the panels will have to be glued up. In choosing the wood for the side and top panels, try to get pieces in which the grain patterns look like they belong together. For the doors, you will want something striking. The figures should be as similar as possible so that the doors match. Another approach for the doors is to create a book-match.

If you've decided to make the doors by book-matching, here is how to go about it. If you've found what you want in one 12"-wide, 2"-thick board, divide it into two 6"-wide pieces. Mark the pieces so that you know how they went together. Joint flat the same face

Drawing 4-1. A handsome cabinet—exploded view.

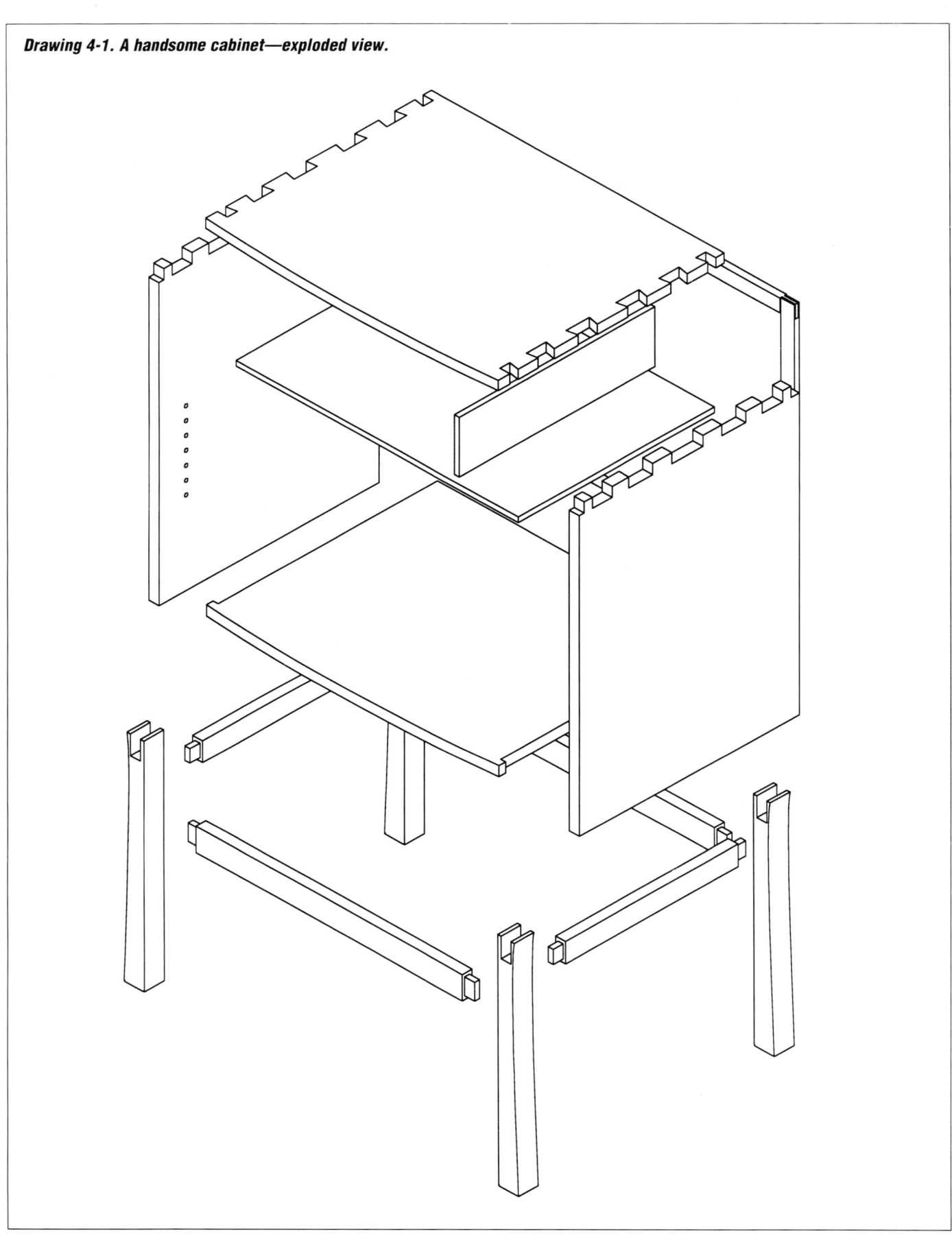

Drawing 4-2. Orthographic views of complete cabinet.

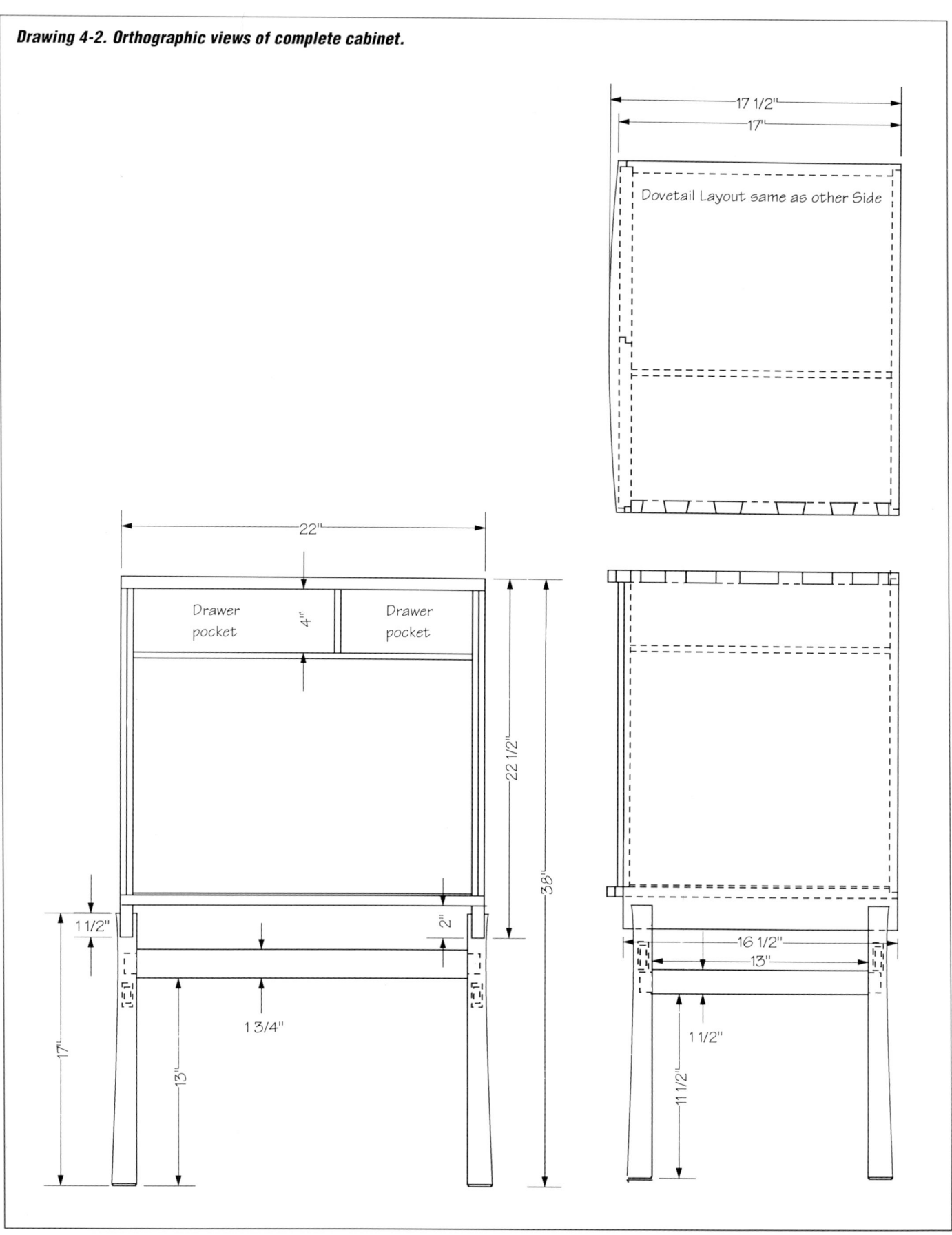

A simple way to keep from mixing up the boards in a panel while working with them.

Marking the pins of the dovetail joint between top and side.

on each piece, then joint both edges on each piece square with the flat face. Set your saw blade at just over 3″ high. (Be sure it's exactly perpendicular to the table. Don't depend on the saw gauge, use a try square.) Set your rip fence at ⅞″, and rip both pieces, one edge, then the other. Lay them open and you have your book-match, in the rough. That's as far as you go with it for the moment. Mark them so you know how they go together, and put them aside on sticks.

Making the Panels

The four main case panels are the same rough size, 1″ x 18″ x 24″. If you can, use three 6″ boards to make each panel. Joint flat one surface of each piece, then joint both edges square with the flat face. Now set your rip fence to ½″ over ¾″ and rip all pieces to that thickness, then joint the cut face lightly. (If you have a planer, you can do everything after the first jointing on it.) When you have assembled each panel to your satisfaction, mark it with a chalk triangle as shown. This system allows you to work with a panel and get it back in the same order you started with. To make the door panels, lightly joint the faces you've opened, just enough to clean up the saw marks. The more you take off, the more of the book-match you'll lose. Rip and joint them to proper thickness as you did the other panels. Now you can carefully fit the edges and glue up all the panels. The fitting of the edges is important because if you've done it carefully and have chosen the patterns on the boards carefully, you won't be able to see the joints. (See chapter eight.)

The Case

As you start building the cabinet, study the drawings carefully. You'll come across a few tricky spots in this project. Try to visualize how the different parts look and fit together.

In making the case, start with the two side panels.

(See Drawing 4-3.) Cut them to finished size, and be sure that the corners are truly square and that they are both exactly the same size. Decide which face of each is to be the outside face and mark it boldly with chalk. Also mark boldly which end will be the top. The reason for this is that each panel will have two dadoes and two rabbets cut on the inside face; none of the cuts is the same and if you haven't marked the faces and ends you could get confused and ruin a panel.

The first cut will be the dado for the case bottom. It's ⅜″ wide by ⅜″ deep, and it's a through dado; therefore, you can cut both sides with the same setup. Always test a setup with scrap wood before committing your work. Depth gauges on saws should never be relied on.

Next cut the two rabbets. Notice that they are different in size and that they are blind, running from the dado you've just cut to the top. Therefore, you will have to cut them with a router. The dado for the drawer shelf is also blind and will have to be routed. Stop it about ½″ from the front rabbet. Be sure that this cut is in exactly the same position on both sides. If it's even a little bit off, the drawer pocket won't be square and the drawers won't fit properly. The best way to be sure is to cut one side, then place the two sides back edge to back edge and even at the bottom; then, with a sharp knife, mark the uncut panel. (Mark anything important with a sharp knife. An X-Acto with a #11 blade is especially good for marking mortices and dovetail cuts.)

Now is the time to drill the shelf support holes on the inside faces of the sides. Just follow the pattern shown in Drawing 4-3. Put the sides away for the time being and go on to the top and bottom panels.

First the top: Cut the panel to its exact length and the width to 17½″. Do not curve the front edge at this

Drawing 4-3. The side panels.

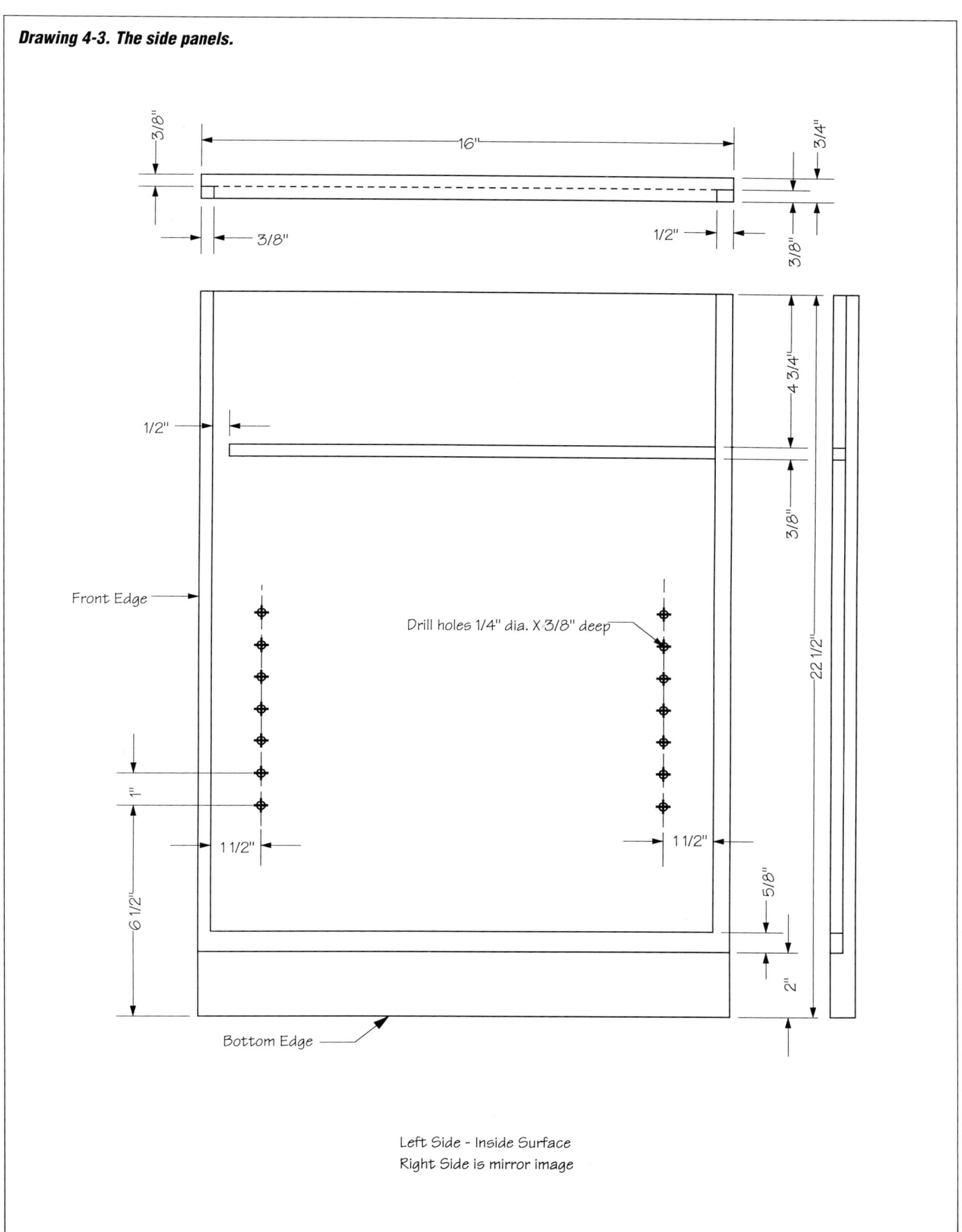

16"

3/8"

3/4"

3/8"

3/8"

1/2"

4 3/4"

1/2"

3/8"

Front Edge

Drill holes 1/4" dia. X 3/8" deep

22 1/2"

1"

1 1/2"

1 1/2"

5/8"

6 1/2"

2"

Bottom Edge

Left Side - Inside Surface
Right Side is mirror image

Drawing 4-4. Front of cabinet—joint detail.

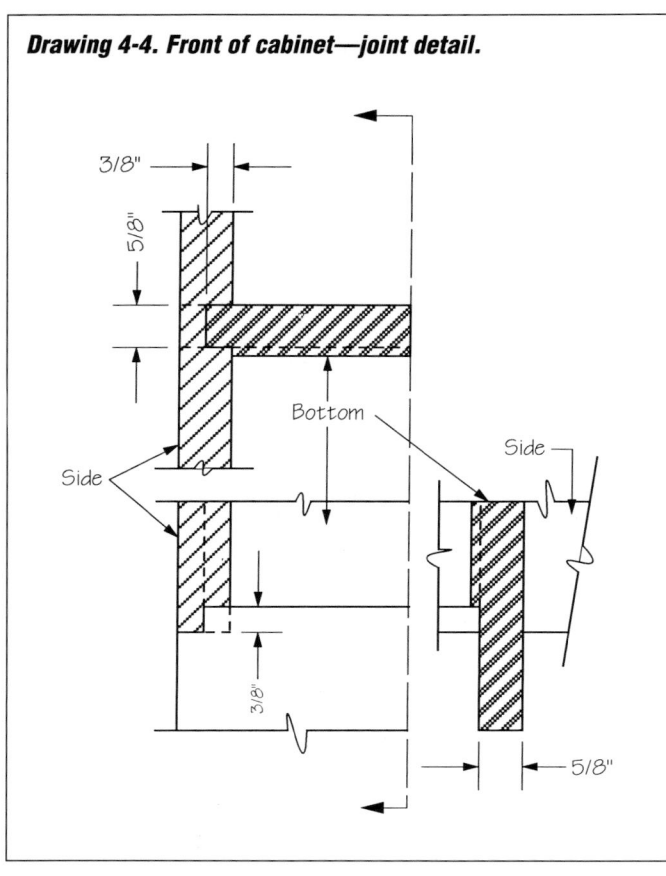

3/8"

5/8"

Bottom

Side

Side

3/8"

5/8"

Drawing 4-5. Rear of cabinet—joint detail.

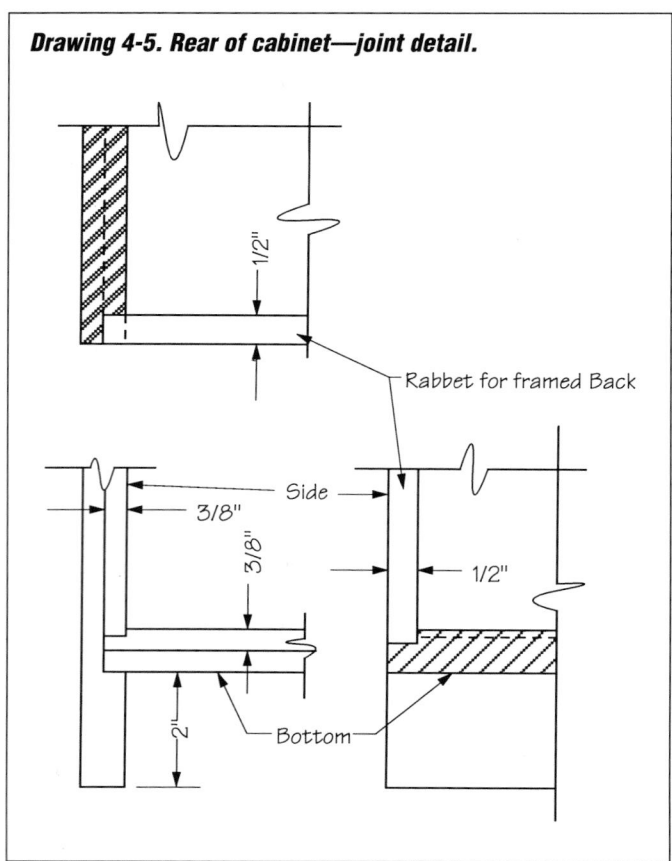

1/2"

Rabbet for framed Back

Side

3/8"

3/8"

1/2"

2"

Bottom

Rabbeting the bottom of the case on the table saw, using the auxiliary fence described in chapter six.

time. Decide which face is to be up and mark it; then decide which edge is to be the back and mark it. Starting from the back edge, lay out, on the top face, the dovetail joint between the top and sides. The top panel will have the tails, and the sides will have the pins. The arrangement can be any way you want. There are only two prerequisites: the hole for the rearmost pin must not overlap the rabbet for the back panel, and the most forward hole must have the front edge straight and exactly matching the inner face of the door rabbet. This is clearly shown in Drawing 4-2. Lay out the sides of the tails first (use the gauge from chapter eight). Then, with a marking gauge set at the exact thickness of the side panels, lightly mark the back edges of the pinholes. Do this on both faces of the panel and at each end. Using a straight edge as a guide and a sharp knife, cut those light markings as deep as you can with one or two strokes. Now go ahead and cut the tails on both ends of the top panel. In doing this, precision in cutting on the pencil lines is not necessary; however, on the knife cut line it is. The next step on the top panel is to route the blind dado for the drawer divider. It's ⅜" wide x ¼" deep and the same length as the drawer shelf dado in the side panels. Its lateral position has been left for you to determine. You can make both drawers the same size or make one bigger than the other.

Now finish the dovetail joints between the top and sides by cutting the pins in the sides. In laying out the pins from the tails, be sure the back edges of the top and sides are flush. On a long joint like this, you must be accurate. Clamp the pieces in position on the workbench and do the marking with a sharp knife. When you've made the joints fit properly, assemble the top and sides, and mark the limits of the back panel rabbet in the rear edge of the top. Make this cut.

Cut the bottom panel to the exact length and width of the top. Mark the back edge and the face that will be up. Now cut the ⅜″ x ½″ rabbet as shown in the drawing. Next cut the rabbets on the side and front edges. The easiest way to make these three cuts is on the table saw. Attach a high auxiliary fence to your rip fence and use a planer blade. Set the fence at ⅝″ between the fence and the blade, and set the blade height equal to the thickness of the side panels. Now run the side edges through with the bottom face against the fence. Without changing the fence position, raise the blade to 1⅛″, and run the front edge through, again with the bottom face against the fence. The next step is to cut the notches in the side edges. The length of the notch, back to front, should equal the width of the side panels. The width of the notch should be such that the width of the remaining rabbet is equal to the depth of the dado in the side panels. This sounds complex, but if you study the drawings carefully, you won't have any trouble. The last operation on both the top and bottom is to lay out and cut the curve on the front edge. Having done this, assemble (dry) the basic case and set it aside.

The doors come next. Lightly joint the edges you have matched to be the meeting edges. Rip the panels to equal widths so that the overall width of the doors fits into the door rabbet on the case. Cut them to a length ³⁄₆₄″ shorter than the height of the door opening in the case. Be sure the case is absolutely square. Cut a ⅜″ x ⅜″ rabbet on the inner-meeting corner of the right-hand door. Now cut a ⅜″ x ⅜″ strip and glue it to the inner-meeting corner of the left door so that it fits into the rabbet you just cut in the right-hand door. This way you won't spoil the matching grain pattern you created on the doors.

Time to hang the doors. Because they are recessed into the sides by half their thickness, use L-shaped knife hinges. Mark, with a knife, the position of the hinges as shown in Figure 4-7 while the case is still assembled (use the hinge as a template); then disassemble the case, and mortice one blade flush with the surface. Position them on the doors in line with the back edge; mark; then mortice one blade flush. A tip: When the mortices have been cut, screw the hinges in place in each mortice, then remove them. Doing this with all pieces disassembled will make it much easier to put everything together later on.

The drawer shelf and divider come next. Resaw the necessary pieces to finish ⅜″ thick. Glue up the shelf as you did the major panels. The grain should run across the cabinet. For a thin panel like this, use the technique outlined in chapter eight. The shelf should be a sliding fit in its dado. Notch the front corners so that the shelf will come forward flush with the door rabbet. Dry assemble and square up the case with the shelf in

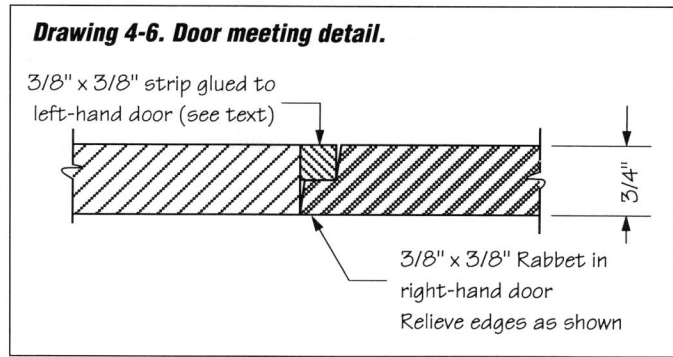

Drawing 4-6. Door meeting detail.

3/8" x 3/8" strip glued to
left-hand door (see text)

3/4"

3/8" x 3/8" Rabbet in
right-hand door
Relieve edges as shown

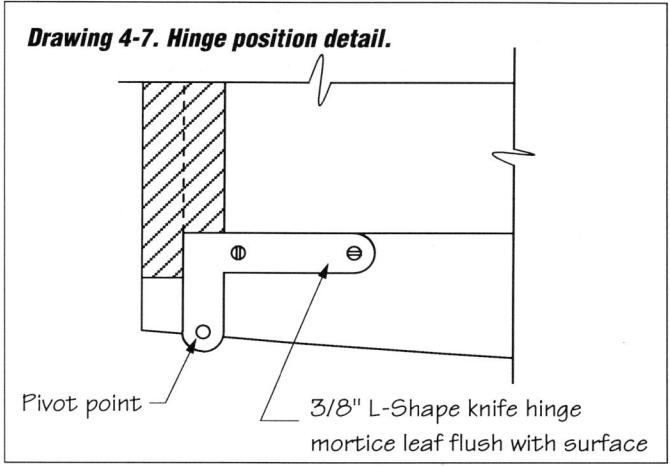

Drawing 4-7. Hinge position detail.

Pivot point

3/8" L-Shape knife hinge
mortice leaf flush with surface

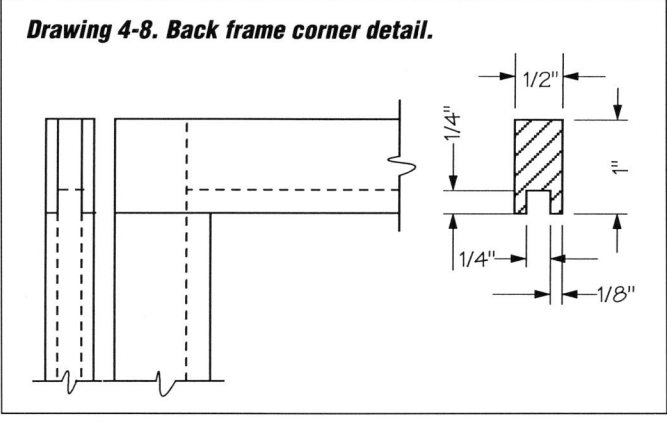

Drawing 4-8. Back frame corner detail.

1/2"

1/4"

1"

1/4"

1/8"

place. Mark for the divider dado on the shelf: Using a try square, transfer one edge of the divider dado in the top, to the shelf. Cut this dado the same length as the one in the top, but only ⅛″ deep. With the shelf in place, measure the width and length of the divider, and cut it to size. Also, notch the front corners so that it will come flush with the front edge of the shelf.

At this point, you will want to finish sand all of the parts you have made so far. Lightly round all exposed corners—⅛″ radius is too much; aim for more like ¹⁄₁₆″. Do this with sandpaper or a spokeshave. You can now glue the basic case together. Be sure it's absolutely square. I say this because experience has shown me that when setting clamps, the case sometimes gets pulled out of square. Don't wipe any excess that squeezes out of the joints. Let it harden and then clean it. If you haven't created perfect dovetail joints (few of us do), here is salvation. Mix some fine sawdust from your pieces with glue so that it's heavy on the sawdust. Press this putty into the gaps so that it stands above the surface. When dry, lightly and carefully plane the entire joint so that the sides and top are smooth and flush. Finish sand the area you have planed.

Now that the basic case is in finished form, you can rehang the doors and fit them properly. If you haven't worked with knife hinges before, here is a setup to make the fitting easy. Screw the bottom hinge to the door and the top hinge to the case. Now with the hinges open 90°, tilt the bottom hinge into its mortice on the case and slide the top hinge into its mortice on

the door. Run the screws into the top hinge and your door will function properly. You should slightly relieve the meeting edges of the right-hand door. This is the time to cut the finger recess. You will also want to put a ¼" friction catch under the right-hand door. Put it about 1" from the meeting edge.

The Back Panel

The final part of the case is the back panel. The four frame members are cut to finish ½" x 1". Cut them to exact length. (Get this from the case, not the drawing.) In doing this, make an extra length, and cut this length into at least three pieces. You will use these to test the setups that follow. Put the high auxiliary fence on the rip fence, and put a ¼" dado blade in the saw. Set the dado blade at ¼" high and the fence so that you cut the groove in the exact center of one edge of each frame member. Now raise the blade to ¾". Decide which pair of frame members will have the open mortices, and

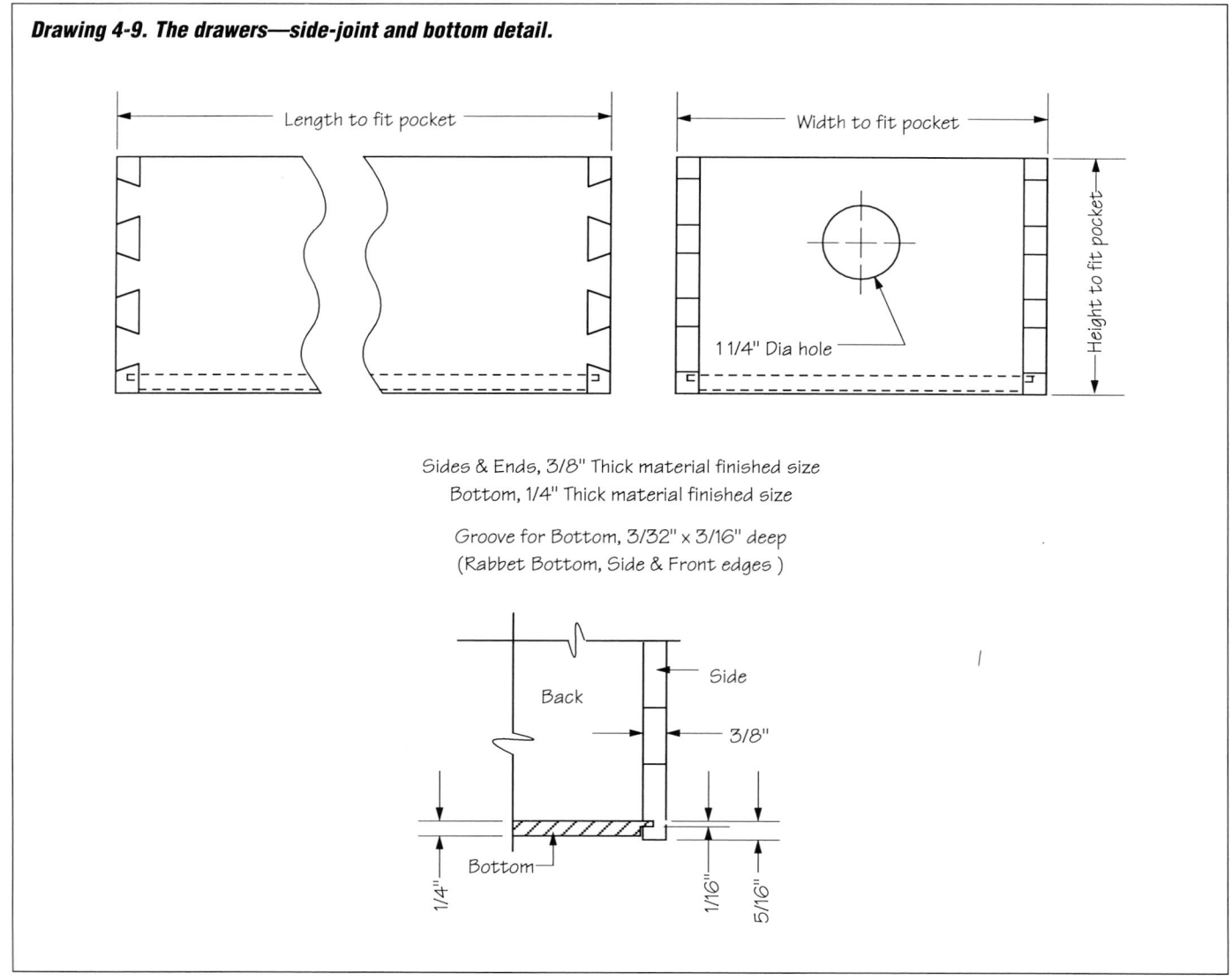

Drawing 4-9. The drawers—side-joint and bottom detail.

Length to fit pocket

Width to fit pocket

Height to fit pocket

1 1/4" Dia hole

Sides & Ends, 3/8" Thick material finished size
Bottom, 1/4" Thick material finished size

Groove for Bottom, 3/32" x 3/16" deep
(Rabbet Bottom, Side & Front edges)

Back

Side

3/8"

Bottom

1/4"

1/16"

5/16"

Mark the leg tops to identify their position in the base, and draw the position of the through mortice.

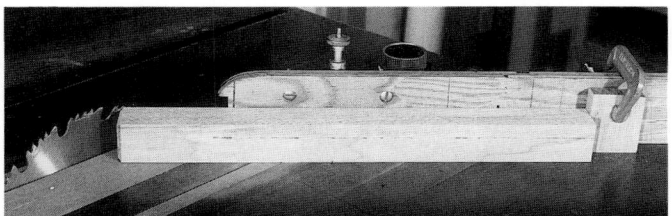

Putting the small bevel on the bottom of the legs.

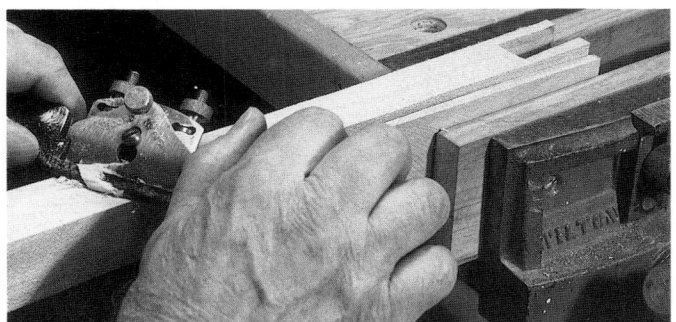

Finish the sawn surface to shape with a spokeshave. Notice the waste from the leg used to help hold it in the vise.

Cutting the through mortice on the top of the leg. It must fit the side snugly.

cut them on each end. (See Drawing 4-8.) Cut the tenons as described in chapter eight. If you have tested as you've gone along, your joints should fit snugly without much adjustment. If they're too tight, it's easier to make the adjustment on the tenon rather than the mortice. Assemble the frame dry, and see that it fits into the rabbet on the case. If it's a little tight, don't worry about it now; you can clean it up later when the frame is glued up.

To make the panel, resaw and finish to ⁵⁄₁₆″ thickness the necessary number of pieces (the grain should run vertically). Glue them up as you did the shelf panel. The finished size should be ¹⁄₁₆″ narrower and shorter than the space in the frame measured from bottom of groove to bottom of groove. Fitting the panel to the groove is done by setting the saw blade at ⁵⁄₁₆″ high and the fence about ¹⁄₆₄″ under ¼″ from the blade. Now run

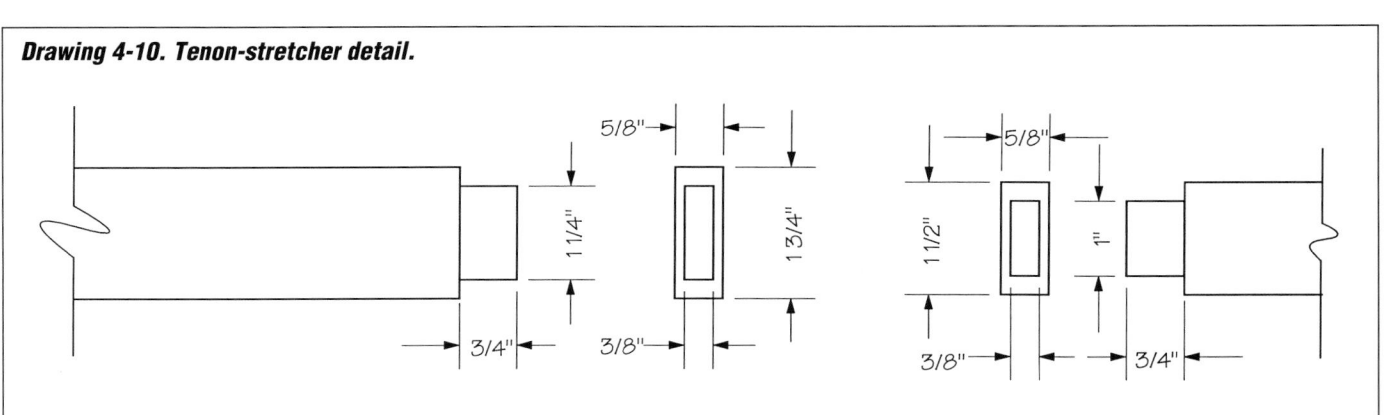

Drawing 4-10. Tenon-stretcher detail.

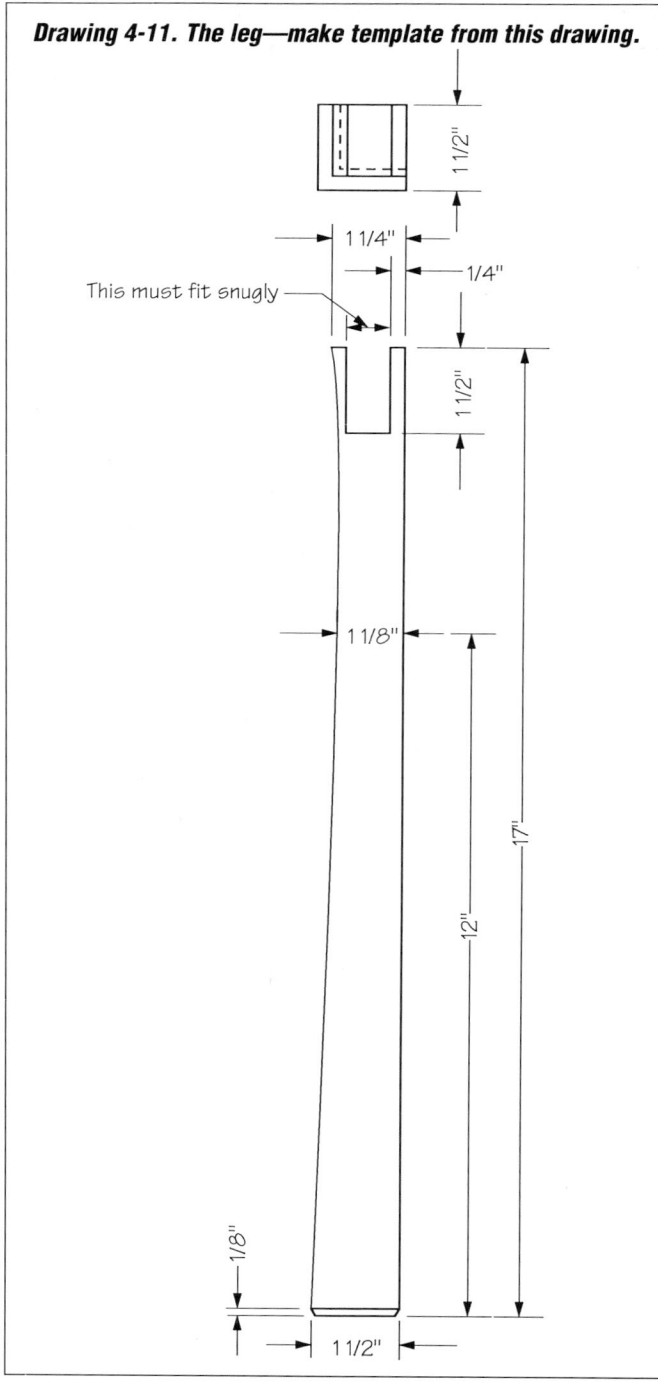

Drawing 4-11. The leg—make template from this drawing.

1 1/2"

1 1/4"

1/4"

This must fit snugly

1 1/2"

1 1/8"

17"

12"

1/8"

1 1/2"

Clamping the stretchers. A cocked clamp is often necessary to maintain squareness. Notice use of leg waste as clamp pads.

for a television or stereo, drill a 1½" hole for the cord in one of the bottom corners of the panel, not in the frame.

Making the Drawers

For the drawers in my cabinet, I used walnut. Whatever wood you use, finish the pieces to ⅜" thick. The size of the drawer pockets you have created will determine the length and width of the fronts, backs and sides. (See Drawing 4-9.) Note that we are using through dovetails here as in the case, so cut these pieces accordingly, and fit them to the pockets. It should be an easy, but not sloppy fit. As for the dovetails, the tails will go on the sides and the pins on the fronts and backs. In laying out the tails, note that they are not the same front and back. This is important; be sure and do it as shown. Cut the tails first (see chapter eight), and from them mark the pins, using a sharp knife. When the joints have been cut and fitted, it's time to cut the groove for the bottom. This is ³⁄₃₂" or ⅛" wide x ³⁄₁₆" deep, and it's located with its upper edge ⁵⁄₁₆" from the bottom edge of the drawer. Please note that while on the sides and back the groove goes all the way through, on the front it must be stopped off or it will show on the outside. When the grooves have been cut, rip off the bottom edge of the backs to the top of the groove. This is the time to drill the 1¼" hole in the fronts. These pieces of the drawers should now be finish sanded, assembled and tried in the drawer pockets. When you have an easy fit, glue the pieces together. (Be sure they are square.) After assembly, lightly round all exposed edges, including both edges of the holes. In making the bottoms, finish the pieces

all four edges through with the inside face of the panel against the fence. Be sure and test this setup before cutting the panel. You want an easy, but not sloppy, fit in the groove. Assemble the frame and the panel dry, and make sure everything fits and is square. Take it apart and apply glue to the frame joints. Do not put any glue between the panel and the frame: the panel must float in the frame. Assemble, clamp if necessary, and let dry. When dry, clean it up and fit it in place. It should be fastened with #5 x ¾" flat-head brass screws, say three to a side. If you're going to use the cabinet to ¼" thick. Glue up the necessary panels and size them as before. Rabbet the two side edges and the front edges to fit the grooves. Slide the bottoms into place, and fasten them at the center of the back with a #3 x ½" flat-head brass wood screw.

The case is complete except for finishing. If you are going to use it with the shelves, now is the time to make them. They can be anywhere from ½" to ¾" thick, depending on what you plan to put on them. Glue them up as you did the panels and cut them to size so that they fit easily. Use the shelf supports described in chapter thirteen.

The Base

The legs start as 1½" square x 17" long; two adjacent faces of each are jointed and all faces are square with each other. Decide which end will be the top. On each leg the corner common to the two jointed faces will be the inside corner. Assemble the legs with the tops together and the inside corners at the center of the square. Now, number the legs, starting with the right rear one, 1, 2, 3, 4 in a clockwise direction. Also mark 1 and 2 to indicate the mating faces; do the same with 3 and 4. Legs 1 and 2 will be the rear and front legs on the right side and 3 and 4 will be the front and rear legs on the left side. This is very important: in each leg, you will cut three mortices, and if they are not properly placed, you will have ruined the leg. Right now is the time to cut the large, through mortice that fits over the case-side panel. Do this with your dado blade. Measure the thickness of your panel, and if it's ¾" or more, use ¾" width in the dado blade. If it's less than ¾", use 1¹⁄₁₆" width in the blade. The reason for this is that this mortice must fit snugly over the panel, and you will want the cut to be a little undersize so that you can create the proper fit. Set the blade at a height of 1½". With the high auxiliary fence in place, set the fence ¼" from the blade, and feed the legs through in a vertical position. This is a rather heavy cut, so feed slowly, and don't forget to check your markings so that you get the cuts in the right positions. Do not do any shaping of the legs at this time; just set the legs aside for the time being.

Finish the side stretchers at ⅝" x 1½" x 14½" long. Finish the front and rear stretchers at ⅝" x 1¾", but do not cut them to length yet. Place the two front-leg blanks in position on the case. Measure the distance between them where they fit over the sides. This is the distance between shoulders on the front and rear stretchers. Add on 1½" for the tenons and cut the stretchers to that length. Now you can cut the tenons, as described in chapter eight. (See Drawing 4-10.)

Using the tenons you have just cut as guides, lay out the mortices on all four leg blanks, marking them with a sharp knife. Again be careful to get each mortice in its correct position. The inside corner is the only straight corner on each leg. All the stretcher mortices, whatever their position vertically, should be ⅜" from this corner. Cut the mortices. (See chapter eight.)

Finally, cut the small bevels at the bottom of the legs. Set this up with the miter gauge at 45° and a stop to position the leg correctly. Make the four cuts on each leg. At this point, assemble the base dry and see that it fits properly on the case.

At last it's time to shape the legs. Make a full-size template as shown in Drawing 4-11. Place this on one of the rough faces of the leg (the ones without mortices), and mark the curve. Saw to the curve. Now place the template on the newly sawn surface and draw the curve, then saw to this curve. Save several of the waste pieces, and cut one in two. These pieces will be very helpful in holding the legs in the vise while working on them. Smooth the sawn surfaces; the fastest and easiest way is with a spokeshave. If you don't have this tool, you'll have to use a file followed by #50 then #80 sandpaper. (My advice is to get yourself a spokeshave. They're not expensive and they're very handy.) The next step is to slightly round all the edges. This step also will proceed much faster with a spokeshave. As a last step, sand all over with #150 paper. Be careful around the stretcher mortices not to alter the flatness of the surface.

Again, assemble the base dry and put it on the case, just to be sure everything fits properly. Now glue up the base. I suggest gluing the side stretchers first. Be sure the legs are square with the stretchers. When they are dry, apply glue to the front and rear stretcher joints and place the assembly in position on the case, then clamp across each stretcher, front and rear. (The waste pieces from the legs work well as pads under the clamps.) When this has dried, you can glue the base to the case. However—and this is important—glue only the front legs. The reason for this is that with changes in climate conditions, the case sides will expand and contract across the grain. The side stretchers will not move in this direction. Therefore, if the base is glued front and back, you will get either distortion of the base or splitting of the side panels when movement takes place. If the back legs are not glued, then the side panels are free to move relative to the legs. In order to compensate for the lack of glue, the fit between the legs and the side panels has to be very snug. Your cabinet is now ready for finishing. Chapter fourteen contains my thoughts about finishing. If you haven't done so, you may find it worth reading before going ahead.

SHOW OFF YOUR TREASURES

The cabinet should be as much a showpiece as the things in it.

Most people have treasures, small things they've gathered over the years, that they value. What they usually *don't* have is a proper place to display these treasures so that they, and others, can enjoy them. Well, here's a chance to create such a place. This showcase cabinet is a comfortable size for most homes, and it's really not very difficult to put together. It will test your skill a bit because it has a few interesting departures from the ordinary. See page 151 for a cutting list for this project.

You can make it out of any kind of wood you want to, but it's my contention that the case should be just as much a showpiece as the things in it. If you agree with me on this, then you'll be much more particular about the wood you choose. The cabinet in the pic-

tures is made from black walnut and English walnut. English walnut is good for this type of piece because it has such a strong contrast between the sapwood and heartwood; thus, you're apt to find interesting and distinct grain patterns, as I did for the sides and back. Other woods have this contrast; Oregon big leaf maple is one. You might also try red gum if you can find it. The pieces you want aren't easy to find—you have to dig for them and it takes time—but the result is worth the effort.

The Case

The two most important parts of this showcase are the top and the bottom. If they're not done correctly, you will never be able to square up the case. The key here

Drawing 5-1. Assembly.

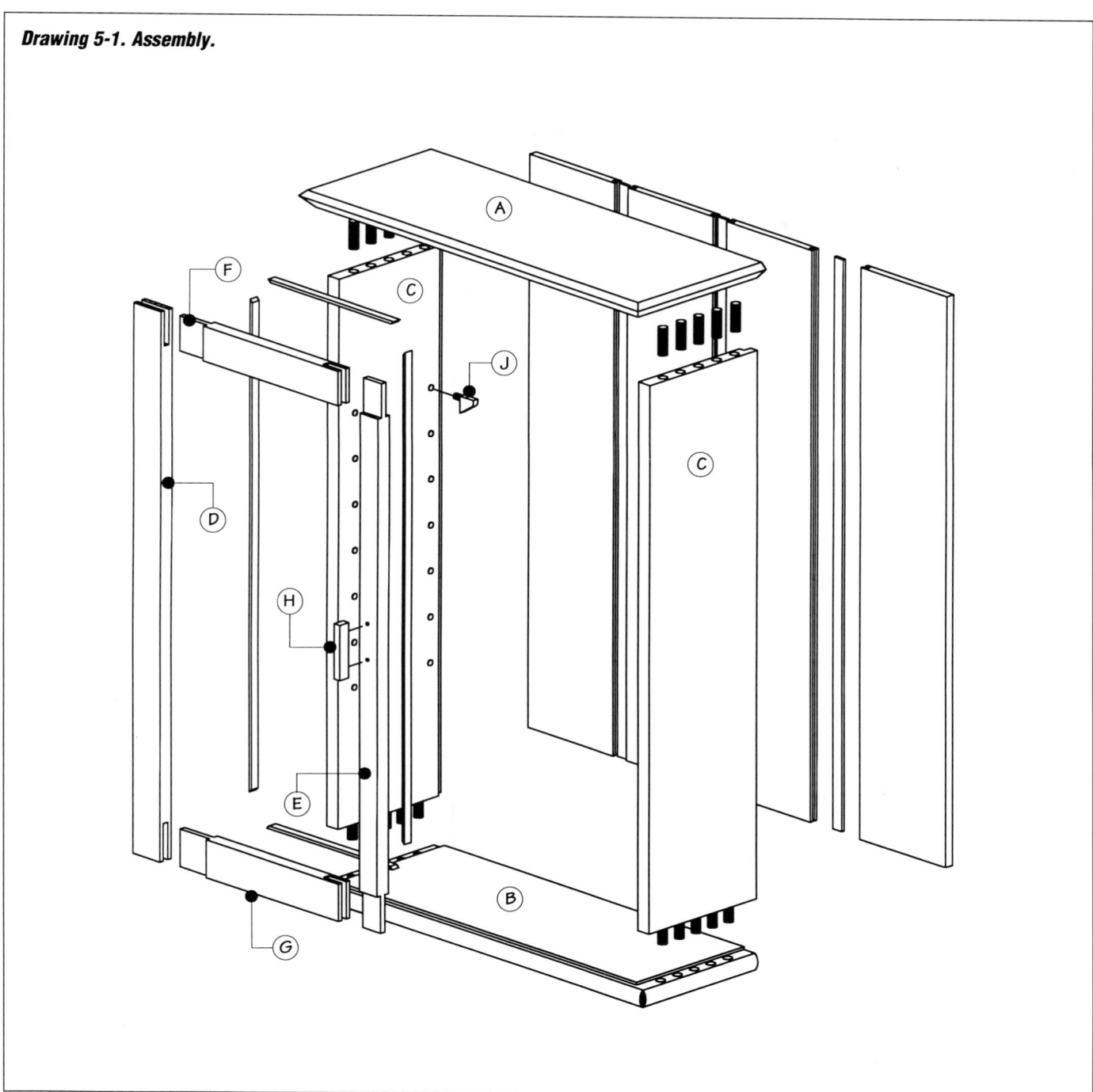

is the dimensions of the area left after the rabbets have been cut. They must be exactly the same on both parts, because the shoulder of the side rabbets positions the sides, and the shoulder of the front rabbets positions the doors. However, as you can see in Drawing 5-2, the overall dimensions of the parts are different. This means that while the depth of the rabbets on each are the same, the width is different. Cut the parts to their overall sizes and joint the top and bottom faces smooth. The rabbets are best cut on the table saw. Use a high auxiliary fence and a planer blade. Set the fence

at ¾″ from the inside of the blade and the blade height at ¾″ for the bottom and 1⅛″ for the top. Test each setup with a piece of scrap. Run the side rabbets first and then the front. If you've been careful to cut to the overall dimensions shown in the drawings, the result will be right. Check it to be sure, and if there is a discrepancy, correct it now.

The next step is to put the bevels on the edges of the top. Notice that they are not the same size. The easiest way to do this is with the table saw, using the planer blade. Move the rip fence to the left side of the blade

Cutting the rabbets on the top.

and put the auxiliary fence on the side toward the blade. Set the blade to make a 45° cut. Set the fence so that the distance between the fence and the blade at the table surface is slightly more than ¼". Run a piece of scrap through to make sure your setup is right. Now, with the top face of the top against the fence, make the three cuts. Run the long edge first and then the two short ones. There is a small problem with the short sides on this cut. The piece is riding on a narrow edge, and because of its short length, it will drop into the blade slot if it isn't supported. The easiest way to provide this support is to clamp a piece of scrap wood to the back side so that it will ride on the top of the rip fence; then, holding the cabinet top firmly against the fence, make the cut. The top bevel is cut the same way except that the fence setting is slightly more than ⅜".

The cabinet-bottom edges are slightly rounded, as

Drawing 5-2. Dimensions of the top and bottom.

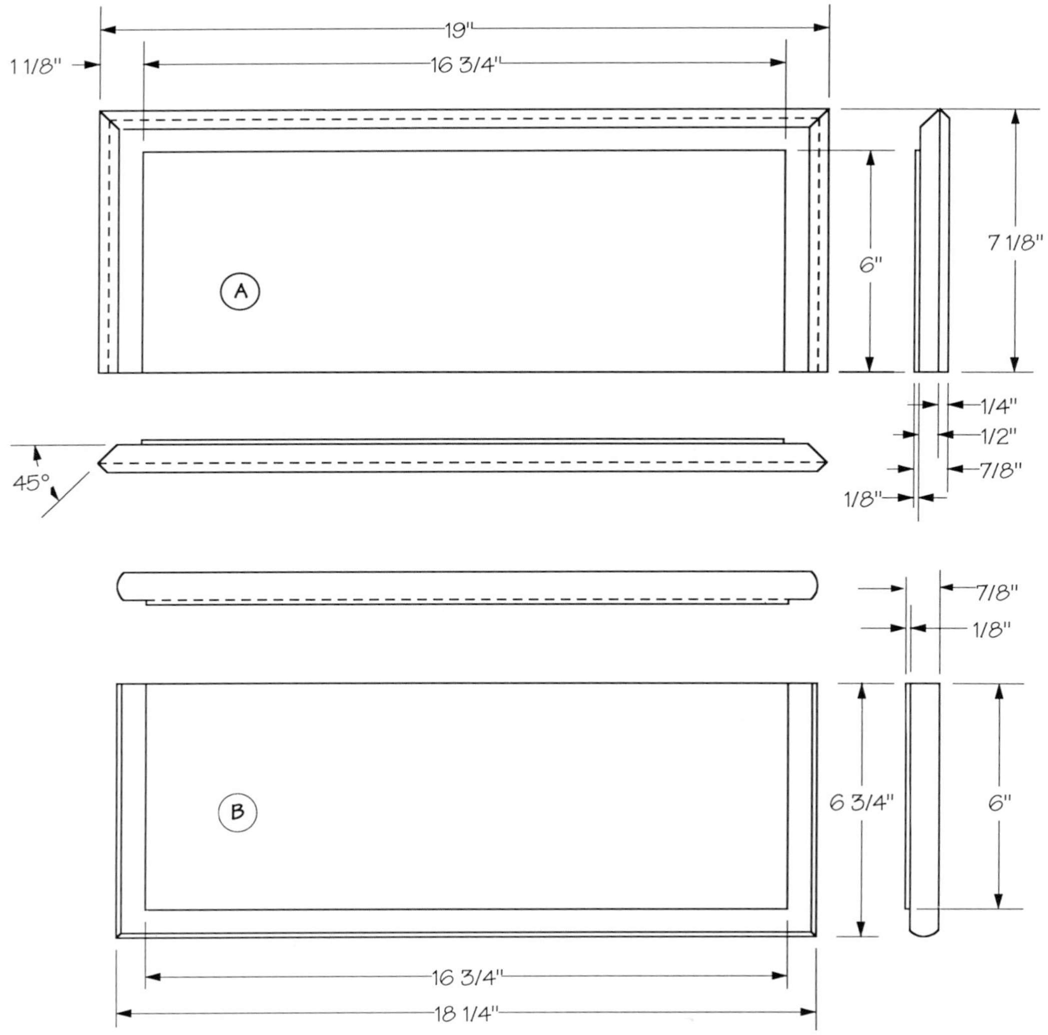

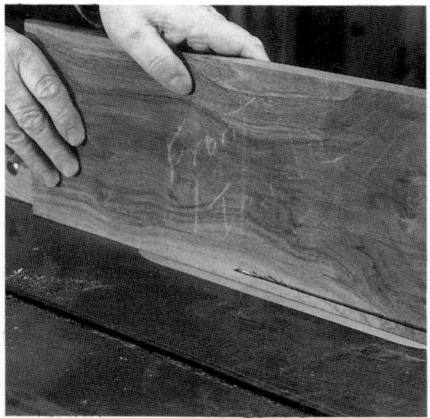

Rounding the edges of the bottom. Notice this is done with the piece flat on the saw table.

Cutting the large bevel on the front edge of the top.

Cutting the large bevel on the ends of the top. Notice the special support necessary.

shown in the Drawing 5-2. I do this with ½" radius concave cutters in a molding head on the table saw. My cutters are ground so that I have to make this cut with the rip fence on the left side of the cutter. Use the auxiliary fence, and set it so that only the curve of the cutter is exposed. Set the height so that it covers slightly less than half the thickness of the bottom. You will need to use two different settings because of the rabbet. (Be sure to test these setups before committing your part. If you cut too deeply, you won't have enough room left for the sides and doors before the curve starts.) These cuts are made with the cabinet bottom laying flat on the table. This is as far as you go with these two parts for the moment.

The sides come next. It is with the sides that you get the chance to create a distinctive cabinet. You may not want to bother with this suggestion, but if you do, here it is: Look for a 2"-thick piece of suitable width and length that has a very distinctive grain pattern, such as the one in the picture. Resaw this piece down the middle and joint smooth the resulting faces. These will be the outside faces of your sides. Now, leaving these faces alone, finish machining the sides according to Drawing 5-3, including cutting the rabbet and drilling the holes for the shelf supports.

It is now time to put the case together. Do this with a dowel joint. (See detail, Drawing 5-4). To get the necessary accuracy and proper positioning of the parts for this joint, it is best to use the jig illustrated in chapter six. The positioning of the jig on the pieces is very important. Mark the sides with chalk to indicate the inside face and the top and bottom edges. Place the jig on the top edge of one side, with the gauging piece at the back. The side of the jig should be flush with the inside face of the side. Push two #6 finishing nails through the small holes, and tap them into the side far enough to hold the jig firmly in place. Using a hand

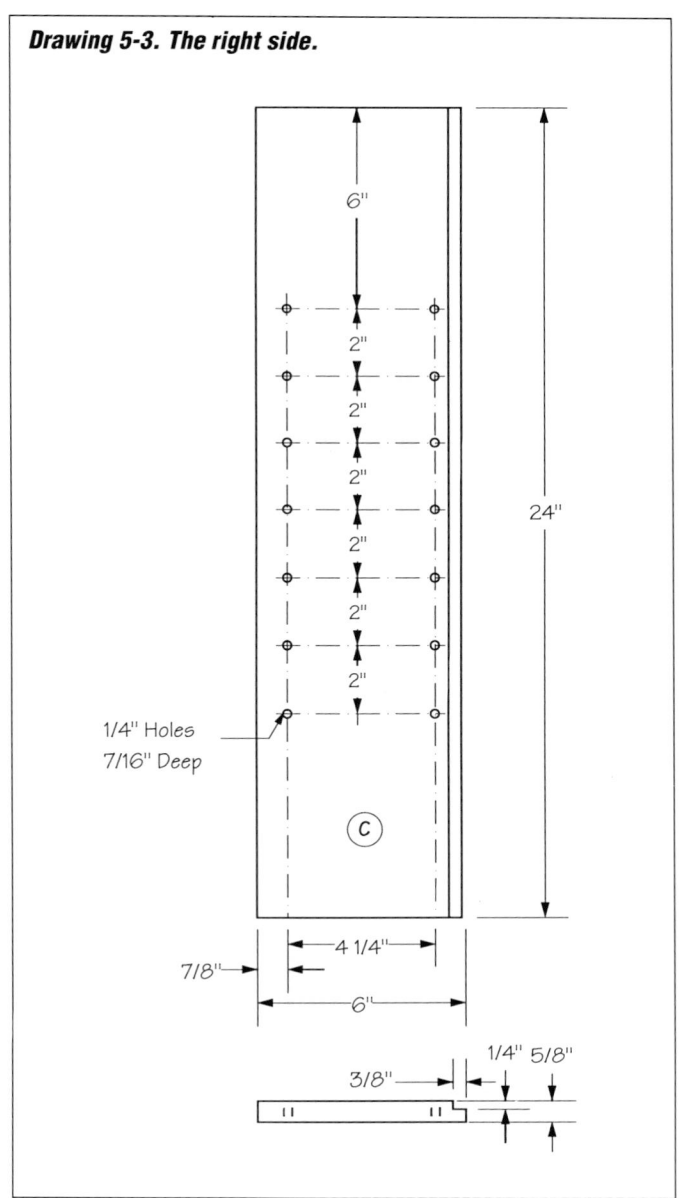

Drawing 5-3. The right side.

1/4" Holes
7/16" Deep

Jig being used to drill the dowel holes in one end of a side.

Drilling dowel holes in top using jig.

Checking the protruding length of the dowels against the depth of the mating holes.

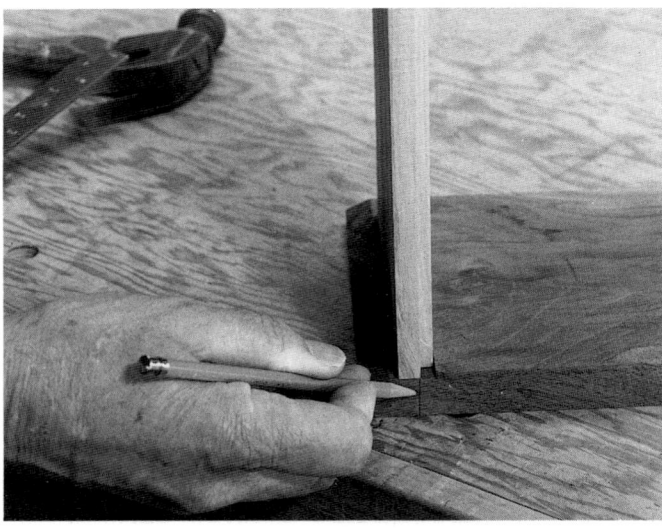

Mark the limits of the top and bottom rabbets for the back.

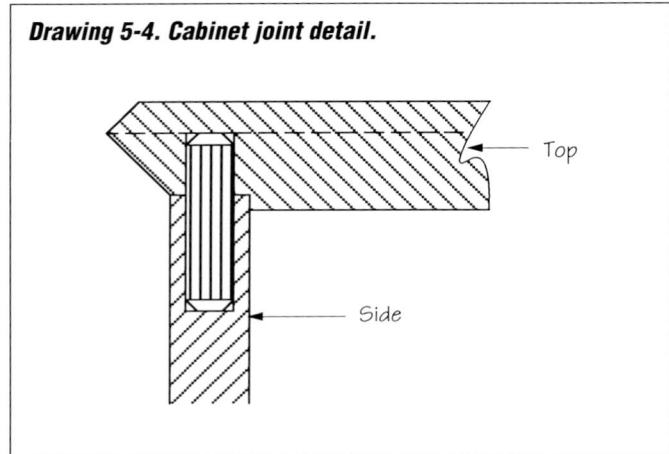

Drawing 5-4. Cabinet joint detail.

Top

Side

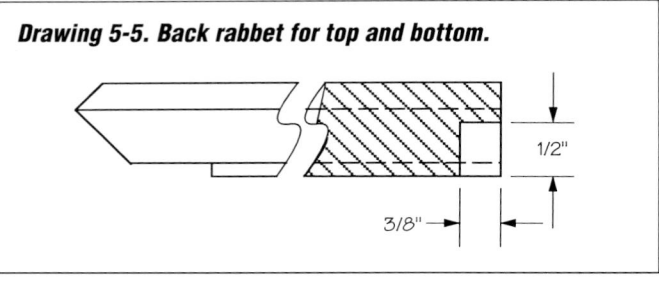

Drawing 5-5. Back rabbet for top and bottom.

1/2"

3/8"

electric drill and a ⅜" brad-point drill bit, drill all five holes ¾" deep. Remove the jig, pull the nails completely out, and push them in from the other side. Position the jig on the matching face of the top, with the gauging piece at the back and the same face as was to the inside of the side tight against the shoulder of the rabbet. Tap the nails home to hold the jig in place, and with your ⅜" drill bit in the drill press, drill all five holes ½" deep.

Now do the other three joints the same way. It is very important that you follow this positioning procedure carefully; otherwise, the holes in the top or bottom and the sides won't match. It is also important to finish drilling each joint before going on to the next one. In other words, don't drill all the holes in the sides and then go back and do the top and bottom. You're very apt to get confused, and then the holes won't match.

Cut twenty ⅜" dowels ¹³⁄₁₆" long. Slightly taper each

end and be sure to put one or two air-escape grooves down the sides of each. They should be a firm, hand-push fit into their holes. Now make a dry (no-glue) assembly of the case, putting the dowels first into the top and bottom. They should be pushed in until they bottom. Using a depth gauge, check the amount of each dowel protruding against the depth of the hole it is to go into. If one is too long, trim the dowel.

Assemble the sides to the top first and then the bottom. Be sure everything fits properly and the two parts of each joint go together completely. Square the case (if you can't do this, make adjustments until you

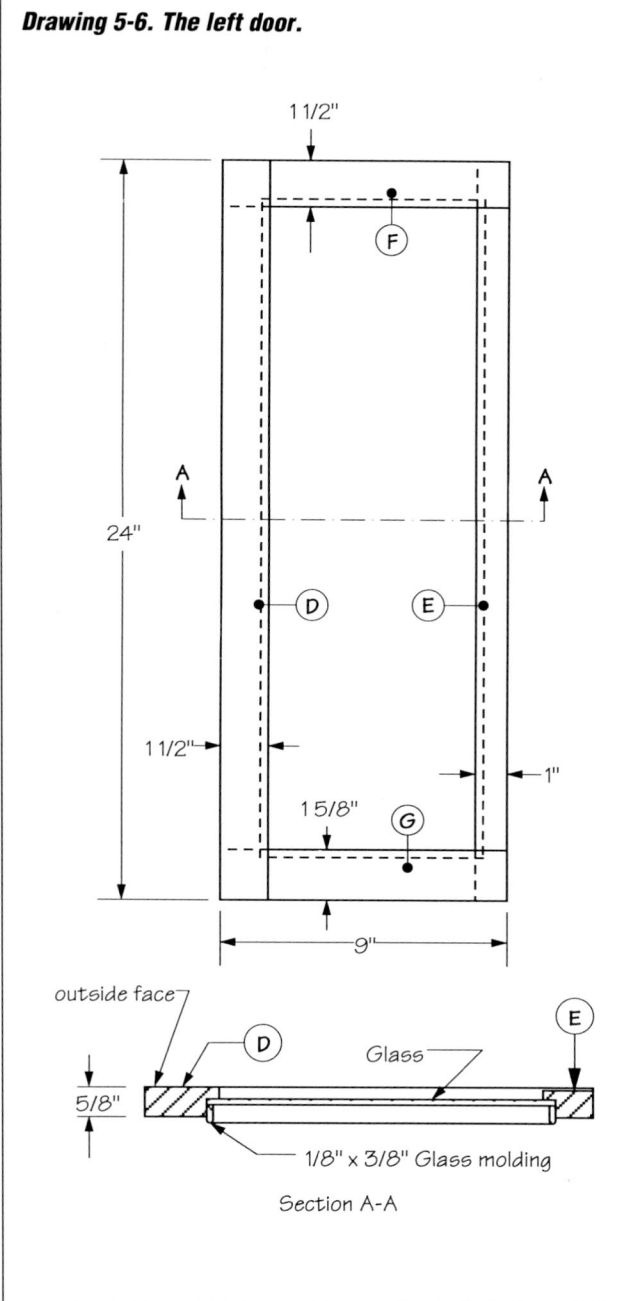

Drawing 5-6. The left door.

1 1/2"

24"

1 1/2"

1 5/8"

1"

9"

outside face

Glass

5/8"

1/8" x 3/8" Glass molding

Section A-A

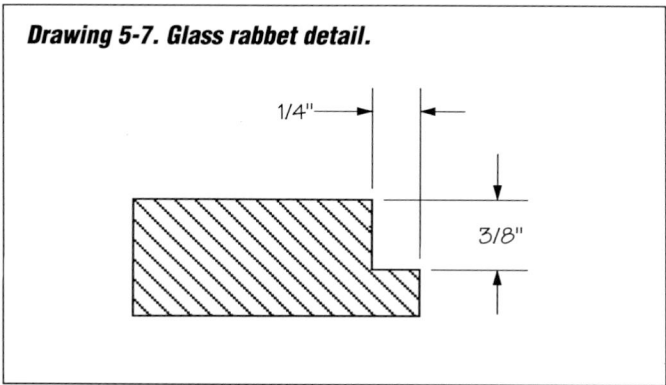

Drawing 5-7. Glass rabbet detail.

1/4"

3/8"

can), and turning to the back, mark the limits of the rabbet in the top and bottom that match the ones in the sides. The dimensions of this rabbet are ⅜" deep by ½" high (see Drawing 5-5). Take the case apart and cut the rabbets with a router, then square the corners with a chisel.

You can now glue the case together. Do this as you did dry, putting the dowels in the top and bottom first and making sure they bottom. Put glue only in the top third of the holes. Do not put any glue on the faces of the joints. When you have the dowels in the top and bottom and before you put glue in the side holes, again check length-against-hole depth on each one, and trim any dowel that's too long. Then finish the assembly. Square the case, clamp it that way if necessary, and set it aside to dry.

The Doors

The doors for this showcase are simple to construct, but as you can see in Drawing 5-6, there are a couple of details that are different. The first is that the outside stiles go over the rails but the inner stiles go inside the rails. The second is that the inner stiles are somewhat narrower and thinner than all the other door-frame members. The purpose of this is to tie the two doors together in appearance. This effect will be further enhanced if you cut both top rails from the same piece of wood so that when the doors are closed, the grain lines will be continuous across both doors. Do the same with the bottom rails. If you look at the picture of the finished cabinet on page 88, you will see what I mean. When cutting the inner stiles, make them the same thickness as all the other frame members to begin with. They will be reduced to proper thickness only after you have cut all the mortice-and-tenon joints. Also notice that the bottom rails are wider than the top rails and the outside stiles. At this point, it might be a good idea to study the drawings (if you haven't already done so) so that you will clearly understand what I've been talking about. Cut all door-frame pieces to the proper finished sizes. (Cut an extra piece about 10" long that you can use later as a test piece in making your mortice-and-tenon setups.) Lay the pieces on the bench top in their relative positions and mark, with chalk, where the mortices go and where the tenons go. Cut the mortices first. Notice that they are open mortices. Set your dado head for ¼" width of cut. The depth of the mortice at the top and bottom ends of the outer stiles is different, so be careful. The depth of the mortices on the inner ends of the top and bottom rails is the same for all but different from those on the outer stiles. Make the cuts in the exact center of the piece. See chapter eight for the way to make the tenons for this joint.

Now put the frames together dry and fit them to the

case. The length of the doors should be about $\frac{1}{32}$" shorter than the opening. As for the width, with the doors tight together, the outer edges should be flush with the outside face of the cabinet sides. Once this is set, disassemble the frames and cut the inner stiles to their proper thickness, $\frac{9}{16}$" finished. Take this cut from the outer face of the pieces. You can now glue the frames together. Remember, in gluing a mortice-and-tenon joint, always put the glue in the mortice, never on the tenon. Use the glue sparingly, and put it in the first third of the opening so that the tenon will wipe it down over the rest of the joint when you put it together. This way you won't have a lot of excess glue to clean up. If some glue does squeeze out of the joint, don't try to wipe it up at this time. Wait until it dries and then clean it up with a sharp chisel.

When the glue has set up, it's time to cut the glass rabbet, which is $\frac{1}{4}$" x $\frac{3}{8}$" deep. (See detail, Drawing 5-7.) You can do this with a router, but it's very tricky, and you could easily ruin a door. I would do it on a shaper, or more likely, a router set up as a shaper. I would use a pin-guide cutter rather than a ballbearing guide because it will leave you with less work squaring up the rabbet. Having made the glass rabbets, turn the doors over, and put a $\frac{1}{8}$" radius on the outer edge of the outer vertical style, then put a $\frac{1}{16}$" radius on the inner edge of all frame members. The first can be done with a router or on the router table, but the latter is best done with a spokeshave and sandpaper. Finally, make the glass moldings. The cross-section dimensions of this molding are $\frac{1}{8}$" x $\frac{3}{8}$"; one edge is completely rounded, as shown in Drawing 5-6. Cut the pieces to length and fit them to the opening. (They should already be mitered at the corners.) They will be held in place with #1 x $\frac{3}{8}$" round-head brass wood screws, which take a $\frac{7}{64}$" body hole. You can drill these now, four in the long pieces and two in the short ones. Please note that when the glass is in place, the molding strip's edges will be above the face of the door frame. This is as it should be.

When it comes to glass, I have learned from experience to leave it to the experts. I take my doors to the glass shop and let them cut and fit the pieces. The shelves are also glass, $\frac{1}{4}$" plate with finished edges. The dimensions should be $\frac{1}{16}$" shorter than the inside width and $\frac{1}{16}$" narrower than the inside depth with the back in place. For the doors, get the thinnest glass you can. You can get the glass now, but don't install it until you have mounted the doors to the case. Mount the door frame on the case using 1" x 1" brass cabinet hinges, two per door. Mortice them into both the door and the case, the inner face of the door and the outer edge of the case side about 1½" from top and bottom. The combined depth of the mortices should be equal to the thickness of the closed hinge across the pin sec-

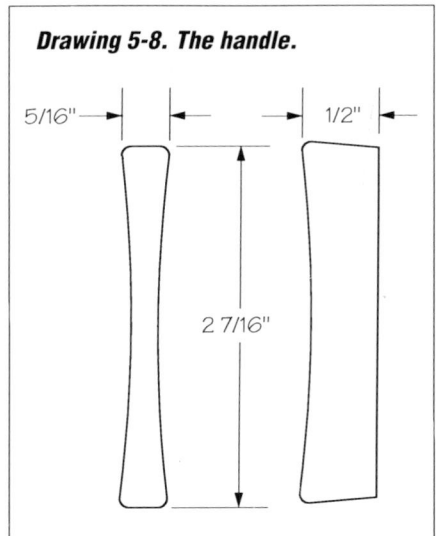

Drawing 5-8. The handle.

5/16"   1/2"

2 7/16"

Brass hangers, fastened with one screw in the top and one in the side.

tion. Mount each door separately. If the door is too tight against the case, place a paper shim under one leaf. If it's still too tight, shim the other leaf. It it's too far away so that there is an unsightly gap between case and door, cut the mortices a bit deeper. You want the door to close smoothly and completely but show little or no gap when closed. Having mounted both doors, you want to fit the mating edges. First, bevel each edge about $\frac{1}{16}$"; if they still won't close, shave a little off one edge and then the other until they do. Ideally, you want them to close with no daylight between them. (Notice I said "ideally." Mine don't.) After two more steps, you will have finished the doors. Step one is to put $\frac{1}{4}$" bullet catches under each door. Mount them in the center of the frame about $\frac{1}{2}$" from the mating edge. Lastly, attach the handles. I used the one in Drawing 5-8. That doesn't mean you

Door hinges installed.

doors; therefore, it should have a distinctive grain pattern that enhances the beauty of the showcase. The number of pieces in the back will depend on the grain pattern you find. Mine was made up of four pieces: the two in the center with the pattern and the two filler pieces on the sides. As I said previously, the individual boards are supported lengthwise with a dry spline joint. Cut a ⅛" x ¼"- deep groove in the center of each mating edge. The splines will be ¾₄" thick x ⁷₁₆" wide x whatever the length turns out to be. These should slide easily in the groove. Put one between each pair of boards. Do not use any glue. The edges of the boards that will be inside the cabinet should have a very slight bevel. The purpose of this is to clearly indicate that they are separate boards and not supposed to be glued together.

The shelves are glass. This means that you will see the shelf supports. You should use the wood ones that are described in chapter thirteen.

For the final finish, see chapter fourteen; it contains my thoughts about this. If you haven't done so, you may find it worth reading before going ahead.

The way this showcase is hung is very important. Because of the dowel joint between the sides and the top, it should not be hung from the top. It should be hung with brass hangers such as those shown in the picture. Place one screw in the top and one screw in the side. Hung this way, there will never be any danger of the joint failing and the case falling.

have to use it. Use anything that you feel enhances the showcase. It should be wood, but beyond that, let your imagination be your guide. If you use the one in the drawing, glue it in place as shown in the picture of the finished showcase. Your own design can go wherever you think it looks best.

The Back

This is the easiest part of the whole project. It is made up of separate boards ⅜" thick fastened top and bottom with #4 x ⅝" flat-head brass wood screws and having a dry spline joint between the boards. Here again, you should take time and care in choosing the wood. Remember that it will be seen through the glass

HAVE A SEAT

Yes, do have a seat. The one I'm offering, you will find to be handsome, versatile, simple to build, and, above all, comfortable. Of course, the last is the most important quality in any chair—and the one so often lacking. The simple design allows this one to fit in as a dining chair, at a desk, or for occasional use in any room in the house. In fact, you'll find it so useful that you may want to build more than one.

To begin this project, I'll take a minute and talk about the wood you'll use. As far as the seat and the top rail are concerned, almost any wood would be suitable. However, this is not true of the spindles and the legs. The spindles must be made from a strong, straight-grained wood that has considerable flexibility. Oak, hickory, ash, maple or walnut will do the job nicely. The legs, because they stand alone, without bracing, need to be strong. Oak, maple or walnut is best here, and it's best to choose a reasonably clear, straight grain. Since the chair will be finished natural, if you decide to use different woods for the various parts, I suggest that you avoid sharply contrasting woods. You might not like the result when finished.

I would also like to suggest that you read this all the way through and study the drawings carefully before

The jig for laminating the top rail.

Laminating jig with clamp blocks and clamps as they are used.

Laminating jig protected from glue with wax paper.

embarking on the project. Also, read chapters six and ten—you will find the work easier and more fun if you do.

There is one difference between this and the other furniture projects in this book: this one does not have an assembly drawing of the piece. There are a couple of reasons for this. An assembly drawing of this chair would be quite difficult to read, and frankly, difficult to draw. However, the real reason is that it isn't needed. If you make the various parts according to their drawings, there is only one way for them to go together.

So, when you've finished reading through the project, start making the parts. Begin with the top rail. The top rail holds the entire back together and gives it strength. Consequently, it must be strong. It's a curved piece, and if you were to cut it from a solid, thick board, it would be weak. The answer to this is to curve it by lamination. (This technique is described in chapter eleven.)

The jig for this is quite easy to make. Drawing 6-1 gives all the details. Use ½" high-density chipboard for the base, and cut the pieces that make the form from pieces of 2x6 fir. Attach these to the base with glue and screws. Be sure that these two pieces present a smooth face when you have put them in place.

The main clamp block is cut from a piece of 4x4,

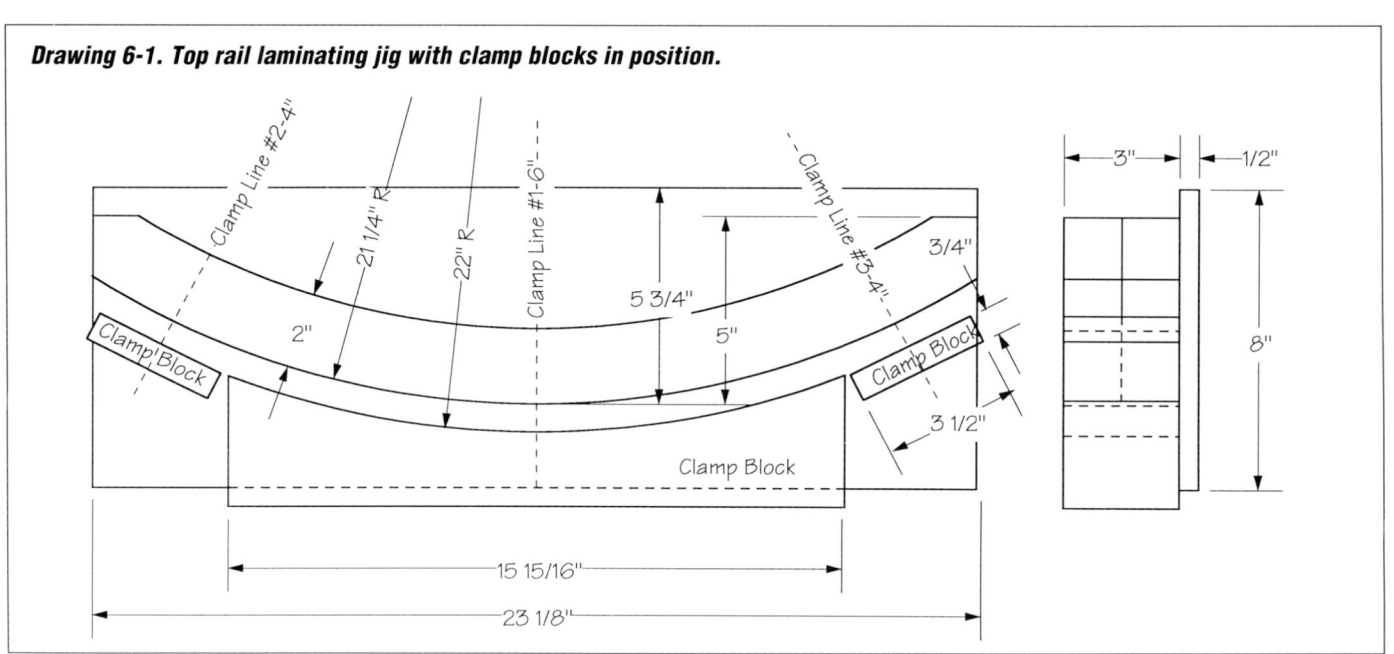

Drawing 6-1. Top rail laminating jig with clamp blocks in position.

Drawing 6-2. Back spindle drawing and table of dimensions.

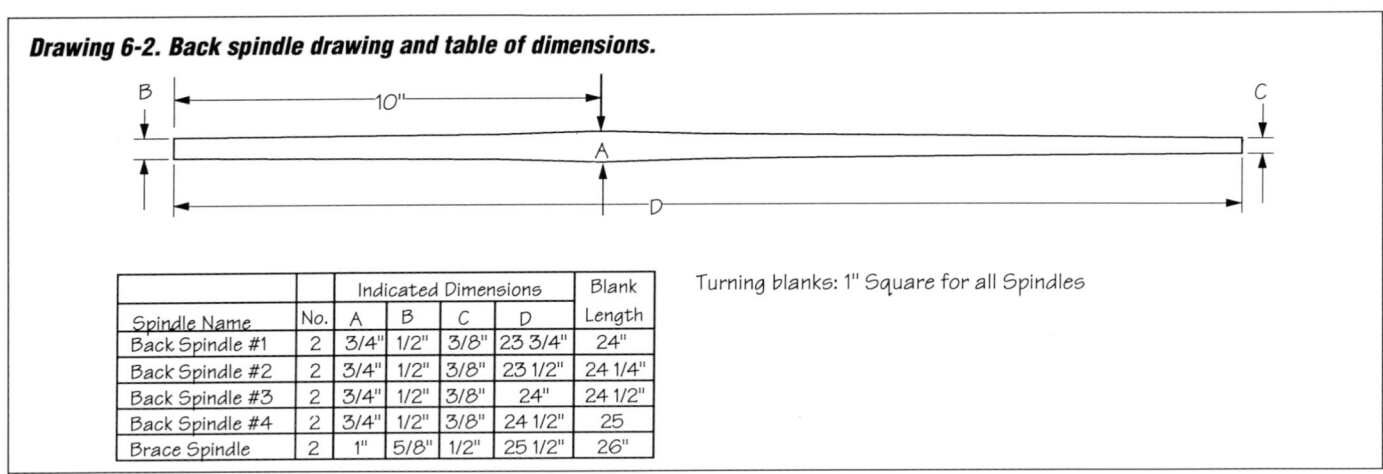

Turning blanks: 1" Square for all Spindles

Spindle Name	No.	Indicated Dimensions				Blank Length
		A	B	C	D	
Back Spindle #1	2	3/4"	1/2"	3/8"	23 3/4"	24"
Back Spindle #2	2	3/4"	1/2"	3/8"	23 1/2"	24 1/4"
Back Spindle #3	2	3/4"	1/2"	3/8"	24"	24 1/2"
Back Spindle #4	2	3/4"	1/2"	3/8"	24 1/2"	25
Brace Spindle	2	1"	5/8"	1/2"	25 1/2"	26"

Drawing 6-3. Leg drawings.

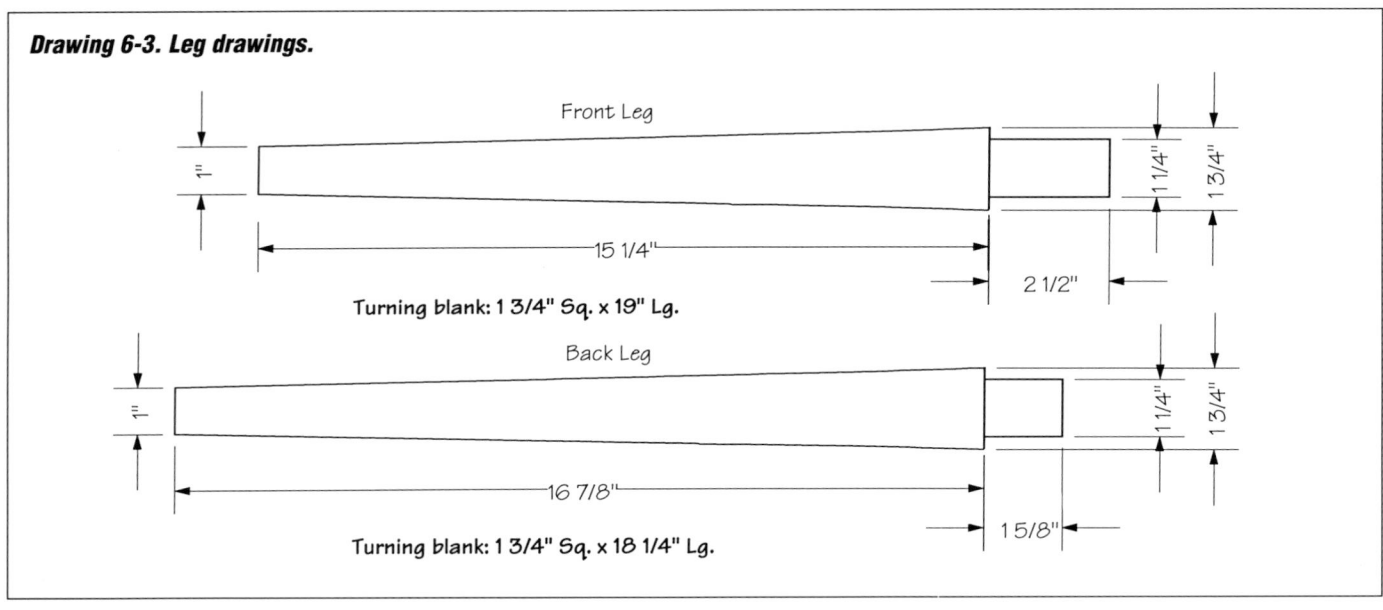

Front Leg

1"

15 1/4"

2 1/2"

1 1/4"

1 3/4"

Turning blank: 1 3/4" Sq. x 19" Lg.

Back Leg

1"

16 7/8"

1 5/8"

1 1/4"

1 3/4"

Turning blank: 1 3/4" Sq. x 18 1/4" Lg.

Drawing 6-4. Top rail.

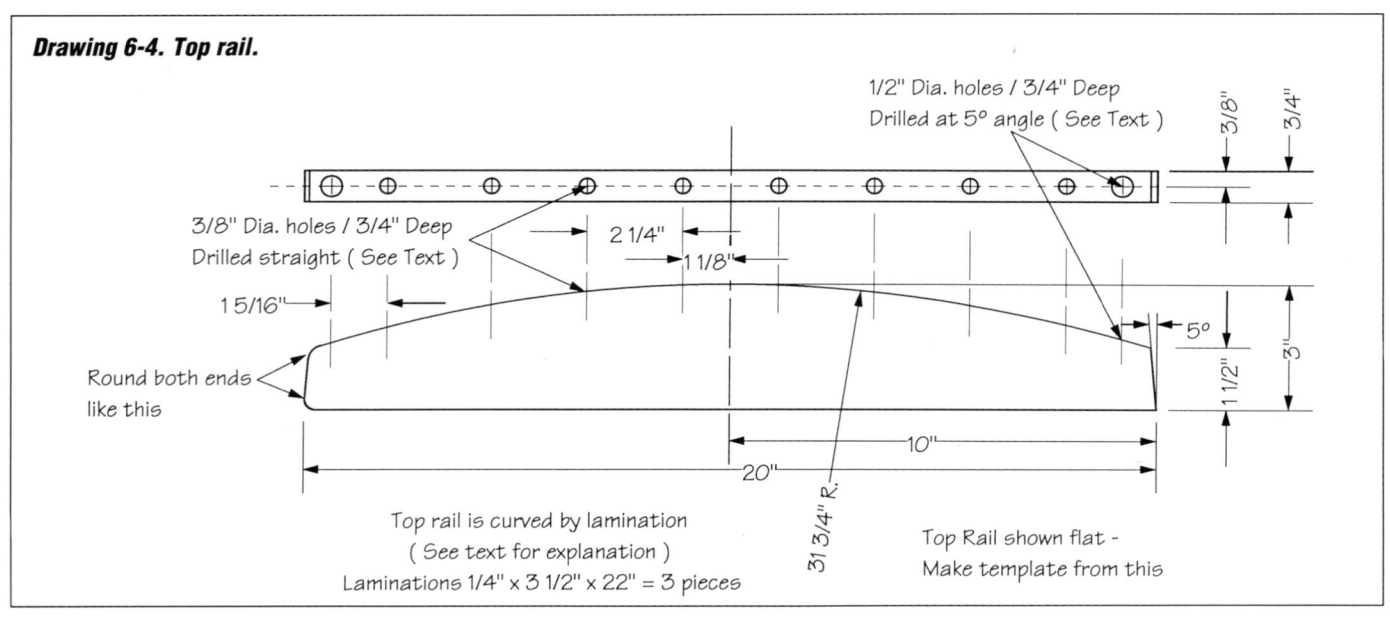

1/2" Dia. holes / 3/4" Deep
Drilled at 5° angle (See Text)

3/8"

3/4"

3/8" Dia. holes / 3/4" Deep
Drilled straight (See Text)

2 1/4"

1 1/8"

1 5/16"

5°

3"

1 1/2"

Round both ends
like this

20"

10"

31 3/4" R.

Top rail is curved by lamination
(See text for explanation)
Laminations 1/4" x 3 1/2" x 22" = 3 pieces

Top Rail shown flat -
Make template from this

Laminating the top rail. Second step.

Drill the brace spindle holes in the top rail using the angle drilling fixture described in chapter six.

and the two smaller clamp blocks are made from pieces of ¾″ plywood. You will need one 6″ and two 4″ C-clamps to complete the setup. Mark a heavy line on the top of the form and the top of the main clamp block to indicate the center of each.

To make the laminations for the rail, cut a piece 1″ x 3½″ x 22″. Joint one face and both edges, and with the jointed face against the rip fence, cut three pieces ¼″ thick. As you cut them, keep them in order so that when you put them together, they will be in the same relative positions as they were before you cut them. Take a light cut, on the jointer, off the outside face of the last piece—just enough to remove the saw marks. Do not do anything to the mating faces.

Before beginning the actual laminating process, it is necessary to line the jig with wax paper and bring together the clamp blocks and clamps ready to use. Lining the jig is necessary if you want to get the finished piece out of it. Applying the lining is difficult to explain but easy to understand from the accompanying picture. Just be sure that the paper comes over the front edge of the base and is taped underneath.

Put the three laminations together, and mark the center of what will be the top edge. Now, apply glue to all the mating faces. Use an old 1½″ paintbrush and sort of scrub it on. Put the laminations back together in the proper order and place them in the jig, matching the center marks. Put the large clamp block in position, and setting the 6″ clamp at the center, begin to tighten it. Keep tightening until you have the form, the laminations and the clamp block all touching each other at the center. If the various laminations try to move relative to each other, push them back in place as best you can. Put the two small clamp blocks in

place with the 4″ clamps, and tighten them as tightly as you can. Set this assembly aside and let the glue dry for twenty-four hours.

While the top rail blank is drying, it's a good time to turn the spindles and legs. There are eight back spindles and two brace spindles. Cut the blanks in accord with the sizes given in Drawing 6-2. Note the five lengths for the spindles. The front and rear legs, too, have different lengths. (See Drawing 6-3.) The technique for turning both the spindles and legs has been thoroughly covered in chapter ten. I won't repeat it here. I will, however, caution you not to remove, at this time, the square left on the turning-jig end of each piece. Also, be sure you mark each piece so that you can put it back in the lathe in the same position as before. This is particularly important for the legs, as you will see when you get to fitting them to the seat.

By the time you get the turning done, the top rail blank will be thoroughly dry. You'll find that the edges and the ends are not flush. Decide which edge is to be the top and joint it flush and square with the back face. At this point, make a full-size template of the top rail from the Drawing 6-4. Make it out of medium illustration board (about .025″ thick). Put on this template the location of the spindles' holes, which you will later drill in the bottom edge. (They are shown on the drawing.) Tape the template to the concave or inside surface of the rail blank. The top edge must be flush with the top edge of the blank, and the centers must match. Trace the outline of the template on the blank, and saw to the shape, leaving the line. Use a spokeshave to clean up the sawn surfaces and to slightly round all corners and edges. Put the template back on the rail, and mark the location of the spindle holes on

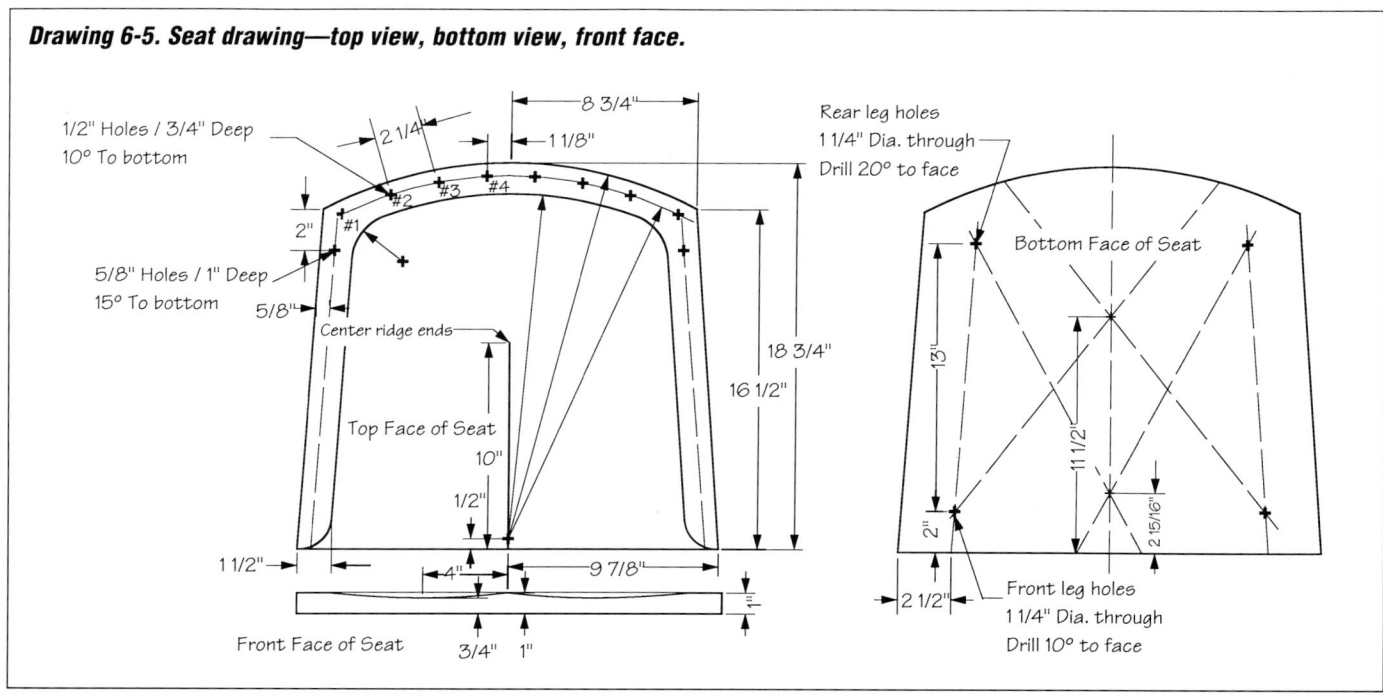

Drawing 6-5. Seat drawing—top view, bottom view, front face.

1/2" Holes / 3/4" Deep
10° To bottom

8 3/4"

2 1/4"

1 1/8"

Rear leg holes
1 1/4" Dia. through
Drill 20° to face

#2 #3 #4

2"

#1

5/8" Holes / 1" Deep
15° To bottom

5/8"

Bottom Face of Seat

Center ridge ends

18 3/4"

16 1/2"

13"

Top Face of Seat

10"

1/2"

11 1/2"

1 1/2"

2"

4"

9 7/8"

2 15/16"

Front Face of Seat

3/4" 1"

2 1/2"

Front leg holes
1 1/4" Dia. through
Drill 10° to face

the bottom edge with a pencil. Set your marking gauge (the end with the pointed marker) to ⅜", and working from the convex or outside surface, make a small indent at each hole marking.

Drilling the spindle holes requires a couple of special setups. For the ⅜" back spindle holes, you will need an auxiliary table clamped to your regular drill-press table. It must be of a size that will allow most of the rail to be on the table no matter which of the eight holes you're drilling. A piece of ¾" x 12" x 36" chipboard held with a C-clamp will do nicely. (I have chosen chipboard instead of plywood because it comes flat and stays that way. Today's plywood rarely does.) In drilling the holes, use a brad-point drill bit instead of a standard taper point. (The latter has a tendency to wander off the mark when starting the hole.) The ⅜" holes should be drilled ¾" deep measured at the marking line. Check this with a depth gauge. Better a little too deep than not deep enough. The ½" brace spindle holes have to be drilled at an angle of 5°. To do this, install the angle-drilling fixture you made in chapter six. Set the table to 5°. Place the rail on the table so that the convex side is facing you and the two ends are parallel with the front edge of the table. Drill the ½" holes ¾" deep at the marking line. Now finish sanding the entire piece.

The Seat

The major and most difficult part of this project is the seat. As you will see from Drawing 6-5, it will have to be made from a glued-up blank approximately 19½"x

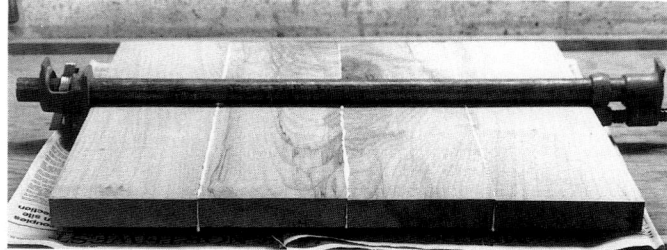

The seat blank glued up.

21". The starting thickness must be at least 1¾".

Depending on your equipment, you can make it from three, four or even five pieces. Cut all your pieces to 19½" long and joint the face that you want to be the bottom of the seat, then joint both edges square with this face. It is important that they be truly square. Now fit them together in the order you want them, and clamp them with one bar clamp in the center. Set the assembly on end and put a light behind it. If you can see the light through any of the joints, rework that joint. (By reworking it, I mean plane the mating edges of the two pieces so that the joint is slightly hollow—enough so you can see light through when the clamp is not pulled up, but no light when it is.)

On each piece, working from the bottom, measure up the edge 1¾" at what will be the rear and 1" at the front. Draw a line between the two points, and cut, leaving the line. The only way that you can saw this taper is on a band saw or by hand. If you don't have a band saw and you don't want to do the job by hand, there is another way, which doesn't involve sawing, that I will describe in a minute. But first, if you have made the cut, it's time to glue the pieces together. To do this correctly, you'll want a flat surface and two uniform sticks about ¾" square and 24" long. Put newspaper on the flat surface and then the sticks, far enough apart so as to support the front and rear edges of the seat. Apply glue to both faces of each joint and put them in position, making sure that the front edges line up flush and that the bottom is flat. Set the clamp that you used to test the joints. Pull it up so that glue is squeezed out all along each joint, and put the blank aside to dry. When it has dried, clean up the bottom face and be sure it's flat.

If you are not able or don't wish to saw the taper, reduce the thickness to the minimum 1¾", and glue the untapered pieces together just as I described above. When the blank has dried for twenty-four hours, clean up the bottom face and be sure it's flat, then draw the taper on the two side faces and across the front face. Clamp the blank between the dog on your vise and one set in one of the holes in your bench top, with a side facing you and the high end of the taper to your left. If you have a roughing plane, start with that and finish with a jack plane set for a pretty good cut. Planing across the grain, reduce the taper to the line. Turn the blank 90° on the bench, and with the high end facing you, finish planing with the grain for a smooth finish. A really smooth finish is not necessary, because this face of the seat has to be carved later to fit one's bottom. This method is not as difficult or as hard work as it seems. In the time before I could afford a band saw, I made many chair seats this way. If you're in my age bracket, it will give you your day's exercise; if you're younger, you will just work up a good sweat.

If you sawed the taper, that surface is apt to be uneven. Even it up with a jack plane, and you're ready to move on.

I just said we'd move on, but I really want to go back for a moment. When you have the seat blank in clamps, whichever way you're going to make it, there is that twenty-four hour period while it dries. This is a good time to make the seat template, which is very handy if you're going to make only one chair but essential if you're going to make more. Using the same weight illustration board as with the top rail template, lay out the outline and top face of the seat from Drawing 6-5. Cut the template to the outline, and turning it over, lay out the bottom face. While you're at it, make the template for the front face, also shown in Drawing 6-5. This template is necessary whether you make one or a dozen chairs.

Beginning the work on the seat, clean up the front face of the blank. Make it straight, flat and 90° to the bottom face. I usually use a smooth plane for this because I get a cleaner cut than with a block plane. Be

If you can't or don't want to saw the taper on the seat blank, plane it.

Drilling the back spindle holes in the seat. Use the angle-drilling fixture from chapter six.

sure you get all the saw marks out and create a smooth finished surface. Tape the template to the top face, and mark the outline, then cut to it, leaving the line. Plane the sides smooth, and clean up and smooth the back face with a spokeshave. Put a small (⅟₁₆"-⅛") radius on the bottom edge. Put the template back on the top face and tape it so that it can't shift. Using a sharp-pointed punch, press through the template, and mark each of the spindle-hole locations. These should be marked as deeply as you can so that you won't lose track of them when the template is removed. Remove the template, and draw on the top face of the blank the inner lines shown on the template. Also, from the center point of the front edge, draw a heavy line perpendicular to the front edge and 10" long. These lines will be your guide when carving the seat contour.

Turn the seat over, then turn the template over. Tape the template in place, and mark the leg-hole centers as you did the spindle holes. With a pencil, mark the points where the lines from the center points intersect the front and back faces. Note that the lines from the

Drilling the front leg holes. Notice the guideline on the seat blank and that the blank is clamped firmly to the drill fixture.

Final rough shaping with a spokeshave.

This is the easy way to cut the wedge slots in the leg ends.

front legs run to the back face and those from the back legs run to the front. Remove the template, and draw those lines on the bottom face of the seat. In each case, carry the line down across the front or back face. These lines are very important, as you'll see in a moment when you drill the leg holes.

All the holes in the seat are drilled with the angle-drilling fixture in place. Be sure that it's fastened firmly; that the centerline of the fixture is exactly under the center point of the drill bit; and that the back end of the centerline is in line with the center of the drill-press column. (See chapter six.) Set the table for 10°. (Use the angle blocks described in chapter six.) Using a ½" brad-point drill bit, position the seat so that with the drill bit at the point of each back spindle hole, an imaginary line between that point and the center point of the front face matches the centerline of the fixture. Drill the hole ¾" deep. (Set the depth gauge on the drill press so that all holes will be the same depth.) Having drilled all the back spindle holes, reset the fixture to 15°, and put a ⅝" bit in the chuck. For the two brace spindle holes, position the seat so that the bottom edge is parallel with the front edge of the fixture. Drill these holes 1" deep.

The leg holes are a bit more difficult, primarily because they're bigger— 1¼". It is best to use either a multispur or a Forstner bit. Do the front legs first. Set the angle for 10°. You will need a couple of C-clamps with pads to protect the seat. Bring the drill bit down so that the point is impressed on the centerpoint, and lock the drill-press spindle temporarily in place. This will hold the seat in place. Using the drill point as a pivot, bring the line on the seat bottom into position, matching the centerline of the fixture, and clamp the seat to the fixture. Release the drill-press spindle, and proceed to drill the hole all the way through the seat. I set the speed to the slowest position on a four-speed pulley and feed slowly and carefully. This is particularly important when breaking through the far side. You may get some vibration as you begin the hole. How much will depend on how sturdy you've built your fixture and how firmly you have it attached to the drill-press table. The vibration will disappear as soon as the entire drill bit is in the hole. Having drilled both front holes, reset the fixture to 20°, and following the same procedure, drill the back leg holes. Because of the greater angle, the vibration is apt to be more pronounced, but unless it's very bad, don't worry about it. However, don't hurry your feed because of it.

The last operation on the seat before assembly is to rough carve the contour into the top face. Tape the front-face template you have made to the front face of the seat. The top edge of the ends of the template should be flush with the top of the seat, and the center of the template should match the center of the seat.

Trace the top edge of the template with a heavy line. This line is the contour depth line you should work to. The line you drew on the top face shows the outer edges of the contour area. It's difficult to draw, or even describe, the contour of a chair seat. You simply make it to fit your bottom. One note: The shape on the front face fades out at the end of the 10"-long line you drew on the top face. From there on, the cavity extends all the way across. For the roughing operation, I use a variety of tools, depending on the area of the contour and how far along I am. For the initial work, I use either a roughing plane or an inshave. For later work, I use a spokeshave set heavy. The roughing plane and the inshave are used with the grain; the spokeshave is used across the grain. Work on this until the shape you want is clearly defined and any heavy roughness is removed. Round the bottom edges of the side faces to a ⅜" radius. Finish sand the bottom, side and rear faces. The seat is now ready to be assembled with the legs.

Seat and Leg Assembly

Begin by fitting each leg to its chosen hole. Do this by putting the leg back in the lathe, and using the straight-faced scraping tool, take the diameter of the tenon down to slightly over 1¼". Take the leg out of the lathe and try it. If it is too big, put it back and take off a little more and try again. Continue this until you have a sliding fit—that is, you can slide the leg in and out of the hole without undue force. When they are all fitted, you can cut the square off the bottom. The next operation is to cut the slot in which to put the wedge that will help hold the leg in place. The slot should be about ⅛" wide and 1¼" deep, through the center of the tenon. You can cut this with a hand saw, but that's a rather tedious job. I prefer to do it on the table saw. It's free-hand cutting and a bit tricky, but if you hold the leg firmly with both hands, you won't have any trouble. The picture on the facing page (bottom) shows the operation better than I can explain it. A blade with about a ⅛" kerf set 1¼" high will make the proper slot in one pass.

Make the wedges as described in chapter thirteen. If you're using a light wood, like maple, in the chair, a dark wood for the wedges makes a nice touch. However, a light wood with a dark chair looks terrible.

As you have undoubtedly found out by now, the legs, when in position, extend beyond the top face of the seat. Therefore, place the seat, bottom up, on a couple of sticks to give clearance. Put glue around the top third of the hole, and push the leg home as far as it will go. The slot should be parallel with the front edge of the seat; otherwise, it would run with the grain, and you'd risk splitting the seat when you drove the wedges in place. Turn the assembly over and set it on its legs. Using a knife or spatula, put glue generously

Drive the wedges all the way home using a soft-headed hammer.

This setup lets you work at bench level with the seat firmly clamped in place.

Final shaping of the seat done with a sanding disc in your hand drill.

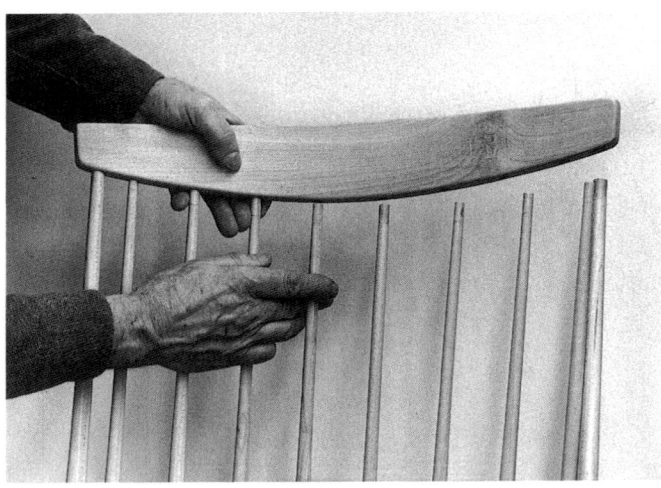

Assembling the top rail to the back spindles.

in the slots, and drive the wedges until you're pretty sure they're bottomed.

When the assembly has dried for twenty-four hours, you're ready to trim the protruding tops of the legs and sand the seat contour to its final shape and finish. For this work, I have developed a special setup so that I can clamp the seat firmly in place while I'm working on it. A piece of 2x12 about 4½' long, clamped to the bench and protruding from it, provides the working surface. The picture on page 103 (center) shows how the setup is arranged. The first step is to trim the leg tops flush with the surrounding area. I do this with a flexible, keyhole-type saw, and if that doesn't get it flush, I clean it up with the spokeshave or a chisel. For the final shaping of the contour, use a flexible rotary sanding disk mounted in your electric hand drill. I use a 5" diameter disk. Start with 50 grit paper and go to 80 grit. Final sanding is done with an orbiting sander like the Porter Cable 330, which fits the palm of your hand. Put an extra sponge-rubber pad under the sandpaper. Start with 80 grit and finish with 150. Be sure to get out all the rotary marks.

Final Fitting and Assembly

The time has come for final fitting and assembly. Take the two brace spindles and saw off the square at the bottom. Fit them into their holes in the seat. They should go in with a light tap, and you should be able to rotate them with your hand when they're in place.

Be sure they're bottomed in the hole. Mark each spindle and the hole it goes into. Remove them from the seat and fit them to the top rail, then put a mark on each spindle at the bottom edge of the rail. Remove the bottom square from all the back spindles, marking them with their numbers as you go. Working from the middle outward to the right and left, number them from 4 to 1 with the shortest being 4. Fit each one to its hole in the seat and in the top rail as you did the brace spindles.

Now, put all the spindles in place in the seat. Put the top rail on the brace spindles positioned in front of the back spindles, making sure that the rail comes down to the marks you previously made on the spindles and that the rail is level. Position each spindle behind its proper hole in the rail, and mark it at the bottom edge of the rail. Remove the rail and the back spindles. Measure each back spindle from the mark you just made to the top end. If it measures more than ¾", cut it to that length. (If all the spindles measure more than ⅛" short, then your brace spindles are a bit too long. Shorten them and remark the back spindles as you did before.) Put all the spindles back in the seat with the marks on the upper ends facing forward. Take the top rail in hand, and starting at either side, carefully start each spindle in its hole. When they are all started, using a small block of wood as a buffer, drive the top rail down until it comes to the marks. To get it all the way down, you may have to hit it rather hard. If it won't come down, something is wrong: one hole may not be deep enough. Take the rail off, find the trouble and do it again. When you are satisfied that everything is right, take it all apart, apply the glue to the holes, and put it together again. In applying the glue, be very careful; put glue only in the top third of the hole, and be rather sparing with the amount you use. If you use too much, you will trap it in the bottom of the hole and the spindles will not go home—and you won't realize it until it's too late.

Well, that's it. You're done, all except the finishing, which I'll leave to you. Just don't spoil it with stain. I think you will be pleased with what you've made, and I hope you decide to make several. You may like them enough to want to build a dining room set around them. Project nine is a great table for this purpose. Four of these chairs fit it nicely.

TO WRITE A LETTER

In the days before fax machines and telephones, people wrote letters, and writing desks were in vogue. Even today, many people still write letters by hand. If someone in your home likes to do this, he or she will enjoy this small writing desk. It has a slightly Oriental flavor, the design is such that it will fit with any decor, and it's easy to build. See page 150 for a cutting list for this project.

The Base
Make the leg blanks, as described in chapter eleven, by laminating curved pieces. Once you have the blanks, the first step is to cut the ¾" square tenons on the top of each leg. The easiest way to do this is to make the three horizontal cuts that can be made on the table saw, using the rip fence as a guide. Then make all four vertical cuts with the waste wood on the outside of the blade. Now you can make the fourth horizontal cut

with a hand saw. Do this carefully so that the shoulder remains true all around. The last operation on the legs is to taper the foot. The single taper is on the inside of the curve and begins at the bottom of it. The double taper on the sides begins at about the same point. (Drawing 7-2 shows 8", but this is approximate.) Rough cut these tapers on the band saw, and finish them with a spokeshave. Blend the beginning so that it's a smooth curve and not an abrupt angle. Do not bevel or round any edges at this time. The outside or back face has a rough-sawn surface. On the straight parts of this surface, take a very light cut on the jointer—just enough to clean up the saw marks. Clean up the curved part with a spokeshave.

The spreader is cut from a solid board that you will probably have to glue up. The overall width is approximately 9". In chapter eleven, I said that sawed curves were often weak. That would be true in this case if the

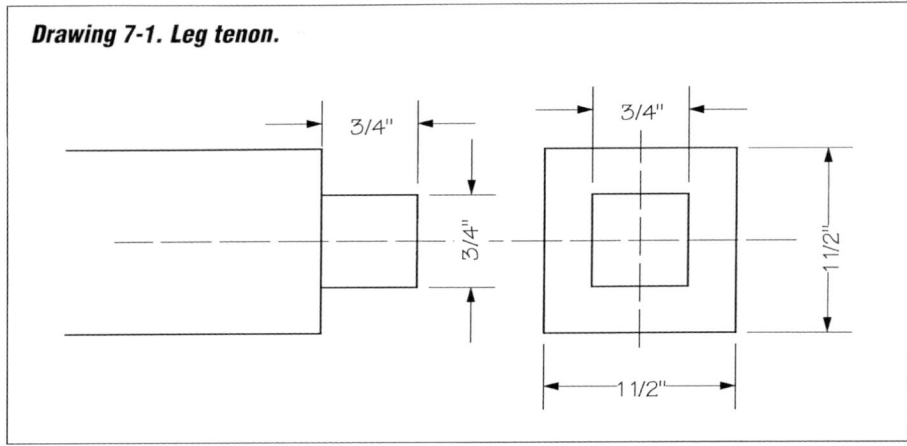

Drawing 7-1. Leg tenon.

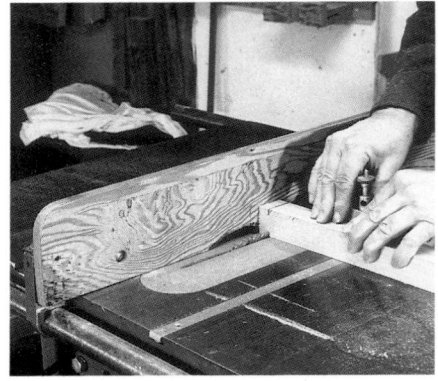

Making the horizontal cuts for the leg tenon.

Drawing 7-2. Three views of the complete desk.

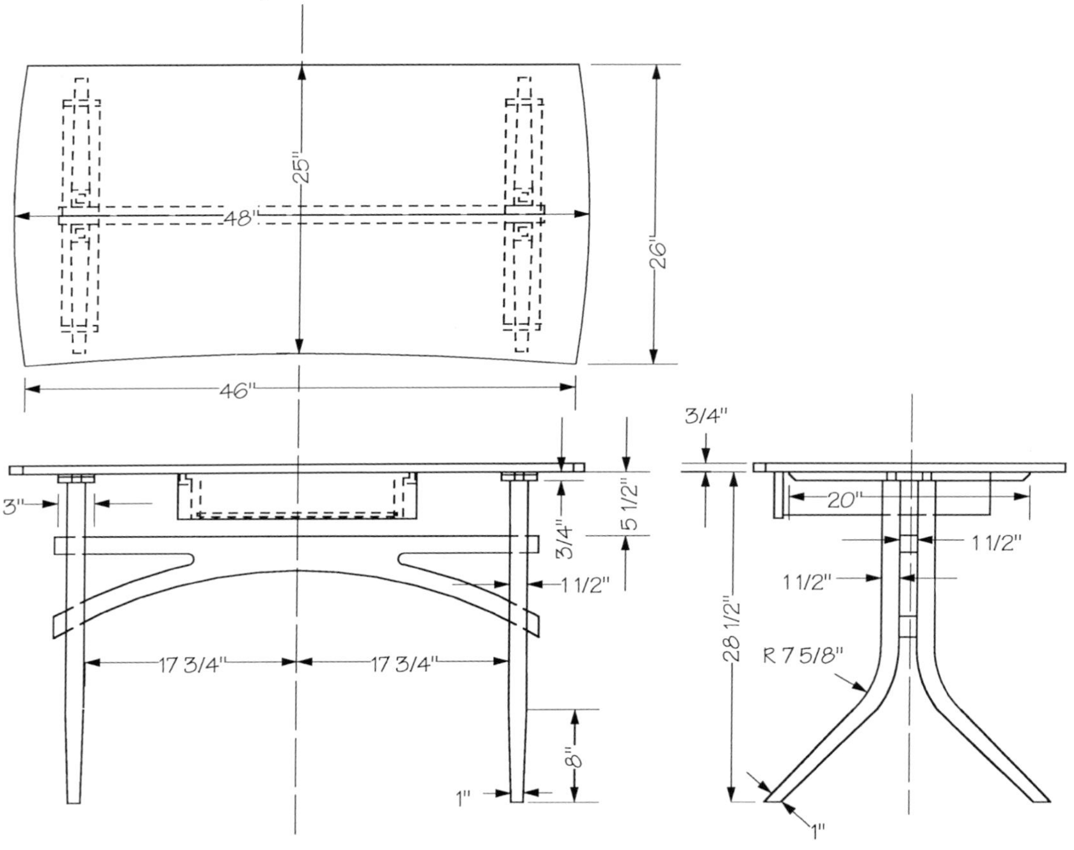

bottom of the curve were not fastened, but since it is, the sawed curve will work very well and is much easier to make. With the glued-up piece finished to 1½" thick and 40½" long, lay out the spreader according to Drawing 7-3. When cutting it out, start with the two small inside curves. Using a 1" Forstner or multispur drill bit, drill holes to give you the curve cut. This will result in a relatively smooth surface that can be finished with sandpaper. Saw the rest of the shape on the band saw, leaving the line. The easiest way to finish is

with a spokeshave. Do not, at this time, round or in any way break the edges. Those sharp edges will be very important in the assembly operation. Another important thing to do now is to cut from the scrap two pieces 1½" wide by the finished thickness of the spreader by 5½" long. Set these aside. They will be vital in the assembly operation.

The top supports are finished to ¾" x 3" x 20" with a ½" bevel at each end, as shown in Drawing 7-2. In laying out the mortices for the leg tenons, do it from the

Making the vertical cuts for the leg tenon.

An easy way to make small curves with smooth surfaces.

Marking the mortice locations.

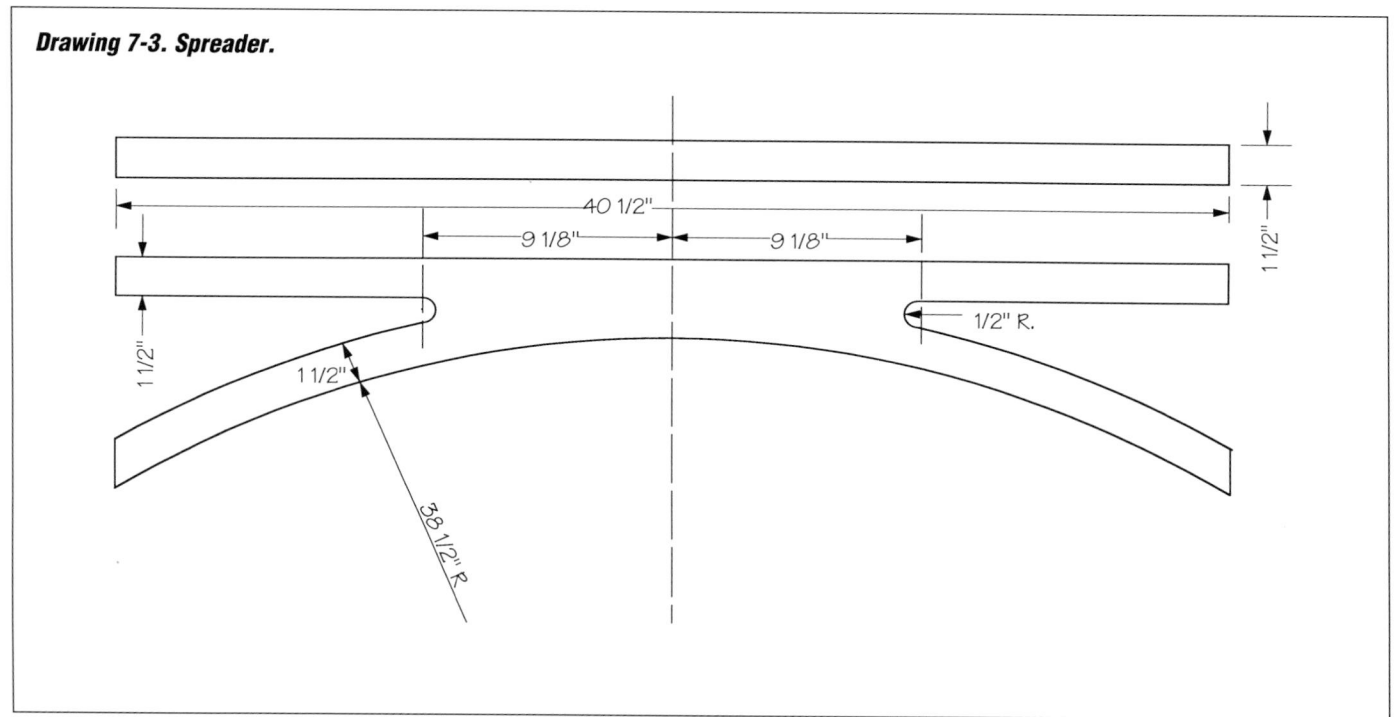

Drawing 7-3. Spreader.

40 1/2"
9 1/8"
9 1/8"
1 1/2"
1 1/2"
1 1/2"
1/2" R.
38 1/2" R.

tenons and not from the drawing. First, number each leg and pair them up. Place between each pair of legs one of those pieces you recently made and set aside. Make sure you position it with the thickness of the spreader separating the legs. Lightly clamp them in this position. Placing them in position on the top support, as shown in the picture, mark the cross lines of the mortices with a sharp knife. Use a marking gauge to mark the other two sides. Notice that these are through mortices; therefore, start your cutting from the side that will show. I take out the waste wood with a drill, picking one that will leave a small amount inside the lines. When you've finished cutting the mortices, fit each pair of legs to its top support without removing the insert or the clamp. This should be a

snug fit. At this time, make the slots that will take the screws that fasten the top in place. There should be two of them on each end of the support between the leg and the outer end. They should be ³⁄₁₆" x ³⁄₈" long to take #10 x 1¼" flat-head wood screws. The reason for the slots is to accommodate the shrinkage and expansion of the top that will occur across the grain with humidity changes.

This next operation is a bit ticklish and requires great care. The legs and spreader are fastened together with blind dowels. Start this step by putting together both sets of legs and top supports with the spacers resting firmly on the top support. Set them up on your workbench with the top supports down and the proper distance apart. Place the spreader in position,

Setup for marking leg positions on spreader.

Setup for marking dowel hole locations on legs.

Base dry-assembled.

and press it firmly down on the spacers. Square everything up, legs with top supports and legs with spreader, and clamp firmly so that they won't move. Mark on both faces of the spreader, with a pencil, the outer and inner edges of the legs. Now, take the assembly apart, and finding the approximate center of the marked spaces on the spreader, drill a ½" hole all the way through in each space. Put one leg of each pair in place on the top supports, and set the spacers in position. Put the spreader on top of the spacers and line up the legs with the line you drew on the spreader. Square everything as before and clamp so that there can be no movement. Take the ½" drill bit (this must be a brad-point drill bit), slide it through the holes in the spreader, and mark the legs with the brad point. Do the same with the other set of legs, and then drill ½" holes ¾" deep on the marks. In putting this assembly together, don't use dowels all the way through the spreader. Instead, use 1¼"-long dowels in the legs, then push the leg dowels into the spreader. Be sure to size the dowels so that they are no more than a tap fit. Put it all together dry to make sure that everything fits and is square. Then take it apart, round or bevel all the edges, finish sand all the parts, and put it back together, this time with glue. Use glue only in the dowel holes, and sparingly in the ones in the legs. (If there's too much, the dowel won't go home.) If you put it on the faces of the parts, it will squeeze out, and you'll have a difficult cleanup job. Put glue only in the top of the top support mortices so that, as the tenons go in, they will wipe the glue over the rest of mortice face and not out the other end.

The Top

The top is simply a matter of gluing up the boards to get the necessary width, finishing the surfaces, and cutting the resulting panel to shape. In choosing the wood for this, try to find boards that go together so that when you're finished it will look like one piece rather than a bunch of boards glued together. Notice that the back edge, which goes against the wall, is straight, while the front is slightly concave and the ends are slightly convex. A ⅛" bevel around the top edge will add a nice touch. The bottom edge can have a ¹⁄₁₆" radius. You can mount it on the base now or wait until you've finished the drawer and hang it at the same time.

The Drawer

The drawer has a slightly different construction. You need extra width on the front to cover the drawer hangers; thus, the standard dovetail joint between front and sides won't work. What we'll use is a running dovetail as shown in Drawing 7-5. There is a rather simple way to make this joint. First, make the front, sides and back blanks to finish sizes according to the drawing. When making one of the sides, make it about 6" longer than required. Cut this off, and we'll use it for a test piece when making the running dovetail. To make this joint, use a standard dovetail cutter. Put your router in the router table so that the top of the cutter is ⅜" above the surface of the table. Set your fence (which should be about 3" high and have no openings in it) so that the distance between the fence and the top edge of the cutter is 1⅛". Make your cut the full width of the drawer front. Now, without moving the router, adjust the fence so that the distance between the fence and the bottom of the cutter (at the table surface) is ½". This can best be measured with a pair of inside calipers. Run the front end of the outside surface of both drawer sides through this cut in a vertical position. Do both ends of your test piece. In making this cut, be sure you feed against the rotation of the cutter, not with it. Now, run the other face of one end of your test piece through the cutter, and try the result in the groove on the drawer front. If it's too tight, move the fence very slightly in and try again. Keep this up until you have a snug sliding fit in the groove, then make the second cut on the drawer sides. The joint between the sides and the back is a standard through dovetail with the tails in the sides. In laying out the tails, be sure that the bottom one is wide enough to cover the groove for the drawer bottom. Cut the tails first, and lay out the pins from them. Fit the drawer together to be sure it all works and is square. Now is the time to cut the groove for the bottom. (See Drawing 7-6.) This is ¼" wide x ³⁄₁₆" deep and is located with its upper edge ½" from the bottom edge of the drawer. Please note that while on the sides and back the groove goes all the way through, on the front it must be stopped off or it will show on the outside. After you have cut the grooves, rip off the bottom edge of the back to the top of the groove.

The drawer bottom is another glued-up panel. The choice of wood is not important here, in that the boards don't have to match. Make it ⁵⁄₁₆" thick, and rabbet the front and side edges so that it slides easily in the groove. It's fastened at the back with one or two #3 x ⅝" flat-head brass wood screws. Glue the drawer together, and slide the bottom in place to make sure that everything is square. While the glue is setting up, you can cut the drawer runners (½" x ½" x 17¼") and make the drawer hangers according to Drawing 7-7. When the drawer assembly has dried, glue the runners to the outside of the sides, flush with the top edge.

The last part to make is the drawer handle, shown in Drawing 7-8. The blank for this is ½" x 1" x 6". Choose wood that either matches the drawer front or

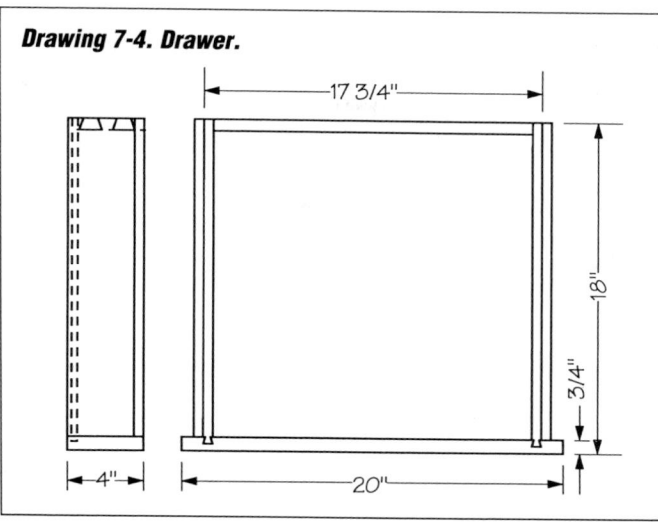

Drawing 7-4. Drawer.

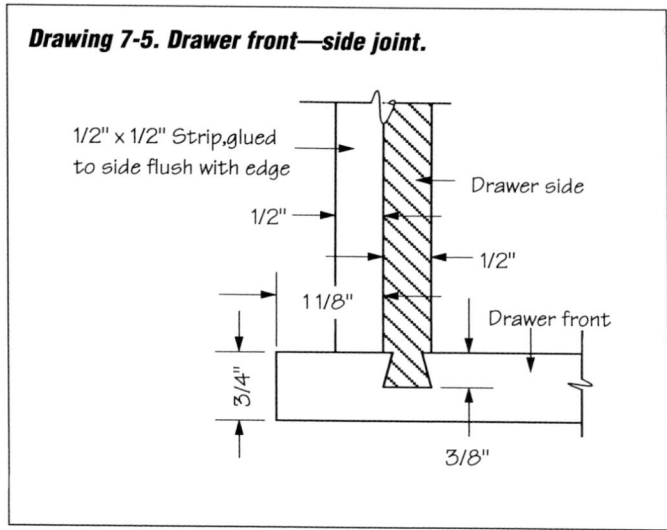

Drawing 7-5. Drawer front—side joint.

Cutting running dovetail on drawer front.

Drawing 7-6. Drawer bottom detail.

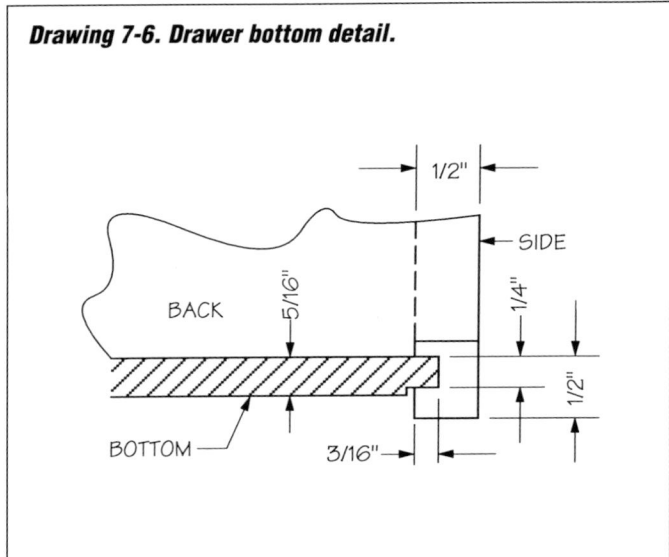

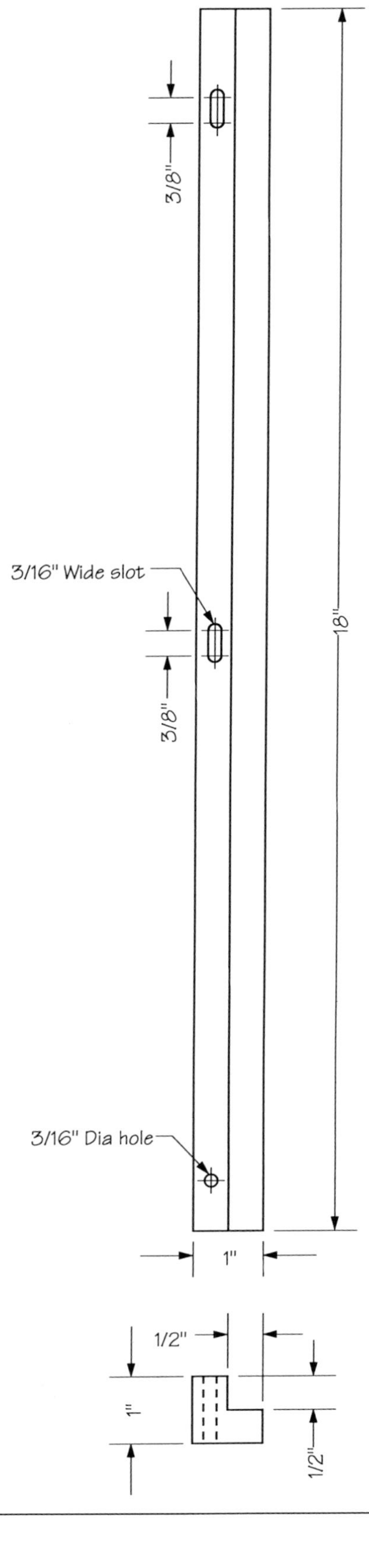

Cutting running dovetail on drawer sides.

Drawing 7-7. Drawer hanger.

is in strong contrast to it. Again, we are going to use the router as a shaper. Use the ¼"-radius cove cutter, and set the top of it ⅜" above the table. The best type of cutter for this job is one with a ball-bearing guide. However, a pin-guide type will work; it just requires more care to keep the guide from burning. Make the cut on all four edges of the blank, doing the ends first. Now shape the top according to the drawing, and recut the sides. After sanding every surface except the bottom, you can fasten it to the front of the drawer. Use a couple of ¼" dowels or simply glue it directly to the front. I don't like the latter method, because in positioning the handle, you invariably smear glue where you don't want it, and it becomes a real problem to clean up. If you use the dowel method, just put glue in the upper part of the dowel holes, and be sure that the amount of dowel protruding from the handle isn't longer than the matching hole is deep.

Drawing 7-8. Drawer handle.

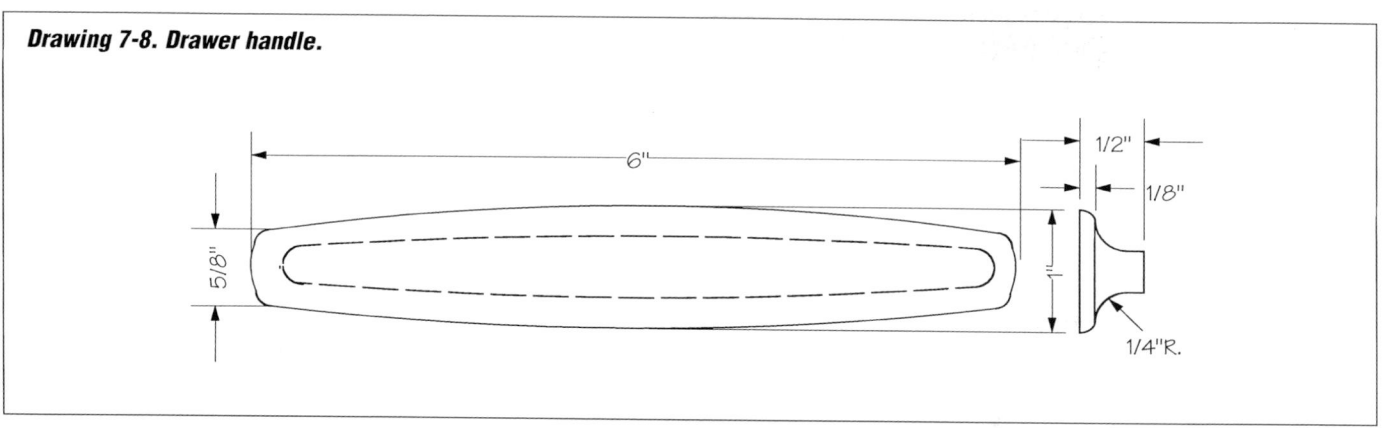

Final Assembly

The final operation is to assemble the top, the base and the drawer. Lay the top upside down on a broad, protected surface. (I use an old blanket.) It's very upsetting to do all this work, get the piece together, set it up on its legs, and find you've scarred the devil out of the top surface. Position the leg assembly on the top according to the drawing and screw it down with the #8 x 1¼" flat-head wood screws. Put one drawer hanger in place and screw it down. Now put the drawer in place, position the other hanger so that the drawer slides easily, then screw it down. Turn the final assembly right-side up, and see that the drawer still works smoothly.

For finishing, I will refer you again to chapter fourteen. I will, however, repeat one thing I said there: Don't use any stain. Use good wood with attractive grain patterns, and finish it natural. If you want a light piece, use light wood, if you want a dark piece, use dark wood, not light wood stained dark. Stain only muddies the picture.

When you have finished this little desk, you'll have a piece that is unique and of which the entire family, especially the one for whom you made it, can be proud.

Shaping the drawer handle.

AN INTERESTING COFFEE TABLE

When it comes to coffee table designs, the only element that they all have in common is that they are low, usually between 16" and 18". Other than that, they vary all over the map, especially in shape and style. As I've said before, the lines of furniture should be simple and relatively plain so that the wood itself provides the beauty in the piece. I also believe that when you make a piece of furniture, you expect to use it and pass it on to your children and possibly your grandchildren. You want it to fit into whatever decor you or they might have now or in the future. The exotic pieces, after the fad has faded, usually end up in the attic or at Goodwill. See page 151 for a cutting list for this project.

Drawing 8-1. Three views of complete table.

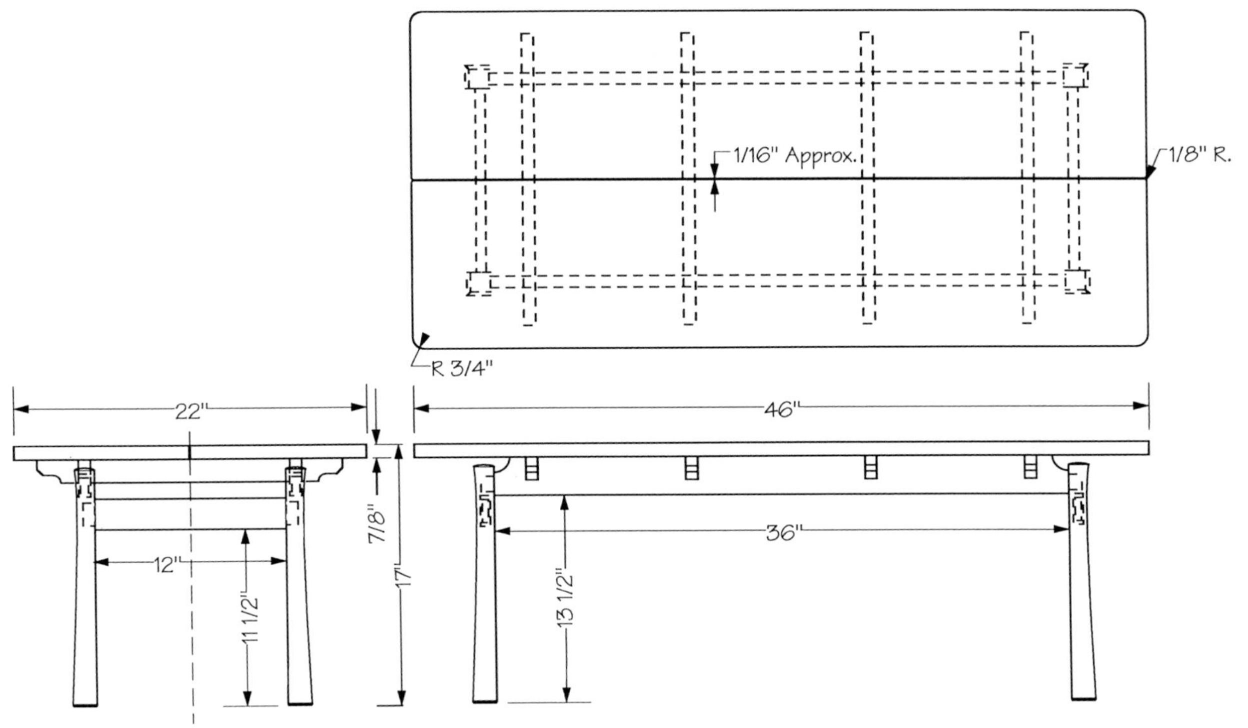

1/16" Approx.

1/8" R.

R 3/4"

22"

46"

7/8"

17"

12"

11 1/2"

36"

13 1/2"

Drawing 8-2. Stretcher, short top support and long top support.

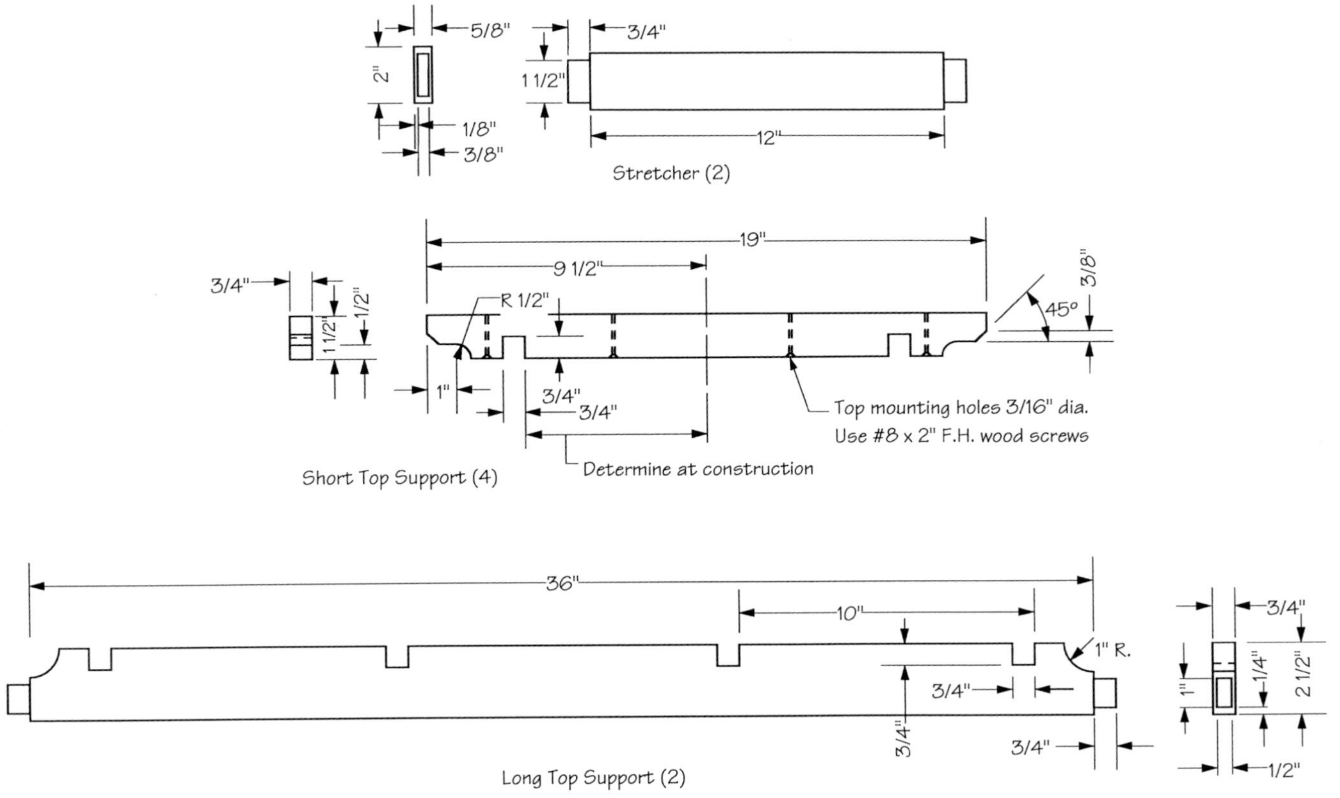

5/8"

3/4"

2"

1 1/2"

1/8"

3/8"

12"

Stretcher (2)

19"

9 1/2"

3/8"

3/4"

1/2"

45°

R 1/2"

1 1/2"

Top mounting holes 3/16" dia.
Use #8 x 2" F.H. wood screws

1"

3/4"

3/4"

Short Top Support (4)

Determine at construction

36"

10"

1" R.

3/4"

3/4"

3/4"

1/4"

2 1/2"

1"

3/4"

1/2"

Long Top Support (2)

Base assembled from roughed-out parts.

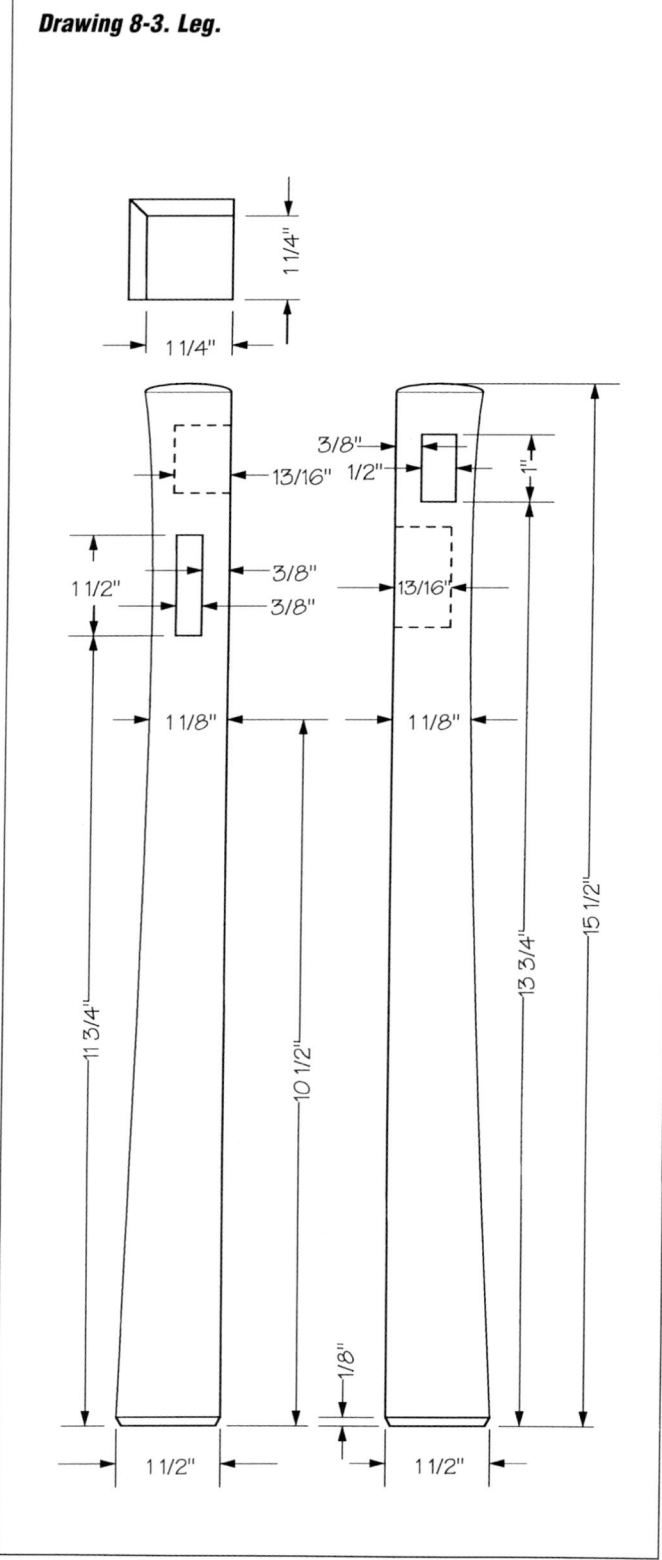

Drawing 8-3. Leg.

If you agree with me, I think you'll enjoy building this table. It's simple and easy to build, yet it has several interesting points that make it a bit more than run-of-the-mill.

The Base

The first operation on the base is to cut all parts to finished size. Start with the legs. Joint two adjacent faces of each, and be sure that these faces are square with each other. Use a try square to check. With the jointed faces against the fence, rip each leg to 1½" square, and cut them all to correct length. Decide which end will be the top, and standing the legs upright with the top end up, form them into a square with all jointed faces touching each other. Now, number the legs, starting with the right rear one, 1, 2, 3, 4 in a clockwise direction. Also mark 1 and 2 to indicate the mating faces, do the same with 3 and 4. Legs 1 and 2 will be the legs at one end, and 3 and 4 will be those at the other end. This is very important; in each leg you will cut two different mortices, and if they are not properly placed, you will have ruined the leg. Do not do any shaping of the legs at this time; just set them aside.

Finish the stretchers at ⅜" x 2" x 13½" long. Finish the long top supports at ¾" x 2½" x 37½". Cut the short top supports to ¾" x 1½" x 19". Now you can cut the tenons on the stretchers and the long top supports. (The short top supports have no tenons.) Do not cut the concave curve on the ends of the long top supports at this time. Cut the tenons as described in chapter eight for the blind mortice-and-tenon joint.

Using the tenons you have just cut as templates, lay out the mortices on all four leg blanks, marking them with a sharp knife. Again be careful to get each mortice in its correct position. (See Drawing 8-3.) There is only one straight corner on each leg. All the mortices, whatever their position vertically, should be ⅜" from this corner. Refer to chapter eight for information on cutting the mortices. The tenons should fit the mortices snugly but not tightly. Too tight a fit wipes most of the glue out of the joint.

At this point, you should finish the long top supports, cutting the concave curves at the ends and the notches as shown in Drawing 8-2. Now assemble the legs, stretchers and long top supports; clamp them together gently but firmly; and make sure everything is square. Carefully measure the distance between the long top supports. This is the distance between the notches on the short top supports. You will note that on the drawing this dimension is marked "determine at construction." No matter how careful the crafter may be, there are usually slight differences between the drawing dimensions and the actual dimensions. Therefore, on a critical dimension such as this, it is best to set it based on the actual dimension. Having obtained this distance, finish the short top supports, and assemble them with the rest of the base to see that they fit properly. Take the base apart, and round all four edges of the stretchers and the bottom edges of the top supports, as well as the edges of all the curved sections. Do the final sanding of these parts at this time. Finally, cut the small bevels at the bottom of the legs. Set this up with the miter gauge at 45° and a stop to position the leg correctly. Make the four cuts on each leg.

At last it's time to shape the legs. Make a full-size template as shown in Drawing 8-3. Place this on one of the rough faces of the leg (the ones without mortices) with the straight edge flush with a jointed face, and mark the curve. Saw to the curve. Now place the template on the newly sawn surface, again with the straight edge against the edge of the jointed face, and draw the curve. Saw to this curve. Save several of the waste pieces, and cut a section from each end of two. These pieces will be very helpful in holding the legs in the vise while working on them. Smooth the sawn surfaces—the fastest and easiest way is with a spokeshave. The next step is to slightly round all the edges. This will proceed much faster with a spokeshave. At this time, you should also round off the tops of the legs as shown in the drawing. As a last step, sand all over with #150 paper. Be careful around the mortices not to alter the flatness of the surface.

Assemble the finished parts, again dry, to make sure everything fits as it should. Take it apart and apply the glue. Remember, when gluing a mortice-and-tenon joint, never put glue on the tenon. Put it around the top half of the mortice; the tenon then will spread it over the rest of the surface as it goes home. Be sparing in the amount you use; otherwise you may

Cutting the bevels on the leg bottoms.

Shaping the leg with a spokeshave. Notice gripping pads made from leg waste pieces.

Top support frame assembled and glued.

trap the excess in the bottom of the mortice and the joint won't go home. (However, if you have a sloppy joint, you can use more to fill the joint and help make it strong.) In gluing the short top supports to the long ones, put the glue in the long support notches (some at the top of each notch face and a little in the center of the bottom). If you use too much, it will squirt out and make a mess that will be difficult to clean up. If it should squirt out, don't attempt to wipe it up at that time. If you do, you'll force it into the pores of the wood and never get it out. Let it dry, and then carefully remove it with a sharp chisel.

I suggest that you glue the legs and the stretchers

first, as two separate assemblies. Make sure the legs are square with the stretchers. I would use clamps across the stretchers. Here is another place where the curved waste pieces you cut from the legs come in handy. They make perfect pads under the clamps. While these are drying, assemble the long and short top supports and glue them together. Make sure the assembly is square, as shown on page 115. When all the subassemblies have dried, assemble the two ends to the top support frame. Use clamps here, too, and be sure that the legs are square with the supports.

The Top

Last, but really the most important, is the top. It's important because it will set the tone of the whole piece. It should be made from wood that has a distinct and interesting grain pattern. Notice that it's two separate boards, each approximately 11" wide, with a slight space between them and all the edges of each board slightly rounded. If you're lucky, by searching through the stack at the lumber yard, you may find two 1" x 12" boards that will do the job. Otherwise you will have to try to get matching pieces and glue them up. However, it's easier to find two pieces to match to make one board than it is to find four to match to make the top solid.

This design has another advantage: Because the boards are relatively narrow, any movement due to changing climate conditions will be slight. Therefore, the mounting screws can be in holes rather than slots. I have made the thickness of the top ⅞" because the extra fullness will look better than ¾". However, you'll have to get 1" rough stock (and a full 1" at that) in order to finish at ⅞". If you can't get the rough stock, you'll have to settle for ¾" finish thickness, which will look okay. Here is another way to get a very striking top. It will take time and searching, but if you can find the right piece, it will be worth it. Look for a piece at least 2" thick by 12" wide and any length over 48" that has a distinctive grain pattern. Joint both edges straight and then resaw it down the middle. Lay it open like a book, and you have a book-match. By the

Mounting top boards to base.

time you have the pieces flat and smooth, you may not be able to hold the thickness to ⅞", but with the beauty and uniqueness of such a top, it will not matter. If you find the board but don't have the resaw capacity in your own shop, find a commercial shop in your town that does, and take it to them. They won't charge you much for doing it, but whatever it is, it will be worth the price to get the top. Remember to look for a really unusual grain pattern.

When mounting the top, put the boards upside down on the bench with a ¹⁄₁₆" shim between them at each end (I used a 3" x 5" file card folded twice), and clamp them together (tighten the clamp just enough to prevent any movement). Mount them as you would a solid top. Next, remove the clamps and the shims, and the construction part of the project is completed.

For the finishing operation, I remove the top boards and finish them and the base separately; it's much easier that way. (When reinstalling the boards, put the shims in place until the boards are screwed down.) See chapter fourteen for finishing ideas, or use your own. If you've been able to find an interesting grain pattern for the top, don't muddy it with stain. So, there you have it: an interesting and somewhat unique coffee table that will elicit comments from your friends. It fits the criteria that I stated in the beginning, but it's different enough that you won't find it in everyone's home.

ABOUT A DINING TABLE

I'm having trouble introducing this project. I suppose I could say, "Here's a nice dining table you can build"—not very eye catching, but true. I could say that it's a differently styled table with several unusual features; that, too, would be true. I could even say that it's just right for a family of four. None of this makes for a very exciting opening, but then you really don't need one. Building this table will generate its own excitement. See page 151 for a cutting list for this project.

The Base

So, let's start building it. It's a rather simple project, but as I said, it has a couple of unusual features. For one, the top floats over the legs. Because of this, braces are necessary between the legs and the frame.

To avoid spoiling the appearance, these braces have to be light and delicate. To have them that way and still strong enough for the job is the trick. We'll come to that later.

For starters, cut the main frame parts to size. There are four legs, four stretchers and four top supports. For the legs, cut four pieces 1¾" square and 27" long, with two adjacent sides jointed square with each other. For the stretchers, cut four pieces ¾" x 3" x 23" long, with all four surfaces jointed square with each other. For the top supports, cut four pieces ¾" x 1½" x 30¾", with all four surfaces jointed square with each other. On the stretchers, it is important that the ends be absolutely square with the edges.

To make the braces, start with two blocks 1½" x 2½" x 13", with one edge and one face jointed square with

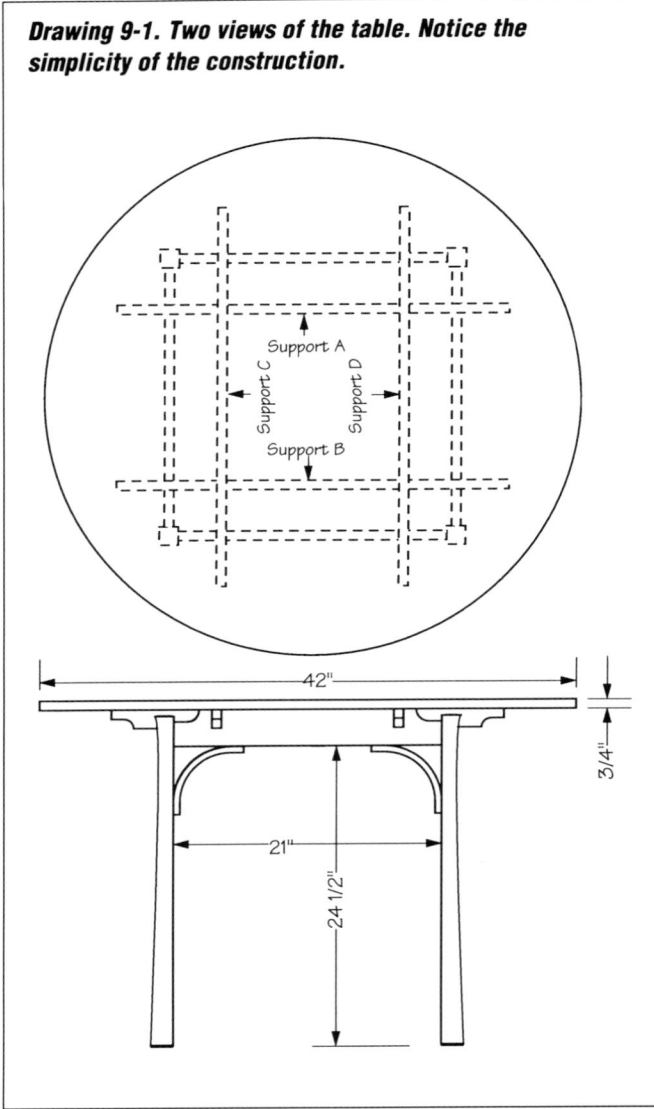

Drawing 9-1. Two views of the table. Notice the simplicity of the construction.

Support A

Support C

Support D

Support B

42"

21"

24 1/2"

3/4"

best to cut them together. Place the top edges down, and with the faces together and the tenon shoulders flush, clamp them together at the midpoint. On the top edge, at the midpoint between the tenon shoulders, draw a square line across all four stretchers. Measure 6¾" on each side of this line and draw lines. Mark the ends of the lines with a knife, so that when the top edge is down, you can see the mark. Put a dado head in the saw set for a ¾" wide cut, and set its height at ¾". Check this width and height on a piece of scrap. Using the miter gauge, set the mark on the stretchers to the left side of the dado head, and make the cuts. Remove the clamp. Lay out and cut the curved sections. If you have a 2" diameter multispur drill bit, there is an easy way to do this. Clamp two stretchers together with their top edges mating and their tenon shoulders flush. On the mating line, make a mark 1" in from the shoulder. With the pieces still clamped together and using the mark as a center point, drill through the pieces. Remove the clamp, and cut the straight section with a dovetail saw or on a band saw. Clean up the face of the cut, and put a slight radius on the side corners of the cut. Also put a slight radius on the corners of the bottom edge of the stretcher. Finish sand all faces that will show, and put the parts aside.

The top supports come next. It's important that they fit in the notches you cut in the stretchers. It has been my experience that dado heads usually cut slightly under the nominal widths, particularly if they have been sharpened several times. If your pieces don't fit or fit very tightly, joint one face lightly until you have an easy slide fit. Please notice in Drawing 9-3 that there are two each of two different top supports. The difference is in the arrangement of the notches. If you don't get them right, the structure won't go together. To guard against error, mark one set of edges top and the other bottom. Also mark the supports *A*, *B*, *C*, and *D*. Now place supports *A* and *B* with their bottom edges down and supports *C* and *D* with their top edges down. Clamp them together as you did with the stretchers and mark the edges that will be down in the same manner as before, making the marks 6¾" from the centerline. This 6¾" must be exactly the same as you marked on the stretchers. Set the ¾" dado head to half the height of the supports, and run a test on a piece of scrap that is the same height as the supports. When you're satisfied with the test, cut the notches. Now remove the clamp and reassemble and clamp with all the bottom edges down. On the bottom edges, measure from the centerline 10⅞" on each side, draw the lines, and mark as before. Set the height of the dado head to ¾". Run a test on the same piece of scrap. As a further test, fit the scrap piece into a notch on one of the stretchers.

each other. Also, be sure that the saw blade is square with the table. Use a square; don't trust the gauge on the saw. This is very important. If these elements are not square, the laminations will not be of uniform thickness. From each block, cut four laminations ⅛" x 2½" x 13". Make the cuts with a planer blade if you have one, and keep the pieces together in the order in which you cut them. Tape each group together, mark the jointed face inside, and set them aside.

The first parts to be made are the stretchers. Mark one edge of each piece bottom. Cut the tenons as shown in the detail drawing, measuring from the *bottom*. (See chapter eight.) Do not cut the bevel on the tenon ends or the curved cutouts at this time. Be sure that the distance between the tenon shoulders is exactly the same on all pieces.

The next step is to cut the notches for the top supports. The location of these notches is vital, and each stretcher must match exactly with the others. So, it is

Drawing 9-2a. Stretcher.

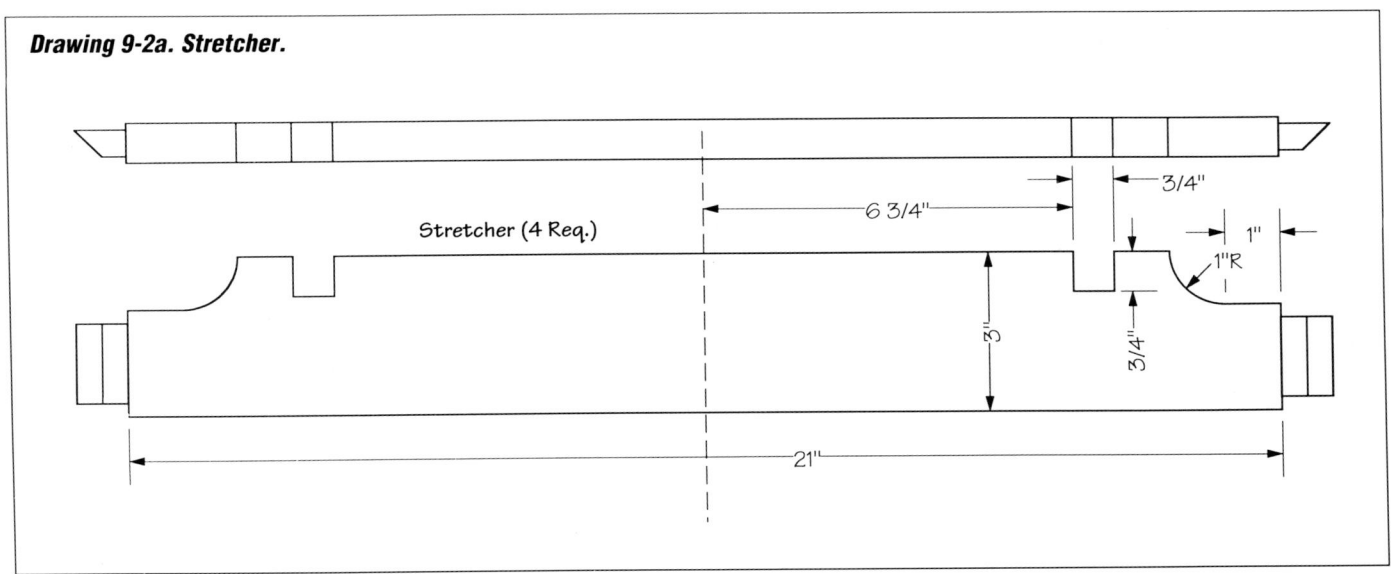

Stretcher (4 Req.)

The top edge of the scrap and the top edge of the stretcher must be flush. If you have made the notches in the stretchers slightly more or less than ¾" deep, you can correct for it with this cut. Having made the necessary adjustments, if any, cut the notches.

You're now ready to cut the curved cutouts. If you have a 1½" multispur bit, you can do it the same way as you did the stretchers. Then, drill a ³⁄₁₆" hole from bottom to top on the centerline of each support and counterbore for a flat-head wood screw. Centered ½" from the outer ends of the supports, drill two ³⁄₁₆" holes, as shown in the drawing. Using a thin file or chisel, make these into a slot. Put a slight radius on the corners of the bottom edge, and finish sand.

Before going any further on the structure, it's a good idea to glue up the blanks from which you will cut the braces. This requires the construction of a

Drawing 9-2b. Stretcher tenon detail.

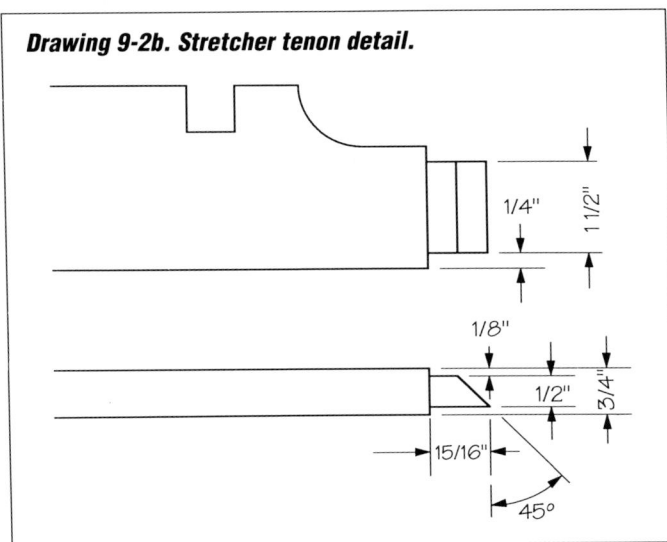

Drawing 9-3. Top supports—notice the difference between Supports A and B and Supports C and D.

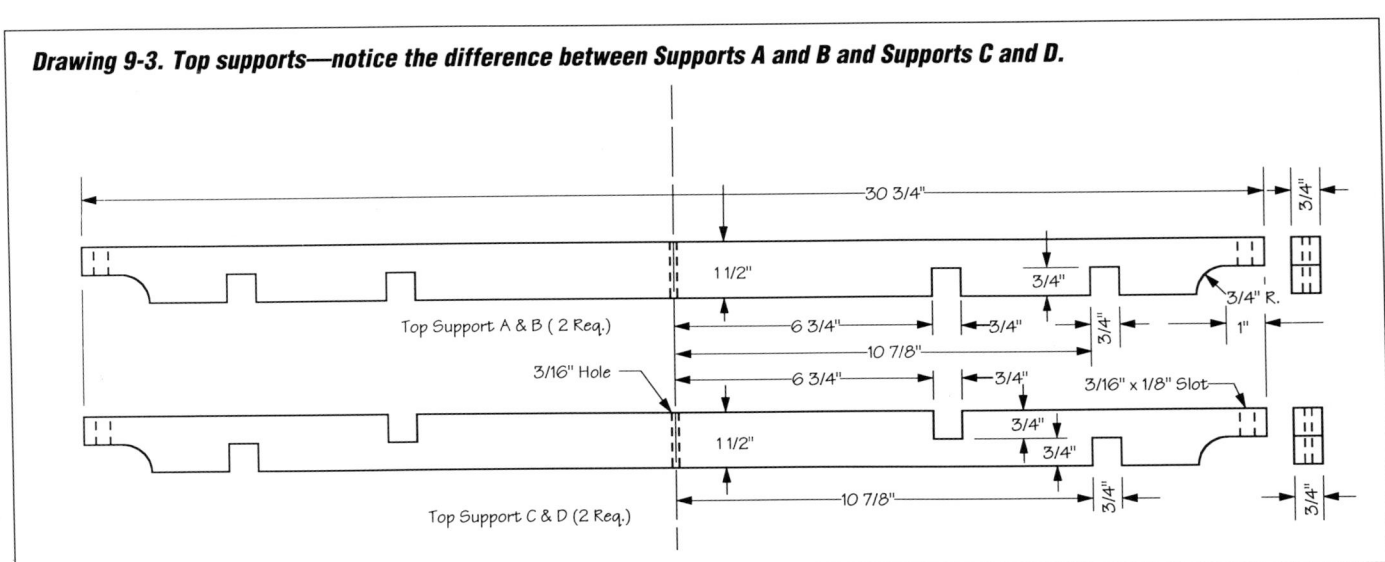

Top Support A & B (2 Req.)

3/16" Hole

Top Support C & D (2 Req.)

Jig for laminating brace blanks—complete with clamp blocks and clamps.

small laminating jig, which is simple to make. (See the detailed drawing of the jig as well as the overall drawing showing the jig with the laminations and the clamp blocks in place and the locations of the three 6″ C-clamps.) This jig is simple to make. Start with the base. You can use ½″-thick material, either plywood or chipboard. Cut the piece to 13″ square, and leave it that way until the jig is built, then cut the corners as shown. The reason for cutting the corners is to allow better positioning in the vise when using the jig. Cut the jig blocks and the clamp blocks from scrap lumber. When laying out the location of the jig blocks, note that the straight sections are at right angles to each other. This is a relatively sharp bend, and a con-

siderable amount of force is going to be required to pull the laminations into place. Therefore, it is best not only to glue the jig blocks in place, but also to drive wood screws through the base into the blocks. Use two #8 x 1¼″ flat-head screws in each block. Cut the clamp blocks to size as shown in the drawing. Be sure to draw on the top and face of the jig blocks the brace cutoff lines shown on the drawing.

The first time a laminating jig is to be used I always suggest a dry run. This is to acquaint you with the jig and how it works. Once you put glue between the laminations, the margin for error is greatly reduced. Take one of the groups of laminations you have previously made; with the ends flush, draw a line across one edge of the group at the center point. Place the group on the jig with this line at the center of the curve, and position the curved clamp block. Place a 6″ C-clamp in position so that it bears about halfway up on the clamp block, and begin slowly to tighten the clamp until the clamp block is all the way home. Place the two side clamp blocks and their clamps in position, and begin tightening, first one then the other, a little bit at a time. When they have come in about halfway, tighten the center clamp as tight as you can get it. Then finish tightening the side clamps. If you have accomplished this without any problems, you are ready to use glue.

Before doing the job with glue, however, there is an additional and very necessary step, which I purposely left out of the dry run. This step is to line the jig with

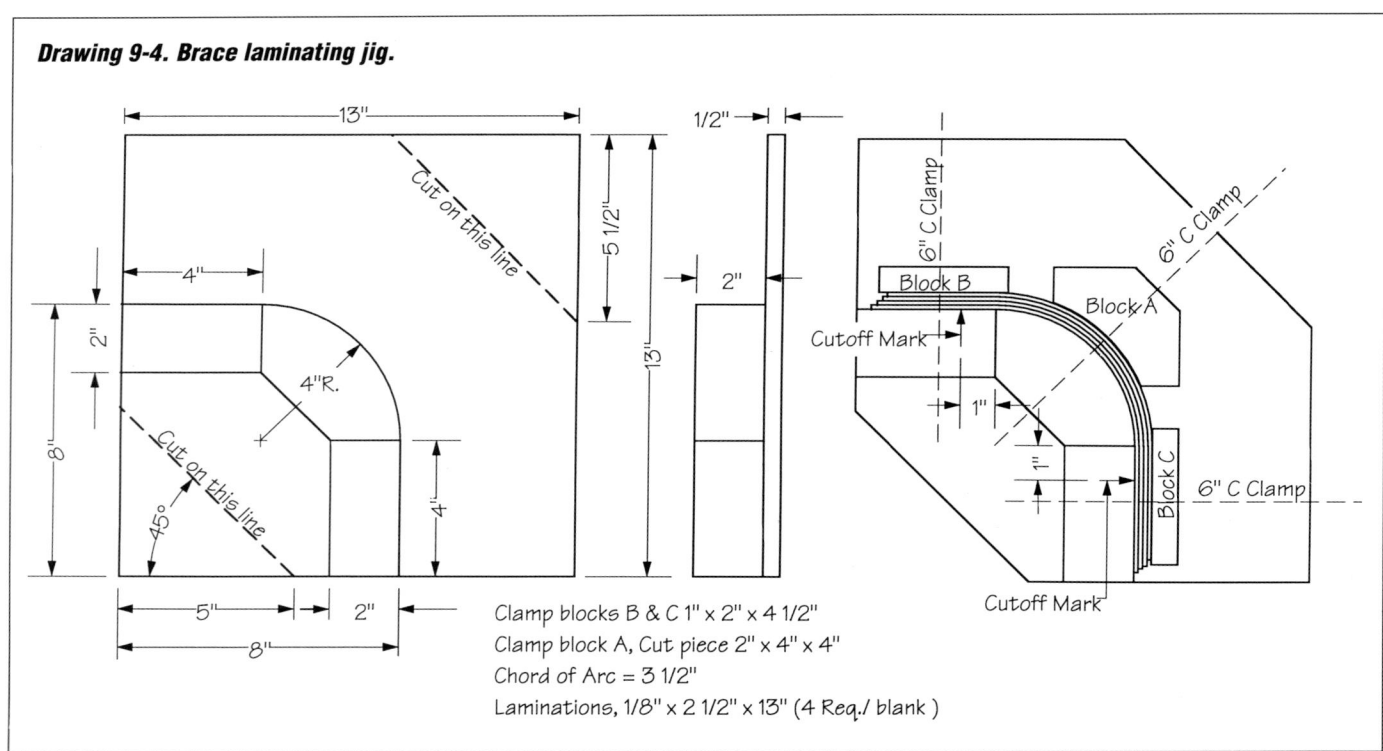

Drawing 9-4. Brace laminating jig.

13″

1/2″

5 1/2″

13″

4″

2″

Cut on this line

4″R.

Cut on this line

45°

8″

2″

4″

5″   2″

8″

2″

Clamp blocks B & C 1″ x 2″ x 4 1/2″
Clamp block A, Cut piece 2″ x 4″ x 4″
Chord of Arc = 3 1/2″
Laminations, 1/8″ x 2 1/2″ x 13″ (4 Req./ blank)

6″ C Clamp

Block B

Block A

Cutoff Mark

1″

1″

Block C

6″ C Clamp

6″ C Clamp

Cutoff Mark

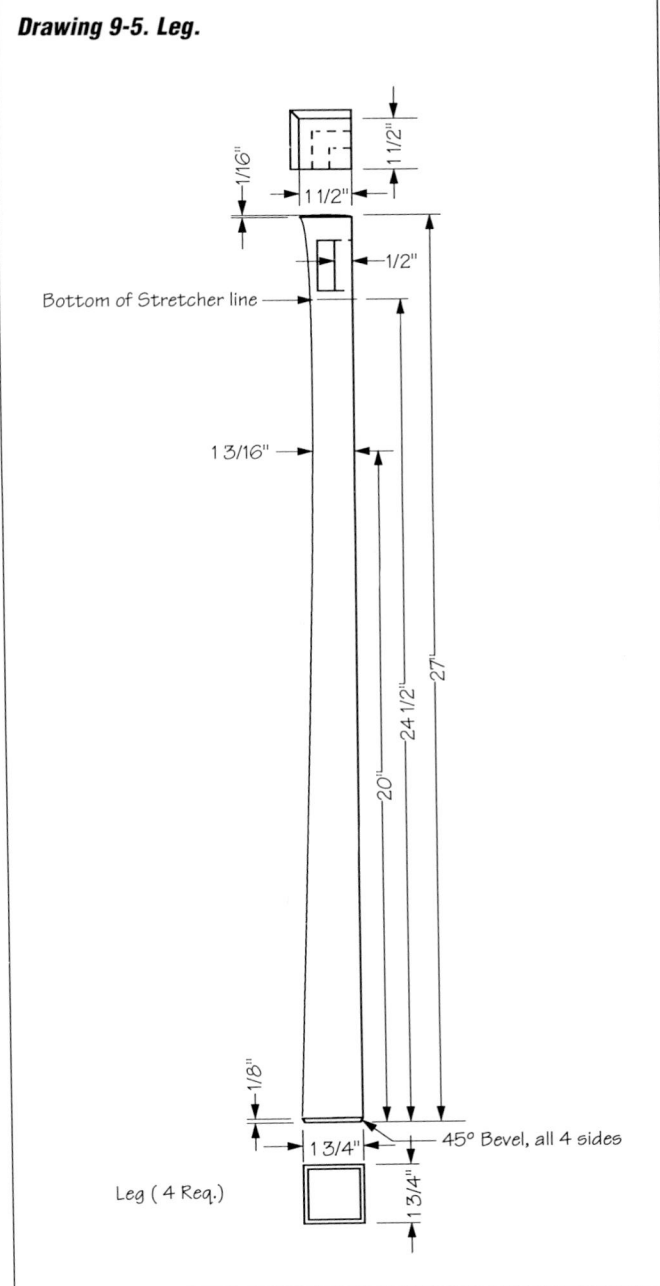

Drawing 9-5. Leg.

1 1/2"

1 1/2"

1/16"

1 1/2"

1/2"

Bottom of Stretcher line

1 3/16"

27"

24 1/2"

20"

1/8"

1 3/4"

45° Bevel, all 4 sides

1 3/4"

Leg (4 Req.)

Here, the dry run has been completed.

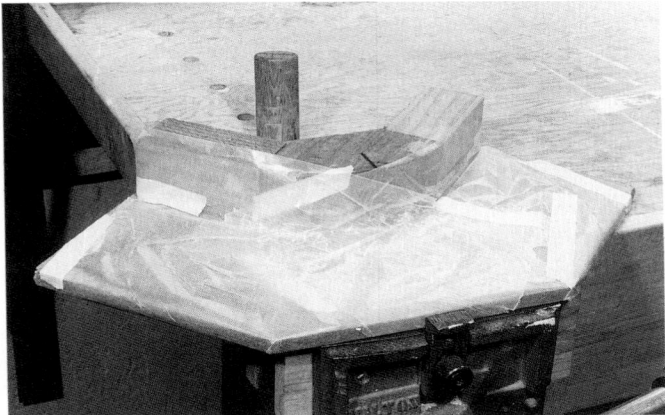

Jig with wax paper in place.

wax paper. If you don't, you'll never get the blank out of the jig. This step is simple: just cut two strips of wax paper the full width of the roll and 10" long. Fasten them in place with masking tape. It's difficult to explain how this is done, but if you will look closely at the picture, I think you'll be able to see what to do. Don't worry about it being smooth, that doesn't matter. Just see that the face of the jig blocks and the entire flat surface of the jig in front of the blocks is not only covered, but also turned under the front and side edges and taped to the bottom.

Apply the glue to all mating faces. Use an old 1"

paint brush, and be sure all of each surface is covered. Put them back together in the same order they were before, and see that the center marks all line up. Place the group in position, and apply the clamp blocks and clamps as before. With the glue in between, the laminations will have a tendency to move around. If they move too much, try to push them back into place. You won't be able to keep them in perfect position, but being a little bit out won't matter. That's why the blank is oversize. Also, don't worry if the glue squeezes out from between the laminations. Just leave it; you can take care of it later. Allow the glue to dry twenty-four hours before removing the clamps. When the blank comes out of the jig, some of the squeezed-out glue will not be dry. Strip away the wax paper, and it will dry more quickly. Apply new wax paper to the jig for the second group.

While the brace blanks are drying, you can work on the legs (see Drawing 9-5). On these pieces, the corner common to the two jointed faces will be the inside corner. Assemble the legs in a square based on this. On the end that is to be the top, mark the mating

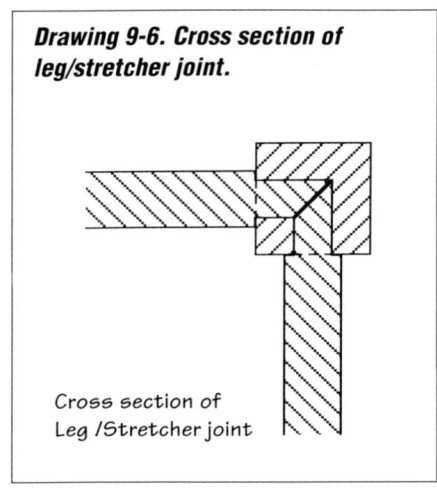

Drawing 9-6. Cross section of leg/stretcher joint.

Cross section of
Leg /Stretcher joint

Mark location of leg mortice from tenon.

Angle-cut location on tenon is marked through opposite mortice.

faces in a clockwise direction from one to eight. Now decide which stretchers go where, and mark, on the tenon at each end, the number of the leg face that it will mate with. The mortices go in the jointed faces. On one leg, measure 24½" from the bottom, and draw a square line across one jointed face. Lay the four legs on the bench side by side and ends flush, with one jointed face of each up, and transfer the line to the other three legs. Carry the line around to the second jointed face on each leg. (This line locates the bottom edge of the stretcher.) Place the tenon on the leg with the bottom of the stretcher on the line, and mark, with a knife, the top and bottom lines of each mortice. Measuring from the inside corner, locate, according to the drawing, the inner vertical line of the mortice. After measuring the thickness of your tenon, locate the outer vertical line. Notice that you do not locate the horizontal lines or the outer vertical line of the mortice from the drawing, but from your tenon. This is very important for a good fit.

When you have laid out all eight mortices, cut them. If you look at Drawing 9-6, the detail drawing of the mortices, you will see that it is very important that they do not exceed 1" in depth. I've found that the easiest way to cut a mortice is to drill out the main waste and then clean up the sides to the lines with a chisel. If you use a spur bit in a drill press with a depth gauge, you can be sure that you won't exceed the 1" depth. Set your gauge so that the cutting edge of the bit, not the point of the spur, gives you your depth. It is also important that the sides of the mortice be perpendicular to the face. I use a depth gauge as a square to accomplish this.

As you fit each tenon to its mortice, draw a line with a sharp pencil on the face of the tenon that shows through the opposing mortice. This is the line to which you cut the 45° angle on the tenon. Be sure, when you make this mark, that you have the tenon in

the right way, because if you cut the angle backwards, you'll have to make a new stretcher. When the mortice and tenon have been properly fitted (be sure both tenons in each leg go home together), there should be a small clearance between the bottom of the tenon and the bottom of the mortice. This clearance allows room for excess glue.

Before going any further, it's a good idea to dry assemble all the pieces and to check that they fit together tightly and that the assembled structure is square in all directions. Assemble the legs and the stretchers first, then add the C and D top supports, and finally the A and B top supports. Putting the parts together in this manner is the only way you can check for interference between the tenon ends in the right-angle mortices. This is your last chance to make adjustments easily, because the next step is to shape the legs, and once that is done, some of the surfaces will no longer be square or flat.

Shaping the legs begins with cutting the small bevels at the bottom. Set this up with the miter gauge at 45° and a stop to position the leg correctly. Make the four cuts on each leg. Next, make a full-size template, as shown in Drawing 9-5. Place this on one of the rough faces of the leg (the ones without mortices), with the straight edge against the edge of the jointed face, and mark the curve. Saw to the curve. Now place the template on the newly sawn surface, again with the straight edge against the edge of the jointed face, and

Cutting small bevels on leg bottoms. Notice extended stop on miter gauge.

draw the curve; saw to this curve. Save two of the waste pieces, and cut a section from each end. These pieces will be very helpful in holding the legs in the vise while working on them. Smooth the sawn surfaces. The fastest and easiest way is with a spokeshave. At this time, you should also round off the tops of the legs as shown in the drawing. As a last step, sand all over with #150 paper. Be careful around the stretcher mortices not to alter the flatness of the surface.

Assemble the finished parts, again dry, to make sure everything fits as it should. Take it apart and apply the glue. I suggest that you glue the legs and two of the stretchers first, as two separate assemblies. Make sure the legs are square with the stretchers. Use clamps across the stretchers. Again, you can use the curved waste pieces you cut from the legs. They make perfect pads under the clamps. When these have dried, assemble the rest of the structure and glue it together. Make sure the assembly is square. Place clamps over the second set of stretchers and legs.

As I've said before, when gluing a mortice-and-tenon joint, never put glue on the tenon. Put it around the top half of the mortice; the tenon will then spread it over the rest of the surface as it goes home. Be sparing in the amount you use. (However, if you have a sloppy joint, then you can use more to fill the joint and help make it strong). In gluing the top supports, put the glue in the bottom notches—some at the top of each notch face and a little in the center of the bottom. If you use too much, it will squirt out and make a mess that will be difficult to clean up. If it should squirt out, don't attempt to wipe it up then. If you do, you'll force it into the pores of the wood and never get it out. Let it dry, then carefully remove it with a sharp chisel.

It is time to make the braces from the blanks that you glued up in the jig. The first step is to clean off any glue that might interfere with the outside face going flat against the jointer fence. Joint one edge of each blank smooth and square with the outside face. Put the thinnest-kerf planer blade you have in the table saw, and set it at about 1" height. Set the rip fence at ½". This is a tricky ripping operation. Start with the leading flat surface down, and feed slowly by hand, following the curve of the blank, until the trailing flat surface is down. Then finish the cut using a push stick. You should get four braces from each blank.

Put each brace back in the jig, mark the cutoff points, and trim the ends accordingly. Sand the braces smooth all over, and except for the first 1" of the outside at each end, break all corners with sandpaper. Now lay out, drill and counterbore the screw holes as shown in Drawing 9-8.

To install the braces, place the structure upside down on your table saw with a leg at the edge, so you

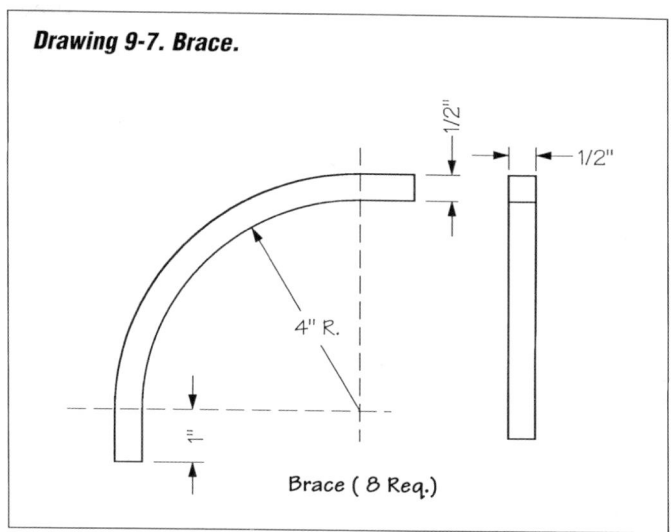

Drawing 9-7. Brace.

4" R.

1/2"

1/2"

1"

Brace (8 Req.)

Finishing leg shaping in vise with spokeshave. Notice leg waste used for holding leg in vise.

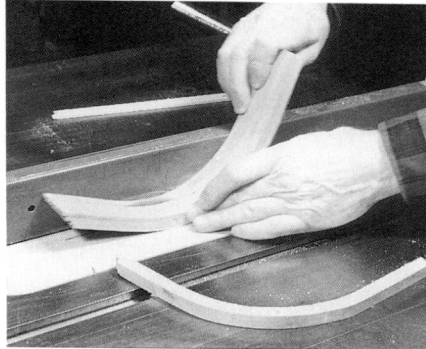

Ripping the braces from the glued-up blank. This operation requires great care.

can easily get at both sides of it. Clamp it there. Put a brace in position with one end against the leg and the other on the edge of the stretcher in the middle. Clamp the end against the leg firmly in place. At the stretcher end, drill ⁵⁄₆₄" pilot holes, and drive the two #5 x ⅜" brass flat-head wood screws. Remove the clamp at the leg end and repeat the process. Now, unscrew the brace, put a dab of glue in the center of each flat surface, and screw it back into place. Don't use too much or it will squeeze out the sides. Install

Setup for installing the braces.

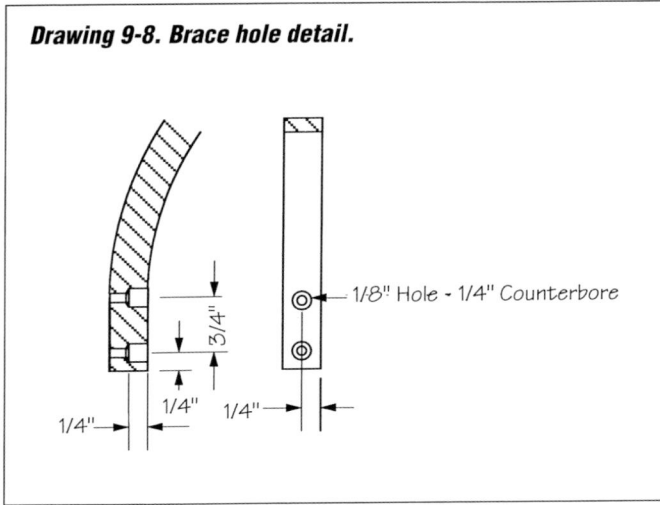

Drawing 9-8. Brace hole detail.

1/8" Hole - 1/4" Counterbore

3/4"

1/4"

1/4" 1/4" 1/4"

the other seven braces in the same manner. The ¼"-diameter holes for the screw heads have to be plugged. There are two ways of doing this. If you have a ¼" plug cutter, cut plugs from the wood out of which you made the braces. Glue them in place with the grain lines matching those of the braces. When the glue dries, trim them and sand smooth. If you don't have a plug cutter, use a piece of ¼" maple dowel (no matter what wood you have used in the table). When the dowel pieces have been trimmed and sanded, it will look like you used wooden pegs to fasten the braces in place—a nice touch.

The Top

Last, but really the most important, is the top. It's important because it will set the tone of the whole piece. Make it from wood that has a distinct and interesting grain pattern, and choose the boards so that their patterns match at least reasonably well. You want the top to look, as near as possible, like it was made from one board.

Glue up a panel about 42½" square. When it's dry, plane both sides smooth. Then draw the diameter of the top using a beam compass. Do this on the surface that is going to be the underside. You make a beam compass out of a long stick and a pair of trammel heads. This is a very handy tool to have around if you draw many curves or circles with a radius larger than your dividers can handle. The easiest way to cut the top to shape is to clamp it to your table saw and use a hand electric jigsaw. I have used a band saw, but a top this size is very difficult to handle on the average band saw, especially by one person.

To clean up the cut edge, clamp the top vertically in your bench vise, and use a spokeshave. This tool will do a neat, fast job, and you can put a radius on the top and bottom corners as you go, thus avoiding a router setup later. If your spokeshave is sharp and you've been careful with it, you can finish the edge with 150 grit sandpaper. Sand the top and bottom surfaces and the job is done.

Installation

To install the top, place and clamp it upside down on the table saw. Position the base structure so that one set of top supports is parallel to the grain lines of the top. This is important because of the expansion and contraction that will occur in the top with the changing of seasons. For fastening, use #8 x 2" flat-head wood screws in the wide part of the supports and #8 x 1¼" in the narrow parts. Place screws in all the holes and slots, and tap them hard enough to make a mark. Remove the structure, and drill 3/32" pilot holes ½" deep at each mark. Use a hand drill for this. An electric drill moves too fast and a slight slip will find you through the top before you know it. It's a good idea to play safe and put a marker on the drill bit at the ½" point. I wrap a small piece of masking tape around the bit. Put the structure back in place and drive the screws. Your table is ready for finishing.

For the finishing operation, I remove the top, and finish it and the base separately; it's much easier that way. Check chapter fourteen for my schedules, or use your own, but keep away from stain.

So, it's done: an interesting and somewhat unique dining table that will elicit comments from your friends, and it's different enough that you won't find it in every one else's home.

A CHAIR FOR ALL REASONS

Many of my clients did not want the high-back side chair that I described in project six. They asked for a low-back chair, with arms, that could be used at a desk or dining table. This was my answer. It seemed to be just what they wanted, and it became quite popular, perhaps because it looks good and is comfortable. I think you'll find it an interesting project, and I hope you'll decide to make several. The first one may be a little difficult, but the second, third and fourth are much easier.

Those of you who built the high-back chair in project six have a leg up on this one. The seat, the legs and the manner of their assembly are exactly the same with one slight exception, which I'll cover later. And

although the top rail is different in shape, the blank can be laminated in the same jig that is described for that part on the other chair. If you haven't built project six, turn to it for the description of how to make the seat and legs and the plan for the jig. Finally, all jigs and accessories for turning the legs and long, thin spindles are necessary here, as is the angle jig for drilling the seat. The jigs and accessories are described in chapter six, and the turning of spindles and legs is covered in chapter ten.

To begin this project, turn back to project six. Turn the legs, and form and drill the seat. Note that in this current project you have arm spindles instead of support spindles. (See drawings in this project.) This is the one place where the seats differ: Instead of one hole for a support spindle, there are three holes on each side for arm spindles. Their location and size are shown clearly in Drawing 10-1, and you should put them on your top surface template. They are the same diameter as the back spindle holes and are drilled at the same angle. When drilling them, be sure that the bulk of the seat is between you and the drill bit and the edge of the seat is parallel to the top edge of the drill jig. Aside from this, you can go ahead and finish, right down to the final sanding, the seat and leg assembly just as described in project six.

Turn the back spindles in the same manner as for the previous chair, using the steadyrest. However, the arm spindles are so short that they don't need the steadyrest. Otherwise, they are turned the same way and in the same order as the longer ones.

At this point, cut the laminations for the top rail, and glue them up in the jig. To make them, cut a piece 1" x 4" x 24". Joint one face and both edges, and with the jointed face against the rip fence, cut three pieces ⁷⁄₃₂" thick. Cut them with a planer blade, and keep them in order so that when you put them together, they will be in the same relative positions as they were before you cut them. Take a light cut, on the jointer, off the outside face of the last piece. (Cut just enough to remove the saw marks.) Do not do anything to the mating faces. Notice that the laminations are thinner than before because the part finishes ⅝" thick instead of ¾". (The gluing process is described in project six.)

The arms come next. I'll tell you right off, these are difficult and tricky parts to make. A band saw and a good spokeshave are necessary tools. As you can see from the picture at right (facing page), they are curved, and we get that curve by lamination. That necessitates a jig, shown in Drawings 10-3 and 10-4. The base is ⅜" CDX plywood. The straight jig blocks are cut from a piece of fir 4x4 and the curved one is made up of three layers of ¾" CDX plywood and/or chipboard. Fasten them in place with glue and screws through the plywood into the blocks. They will be subjected to some strong forces, so they must be securely fastened. The clamp blocks can be cut from scrap material to fit as shown on the clamped-up draw-

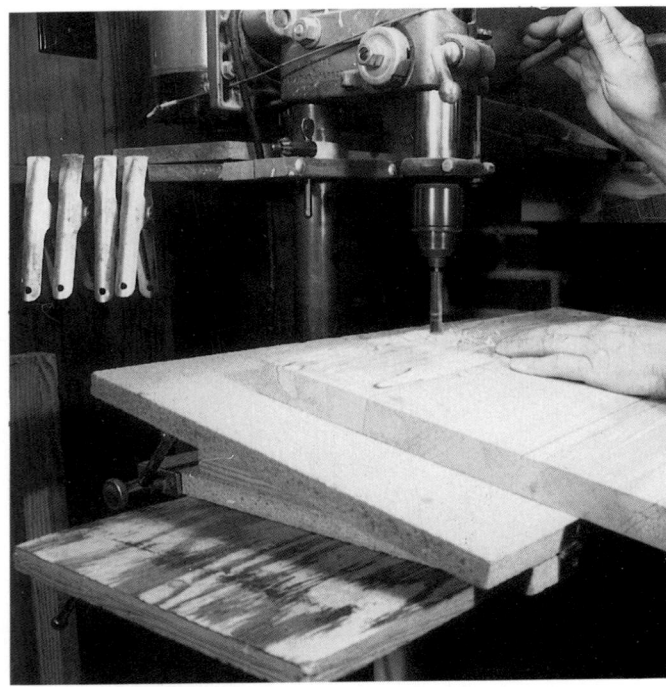

Drilling arm-spindle holes in chair seat—edge of seat is parallel to top edge of drill fixture.

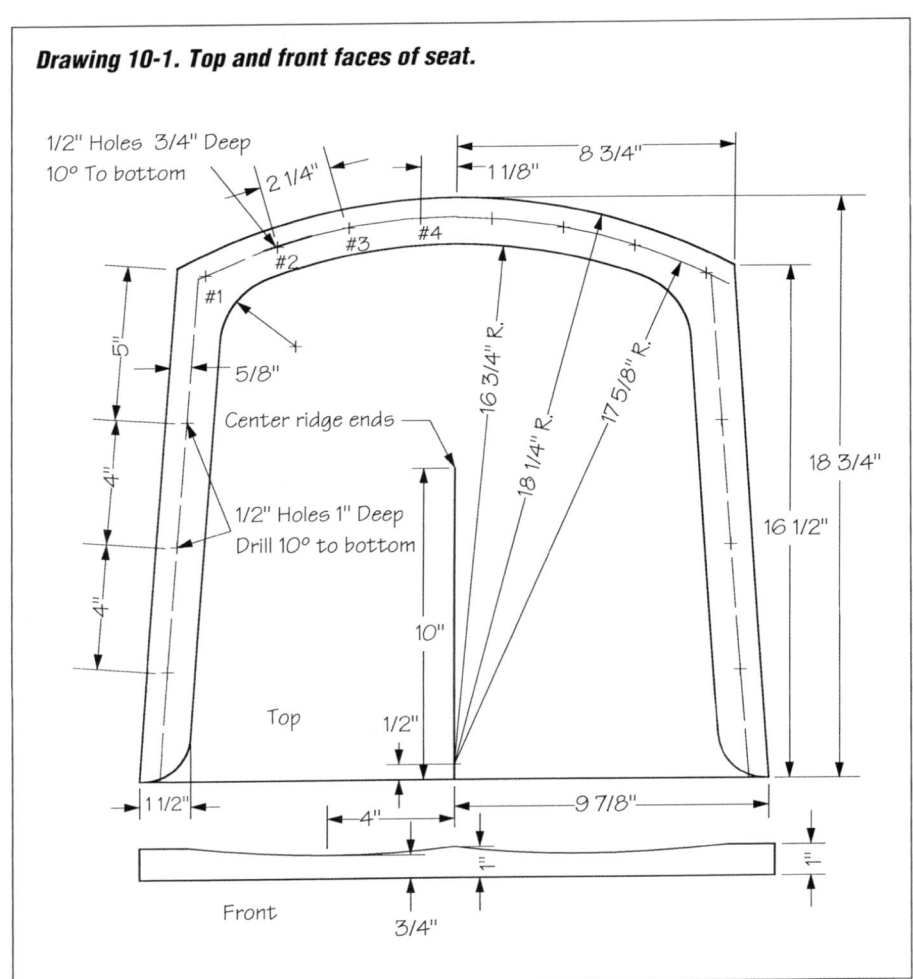

Drawing 10-1. Top and front faces of seat.

Drawing 10-2a. The back spindles.

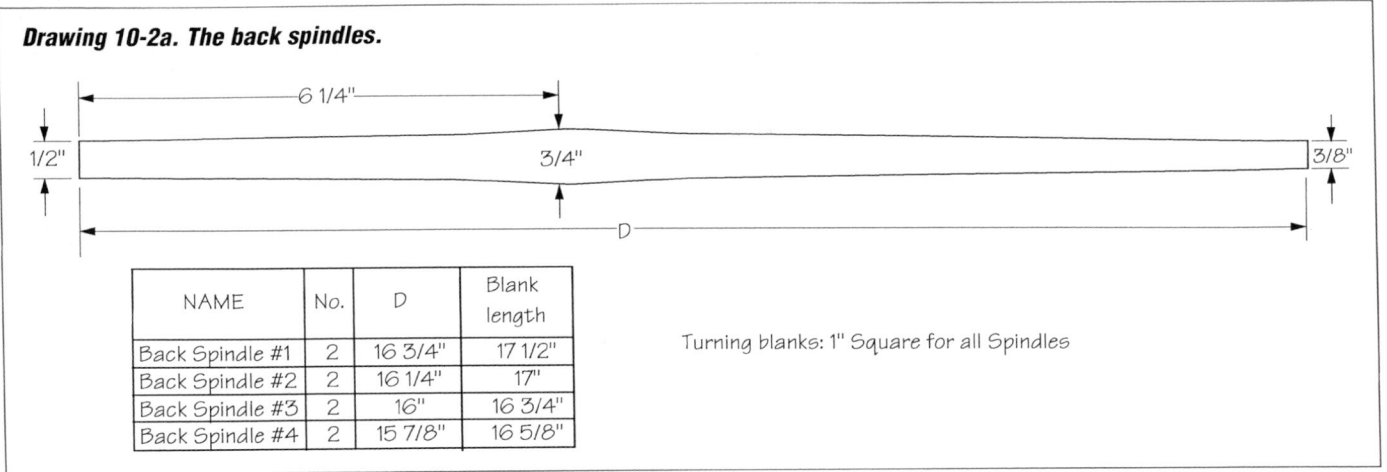

NAME	No.	D	Blank length
Back Spindle #1	2	16 3/4"	17 1/2"
Back Spindle #2	2	16 1/4"	17"
Back Spindle #3	2	16"	16 3/4"
Back Spindle #4	2	15 7/8"	16 5/8"

Turning blanks: 1" Square for all Spindles

Drawing 10-2b. The arm spindles.

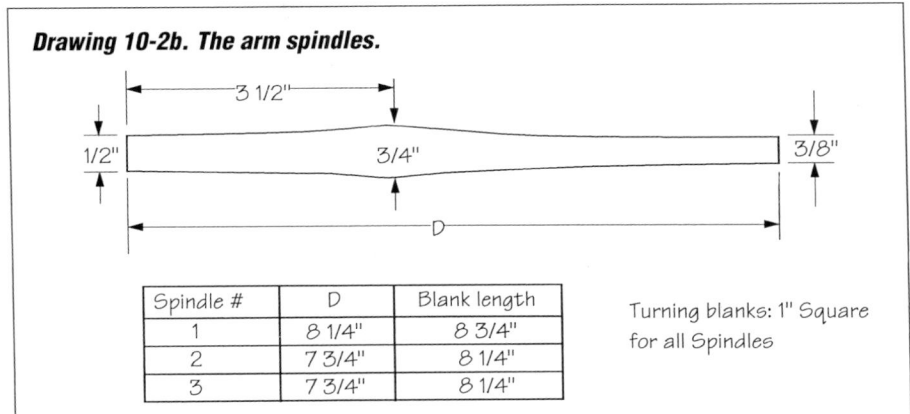

Spindle #	D	Blank length
1	8 1/4"	8 3/4"
2	7 3/4"	8 1/4"
3	7 3/4"	8 1/4"

Turning blanks: 1" Square for all Spindles

Jig to make arm blank, shown with clamp blocks in place.

ing. Don't neglect to put in the top and bottom markers as well as that for the starting point. You will need four 6" and three 5" heavy-duty C-clamps. The laminations are ³⁄₁₆" x 2¼" x 29", and you'll need six for an arm. Cut them from a piece 2" x 2¼" x 29". The 2¼" face that goes against the rip fence should first be jointed smooth and square with the 2" face. This will be the inside of the curve against the jig blocks. As

with the top rail laminations, cut them with a hollow-ground planer blade, and keep them in the order in which you cut them. As each set is cut, tape them together so that they won't get mixed up. It's also a good idea to mark them left and right so you won't get confused later.

I've found that the best way to hold the jig while doing the job is to grip it between the adjustable dog on your vise and put a pin in one of the pinholes in the bench behind the vise, as shown in the picture. Before actually gluing up a set, I think it would be a good idea to have a dry run, to get the hang of things. Once the glue is in place, there isn't much room for error or time to run after something you forgot. Having put a set through the process dry, the pieces will remain somewhat bent. This will make it harder to apply the glue, but not enough to cause trouble.

Measure along the jig blocks from the top marker to the position of the #1 clamp or starting-point marker. Add about 1½", and measure this distance from the top end of your set of laminations. Make a heavy mark across all the laminations at this point on the side that will be up. The weight of this mark is not so important on the dry run, but with the glue in place, a light line can become obscured. Now, place the set on the jig with the mark at the starting-point marker. Put the #1 clamp, with its clamp block, in position, and tighten it, but not entirely. Put the #2 clamp and block in place and pull it up enough to hold it there. Put the long clamp block and the #3 clamp in place and pull it up enough to hold it in place. Now slowly tighten the #2 clamp two or three good turns, then do the same with the #3 clamp. Continue this until you have the

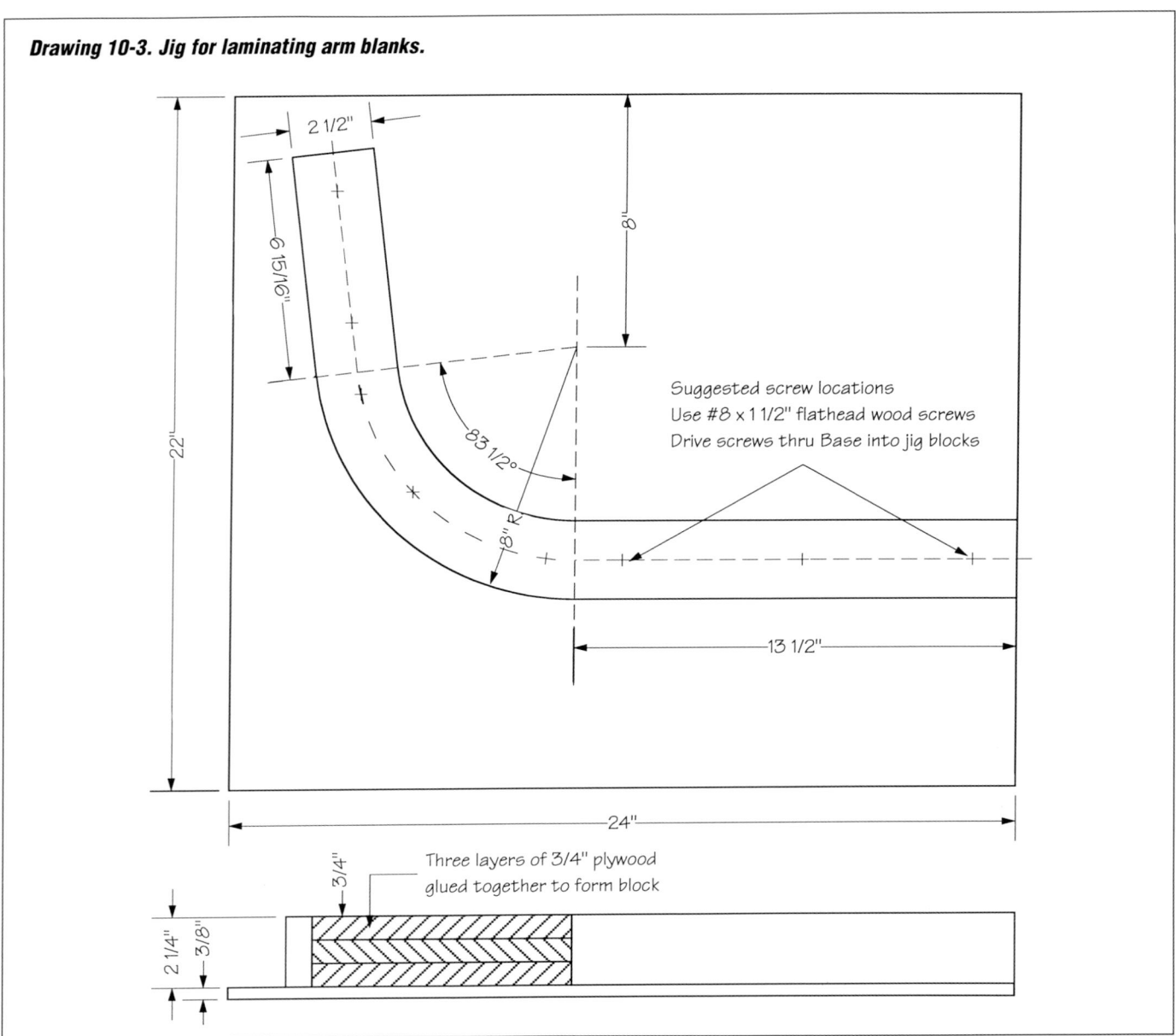

Drawing 10-3. Jig for laminating arm blanks.

2 1/2"

6 15/16"

8"

83 1/2°

8" R

22"

Suggested screw locations
Use #8 x 1 1/2" flathead wood screws
Drive screws thru Base into jig blocks

13 1/2"

24"

3/4"

Three layers of 3/4" plywood
glued together to form block

2 1/4"

3/8"

inner face of the lamination almost touching the jig blocks at these points. Next, put the #4 clamp in place and tighten it until the inner face is almost to the jig blocks, then tighten #2 completely, as tight as you can get it. Do the same for #4 and then #1 and #3. Now put #5 and #6 in place and tighten them fully. Last, set the #7 clamp, and tighten it fully. If everything has gone smoothly, you're ready to glue.

Before doing the job with glue, however, there is an additional and very necessary step that was purposely left out of the dry run. This step is to line the jig with wax paper. If you don't, you'll never get the blank out of the jig. This step is simple: just cut several strips of wax paper about 6" wide and 12" long. Fasten them in place with masking tape. It's difficult to explain how this is done, but if you will look close-

ly at the picture, I think you'll be able to see what to do. Don't worry about it being smooth; that doesn't matter. Just see that the face of the jig blocks and the entire flat surface of the jig in front of the blocks is not only covered, but also turned under the front and side edges and taped to the bottom.

When applying the glue, use a stiff, 2" brush sideways (I sort of scrub it on), and cover both surfaces of the mating faces entirely. Be sure to keep them in order. Line up the ends and sides (they won't stay that way, but they should be so at thé start). Put them in the jig in the proper position, and proceed as on the dry run. There will be a difference now that there is glue between the laminations; they will want to move around relative to each other. You won't be able to control this entirely, but you should push them back

Dry run on arm blank complete.

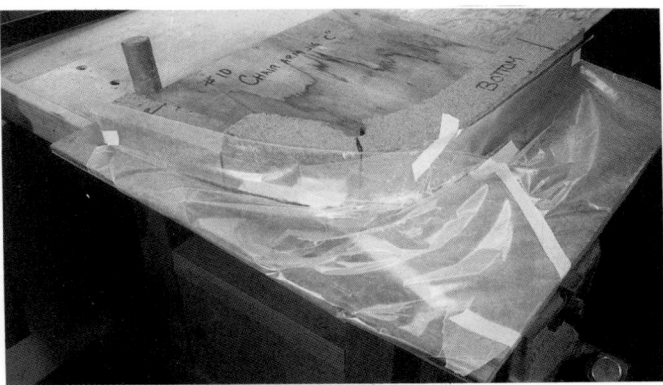

Don't forget the wax paper.

into place as best you can during the tightening process. (That's the reason for the extra width and length.) You will also have excess glue oozing out top and bottom. Don't be concerned about this as it will all clean up later. After about six hours, you can take the blank out of the jig. You can't do any work on it at this time, but you can glue up the other set. When the blank comes out of the jig, the wax paper will stick to the underside, and there will be wet glue between the

paper and the blank. This is some of the excess. Peel the paper away, and using an old putty knife, scrape off as much as you can of the wet glue. It will speed the final drying and save work later on.

While the arm blanks are drying, take the top rail blank out of the jig. Joint what will be the top edge even, and square with the convex face. Rip the blank to 3⅝" wide. When it comes out of the jig, the ends of the blank will be uneven. Find the center of the part

Drawing 10-4. Jig with laminations and clamps in place.

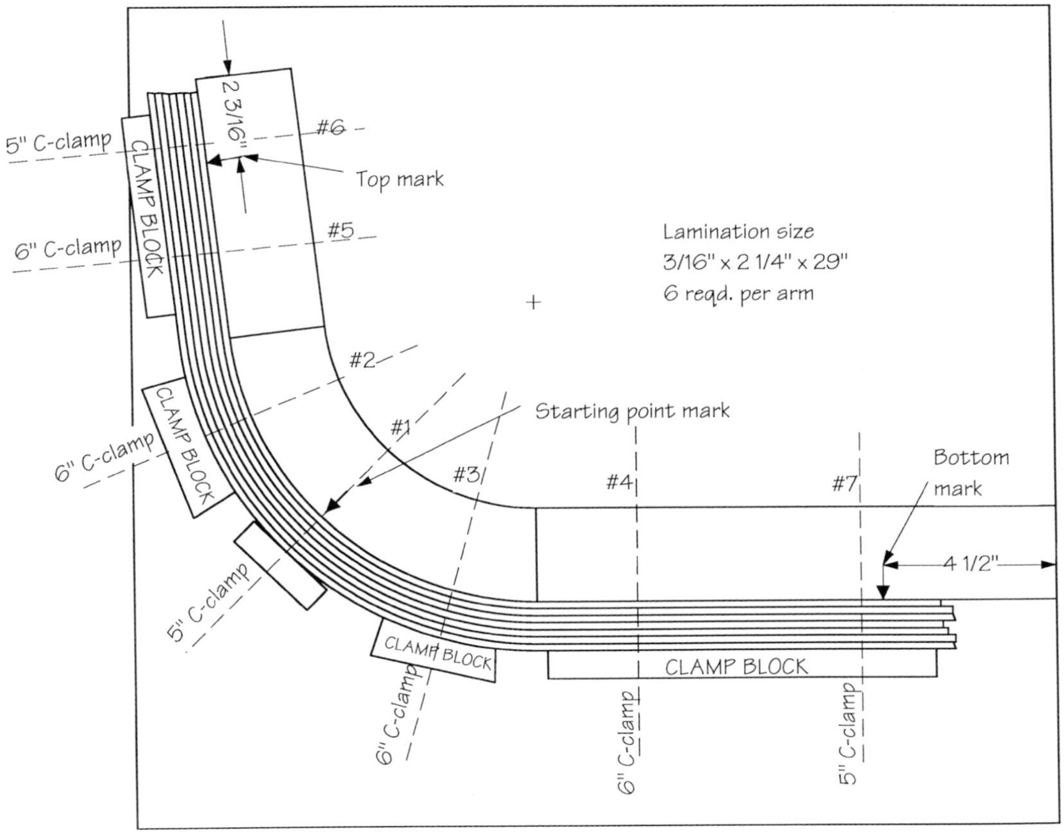

2 3/16"

5" C-clamp

CLAMP BLOCK

6" C-clamp

#6 –

Top mark

#5

Lamination size
3/16" x 2 1/4" x 29"
6 reqd. per arm

#2

CLAMP BLOCK

6" C-clamp

#1

Starting point mark

#3

#4

#7

Bottom mark

5" C-clamp

CLAMP BLOCK

6" C-clamp

CLAMP BLOCK

6" C-clamp

5" C-clamp

4 1/2"

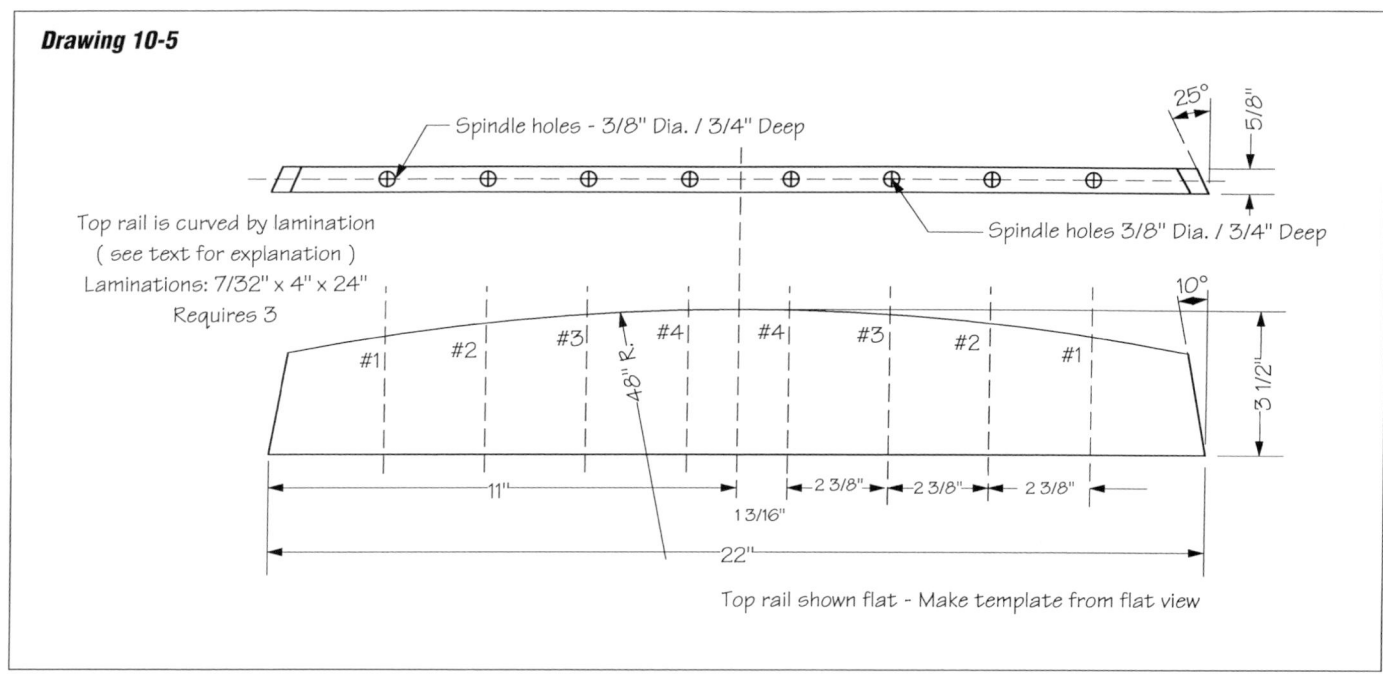

Drawing 10-5

Spindle holes - 3/8" Dia. / 3/4" Deep

Top rail is curved by lamination
(see text for explanation)
Laminations: 7/32" x 4" x 24"
Requires 3

Spindle holes 3/8" Dia. / 3/4" Deep

25°

5/8"

10°

3 1/2"

48" R.

#1 #2 #3 #4 #4 #3 #2 #1

11"

1 3/16"

2 3/8" 2 3/8" 2 3/8"

22"

Top rail shown flat - Make template from flat view

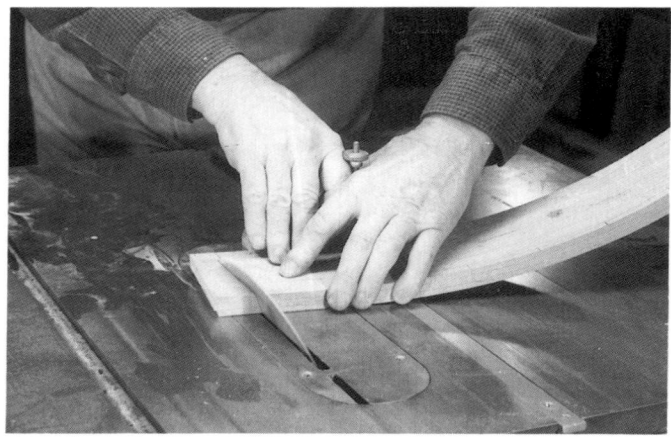

Making the compound cut on the top rail ends.

that is the full thickness. Position the center of the template you have made from the top-rail drawing at this point; make sure the top edge is flush with the top edge of the blank. Tape it firmly in place on the concave face at several points, and draw the other three sides on the blank. The two end lines are very important, so get them accurate and straight. Remove the template, but do not cut the curved edge at this time. The end cuts have a compound angle, and the operation is a bit ticklish. Using the planer blade, set the blade angle at 21° and the miter gauge at 10° to the right. Place the convex face of the blank down and the top edge against the miter gauge; hold the blank flat on the table at the point of the cut, and cut along the line on the blank. Reverse the miter gauge to 10° left, and reverse the blank so that the bottom edge is

against the miter gauge. Make that cut the same way. Now you can bandsaw the curved bottom. Clean up the sawed edge with a spokeshave, and round the corners just a little. Don't touch the end cuts, and don't round the corners of the top edge at this time. On the bottom edge, lay out the positions of the spindle holes from the template and drill them ¾" deep, measured to the centerline of the hole front to back. In this drilling operation, be sure that the top edge is flat on the drill press table and that, regardless of which hole you're drilling, most of the rail is supported by the table. This is to insure that the holes are parallel to the faces of the rail and straight from side to side. Set this part aside for now.

While this has been going on, you will have removed the first arm blank from the jig and glued up the other. As soon as it has dried for twenty-four hours, you're ready to start making the arms. The first step is to joint one edge flat and at right angles to the convex side. In doing this, recognize that the longer straight section, marked *bottom* on the jig, is the main part of the arm, and that, being arms, they must be opposites. Thus, when placed on the bench side by side with the bottoms down, the inner faces must be smooth. Having done this, place back in the jig the arm that will have the smooth side down, and mark the top and bottom cutoff points. Make these cuts, and put the arms together; then mark the other one and make those cuts.

You are now ready to begin shaping. This is where arm making gets a bit touchy. Look at Drawings 10-6 and 10-7, the top-arm template drawing and the side-

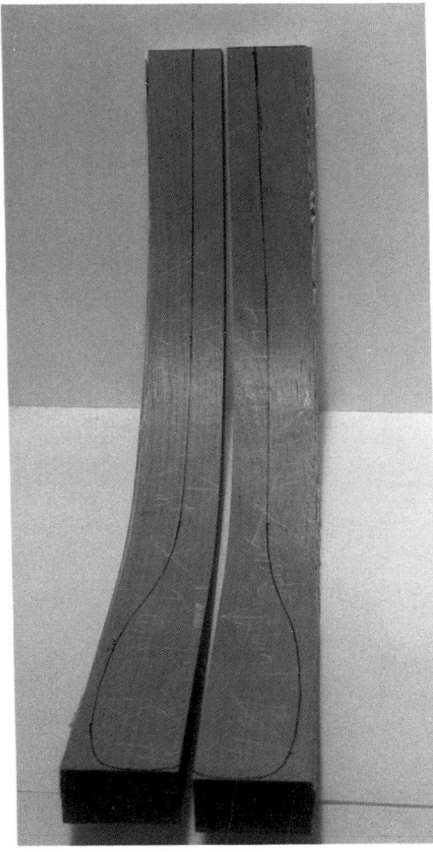

Arm blank with side pattern drawn— mask out background.

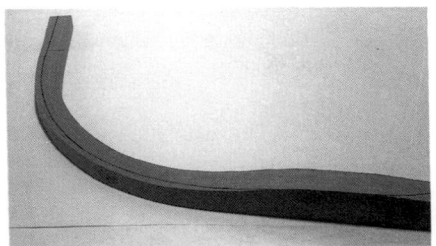

Use templates to mark the shape of the arm blanks as described in the text.

Freehand cutting the bottom bevel.

arm template drawing. From these, make full-size templates on light cardboard. Mark a line 3½" from the top of the side-arm template. This is the location of the bottom edge of the top rail. Place the top-arm template on the top of the arm, straight edge flush with the smooth edge of the arm and the front edge of the template as far forward as possible. Trace the template onto the arm. Go to the top of the arm, measure ¾" from the smooth edge, and make a mark. Connect that mark and the upper end of the outside line of the top template with a straight line. This sounds confusing, but to help you understand, here is a picture of the lines on the arm blank. Bandsaw the shape (leaving the line) except for the front corners; leave those square. (Be sure to keep the convex face of the arm flat on the table while making this cut. There is a tendency to tip it when negotiating the curved section.) Place the side-arm template on the newly sawn edge with its concave edge flush with the concave face of the arm. Trace the outer edge of this template. Now bandsaw the shape, leaving the line. However, do not cut the front part of the shape; leave it as is for now. You will need it to guide you when cutting the bevel I will speak about shortly. Transfer the location of the bottom edge of the top rail to the arm blank. Draw it

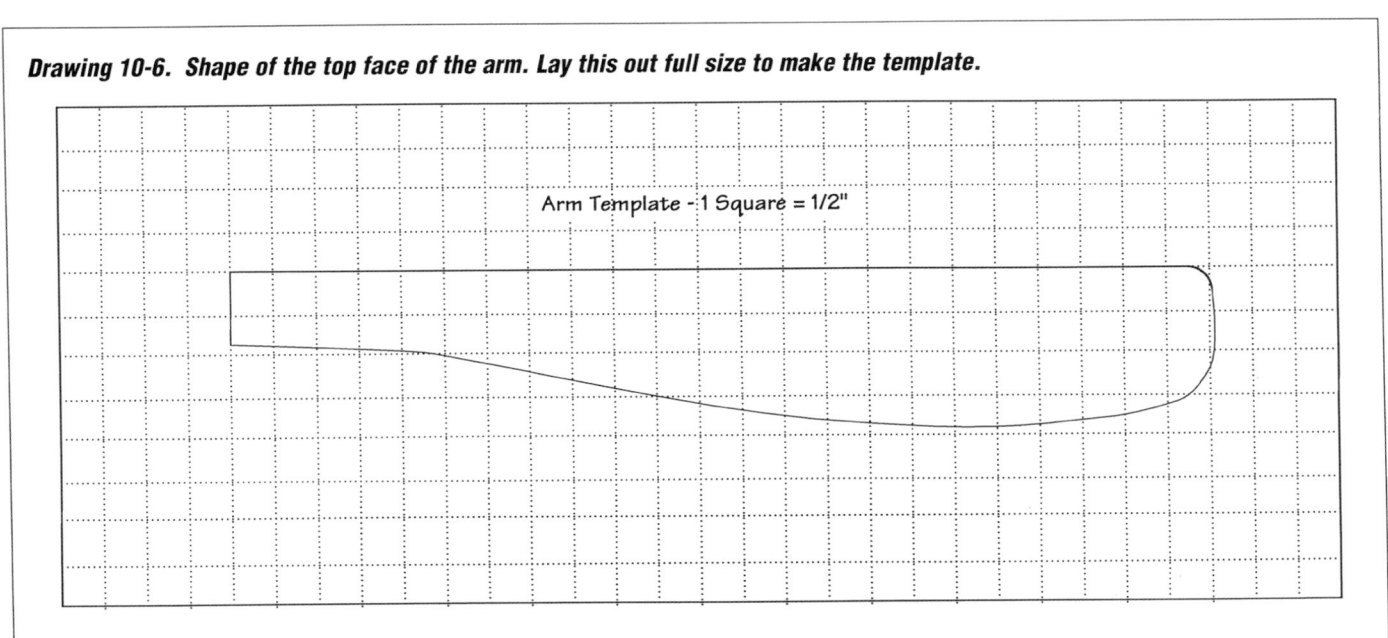

Drawing 10-6. Shape of the top face of the arm. Lay this out full size to make the template.

Arm Template - 1 Square = 1/2"

on all four sides of the blank. This line is important for two reasons: it is where you stop the initial shaping of the arm, and it is vital while assembling the arm to the top rail.

The last of the roughing cuts is the most difficult. It's even hard to explain. It makes a bevel on the bottom face of the main part of the arm. The bevel is from the lower corner of the smooth edge upward toward the top of the shaped face. It is parallel to the top face. The saw blade goes in at the bottom of the second lamination and comes out just above the corner of the smooth edge and the bottom face. The only way to make the cut is freehand on the band saw. When finished, the arm will look like the picture at right (center). I have included the cut-off piece to help you understand just where and how the cut is made. Study these pictures carefully, and be sure you understand them. If you make the bevel in the wrong direction, you will ruin the arm, and you'll have to make a new blank. Remember, the smooth edge (which is the inside edge of the arm) is not cut into. Now, with the inside edge of the arm flat down on the bench, measure 2½" from the front along the bottom edge, and strike a line from there to the top-front corner. With the arm flat down on the band saw table, cut along this line. You have now roughed out the front curve.

The final work of the initial shaping is going to be a matter of using your eye and your judgment. Look at the picture of the finished arms as they should look when they're ready to be attached to the top rail. This will give you an idea of what you're working toward as you proceed with the shaping. It's done with a spokeshave and sandpaper. (As you will see, in this operation, sandpaper does wonders.) Grip the lower part of the arm in the vise with the top pointing up, and shape from the bottom to the top, stopping short of the line you have marked. (The shape goes from oval as it comes out of the flat part of the arm to round at the top line. At this point, it should be slightly over ⅝" in diameter.) When you have the shape to your liking, sand it smooth with 80 grit paper and finish it with 150 grit. Wrap the upper end you have just finished in folded newspaper to protect it, and grip it firmly in the vise with the lower part pointing toward you. Shape toward you, and blend the upper part into the lower as you work. Don't take any more material than is necessary to smooth and blend the surfaces. If you get the arm too thin, there won't be sufficient depth to hold the arm spindles securely. Again, when you have the shape the way you want it, sand it smooth with 80 grit and finish with 150 grit paper. Still gripping the upper arm in the vise, turn it so that you can work on the flat surface of the lower arm. Don't use the spokeshave on the flat itself; just use it to blend the upper flat into the upper arm and to

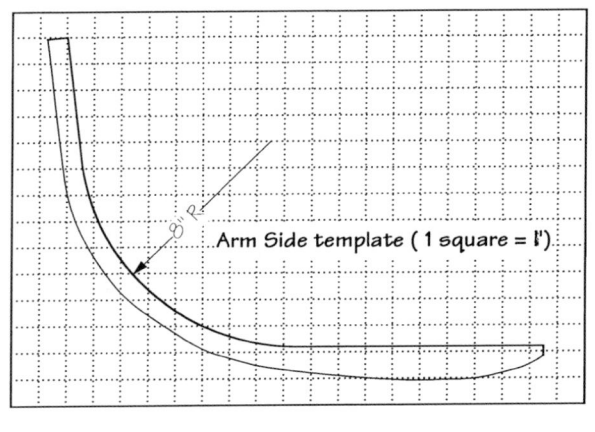

Drawing 10-7. Shape of side of the arm. Lay this out full size to make the template.

Arm Side template (1 square = 1").

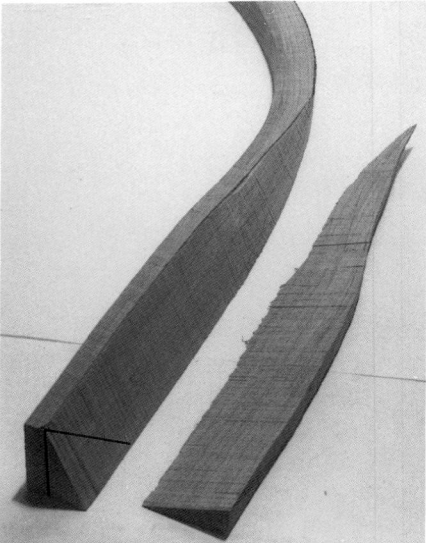

The arm after cutting the bevel—notice the marking for roughing out the front curve.

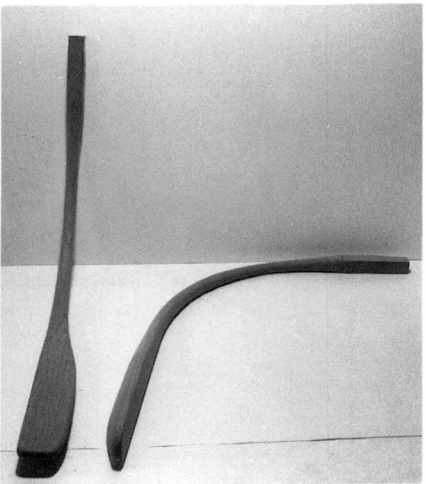

When the arms look like this, they are ready to be fastened to the top rail.

Shaping the upper arm with the spokeshave.

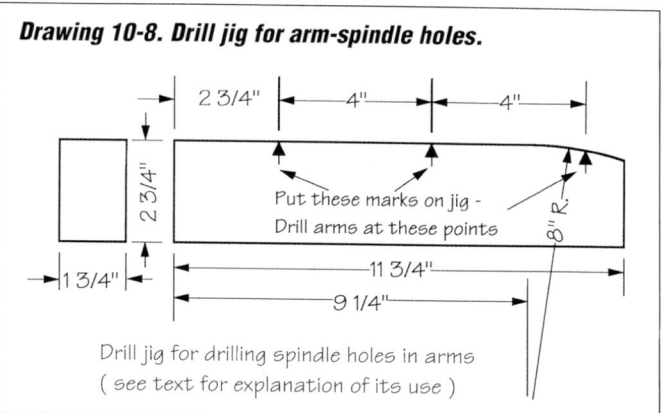

Put these marks on jig -
Drill arms at these points

2 3/4"   4"   4"
2 3/4"
1 3/4"
11 3/4"
9 1/4"
8" R.

Drill jig for drilling spindle holes in arms
(see text for explanation of its use)

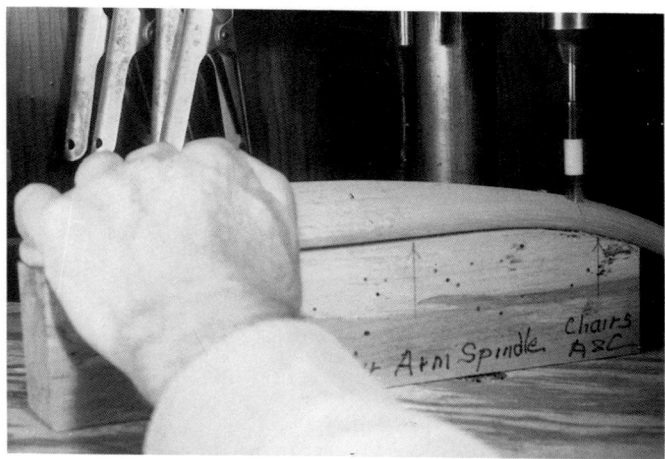

Drilling the arm-spindle holes using a special jig.

round the corners a little. In this position, you can also round the front corners. Then move on to do more finishing with sandpaper. If everything has gone well, the initial shaping is done.

The last step before attaching the arms to the top rail is to drill them for the spindles. Drawing 10-8 is a simple jig to help you do this. Make the jig and mark it as shown. Place an arm with the flat face on the jig and the front flush with the front of the jig. At each marked point, draw a line across the bottom surface of the arm. On the front line, measure 1¹⁄₁₆" from the high side and make a mark. On the rear line, find the middle and make a mark. Lay a straight edge on the two marks, and where it crosses the middle line, make a third mark. Indent the marks with a center punch. Using a pair of calipers, measure the thickness of the arm at each of the marks. You should have a minimum of ¾" in order to get a ⅝"-deep hole. If you haven't got ¾", then reduce the depth of the hole by the difference. Mark this down somewhere, because you will have to shorten the top of the arm spindle that goes in that hole by that amount. By now, you surely understand that there is nothing precise about this arm making. It's pretty much an operation where you feel your way and use your eye and your judgment as I said at the beginning.

Put the jig on the drill-press table and the arm back

on the jig as you had it before. Position it and the table so that the upper part of the arm hangs over the rear of the table and you can reach all three holes without shifting the table. You will need a ⅜" brad-point drill bit. In order to be sure that I don't drill too deep, I measure the depth I want on the drill bit and wrap it with masking tape above that point. On this job, you don't have much leeway, and you don't want to come through the top surface. In the drilling operation, hold the arm on the jig with your left hand, moving the jig and the arm from position to position, and operate the drill press with your right.

It is now time to fit the top rail and arms together. Start with the top rail. First, fit all the back spindles to their holes in the seat and in the top rail. This should be a snug but not a tight fit. Mark them as you go. I always mark each spindle on the bottom 1R, 2R, 1L, 2L, etc. Do the same with the top rail. Put the two outside spindles (#1) in position in the seat and put the top rail on them. Measure the height from the seat at each end, and if it isn't equal, make it so. This fitting operation is going to require considerable trimming of the spindles. It's usually not much, but sometimes it

Final shaping of the upper arm after assembly, with the top rail.

Creating the ear.

Drilling the arm and the top rail assembly after gluing, for dowels to strengthen joint.

Chair assembled for gluing the arms to the top rail.

can be quite a bit. The main reason for this is that the spindle-hole depths will vary. Drilling into tapered parts makes it impossible to use the depth gauge on the drill press, and your eye is not that accurate. At least mine isn't. With the top rail in place on the two outside spindles, put the other spindles in their respective seat holes so that they are behind the top rail. Position each spindle behind its proper hole in the rail, and mark it at the bottom edge of the rail. Remove the rail and the back spindles. Measure each back spindle from the mark you just made to the top end. If it measures more than ¾″, cut it to that length. (This is the same procedure you followed in fitting

together the back of the chair in project six. You can refer back to that project for pictures illustrating the procedure.)

Assemble all the spindles and the rail in their proper positions. The next step is to fit the arm spindles to their respective holes as you did with the back, and then put the arm in place on the seat. When the arm spindles are fully seated in their holes, the height of the bottom edge of the arm from the seat at the front spindle, measured at the inside face of the arm, should be 6½″; the height at the back spindle should be 7″; and the uncarved portion of the arm should line up pretty closely with the end of the top rail. If it's too high and too far forward, trim the back spindle (at the top end). If it's too low and too far back, trim the front spindle. The bottom edge of the top rail should be close to, if not on, the mark you made on the arm for that purpose.

It is now time to glue the arms to the top rail. Do not put glue in any of the spindle holes at this time. To do this operation correctly, you will need two 12″ bar clamps; one 24″ or larger bar clamp; four small, 10° wedges, two spring clamps that will open at least ⅞″; and two thin, flat wooden pads. It is best to do this clamping operation dry first, to make sure you have everything you need and that it all works. Once the glue is in the joint, it's too late to correct mistakes. Using a wedge under the seat and a pad on top of the arm, clamp the arm assembly to the seat with one of the 12″ bar clamps. Place it between spindles 2 and 3. Using masking tape, tape a wedge to each arm opposite the top-rail end. Place a spring clamp across the joint at the bottom of the joint. This will hold the parts in line while you apply the 24″ bar clamp across the joint. The joint faces should mate, but the relative positions of the rail and arms don't have to be perfect. You're going to do quite a bit of final shaping in this area. If everything has worked as it should, take the bar clamp and the two spring clamps off, put glue in the joint, and replace the clamps. Allow this to dry for at least twenty-four hours. This is a naturally weak joint, and while you're going to strengthen it later, you don't want it to come apart in the process.

When you're sure that the glue is thoroughly dry, remove the arm and top-rail assembly from the chair, and remove all the spindles. Be sure that you mark them carefully so that you can get them back in the right places. Using several layers of newspaper, grip the assembly in the vise. With a spokeshave, flatten the top edge of the upper arm parallel with the end of the rail. Draw lines across this flat about ⅜" from the top and the bottom of the rail. Choose a point on these lines that is midway of the thickness of the rail. (You'll have to do this measurement as much by eye as by tool.) Now, with a ¼" spur bit in your hand drill, drill, at each point, through the upper arm and about ¾" into the rail, as shown in the picture on the facing page (top, far left). This takes careful aiming so that you don't come out the side of the rail. Prepare a ¼" dowel of sufficient length that it will extend above the surface when fully in the hole. The dowel should have a breather groove down one side and be a tap fit in the hole. Put glue in the top half of the hole, and tap the dowel in as far as it will go. Now do the other arm the same way.

Allow time for the glue to dry, and you're ready for final shaping of the upper arms. Grip the assembly in the vise the same way you did for the drilling, except the arm should be somewhat higher above the vise to give you more freedom to use the spokeshave. In doing this shaping, the outer edge of the arm should be a straight line; allow no bulge opposite the end of the rail. The front and back of the arm should blend into the rail, and the arm at this point should be the same thickness as the rail. The inside of the arm should be rounded as close as possible to the bottom edge of the rail. This part will take a little file work and considerable sandpaper work. Sand the joint area all over, and use sandpaper to help with and smooth out the final shaping. I find that 80 grit paper is excellent for this.

The last operation before final assembly is the shaping of the ears. Grip the assembly in the vise as shown in the picture. Measure up from the top of the rail about ½" to ⅝", and draw a line around the arm extension. Now draw a concave line from the line at

The top-rail-and-arm assembly in its final form.

the outside of the arm to the top of the rail. Using a coping saw, saw along this line (leaving the line). Using a half round, fine-cut file and sandpaper, shape and smooth the ear as shown in the picture. Now is the time to round the top corners of the rail (use a spokeshave) and sand smooth the top edge.

Now for final assembly. Do this dry first so that you're sure you have all the spindles in the right places and that everything fits properly. The best way to make this assembly is to put the spindles in the arm-and-rail assembly first, then fit that assembly to the holes in the chair seat. Make sure that all the spindles bottom in their holes. You may find that the two front arm spindles want to pop up a little. If this is the case, before you put the glue in, use a bar clamp with pads as before to hold them down firmly. When you're sure everything is OK, take it all apart and start gluing. Glue the spindles in the arm-and-rail assembly first and allow the glue to set for an hour or so, then put glue in the seat holes and fit the assembly as before. Be sure you put glue only in the top half of the holes. If you put it all the way, you'll have too much and the spindle will push the excess to the bottom, which will keep the spindle from going home. The same is true for the arm-and-rail assembly.

Only finishing is left. I will say what I always say: No stain. Finish it natural with one of the schedules in chapter fourteen or your own. When you have finished with this project, I think you will be pleased with what you have made. You will also have acquired a new skill, shaping with a spokeshave, one that you will find most useful in the future.

THAT'S ENTERTAINMENT

Components fit neatly in their section; tape-storage drawers are below.

Home entertainment centers are a worthwhile addition to a home. They provide an attractive way to hide what is usually an awful clutter of equipment and wires, and they can be a fine piece of furniture that's an asset to any room. The one I've designed is long and low, about the size of an average buffet. If you have the amount of equipment that most families have, and it's unhoused, this will take up less room. When it's closed, no one will know what's inside. See page 152 for a cutting list for this project.

This will be an interesting piece to build, but it won't be easy. Several spots require very careful work. I'll emphasize these as I come to them. You may not realize that the finished piece is made up of three units: the case, the top and the base. There are definite reasons for this. As most of you know, wood expands and contracts across the grain but not along it. The grain in the side-base moldings runs at 90° to the grain in the case sides. If they were firmly fastened together, when expansion or contraction occurred, the side would either split or buckle. Therefore, the base is made as a separate unit and fas-

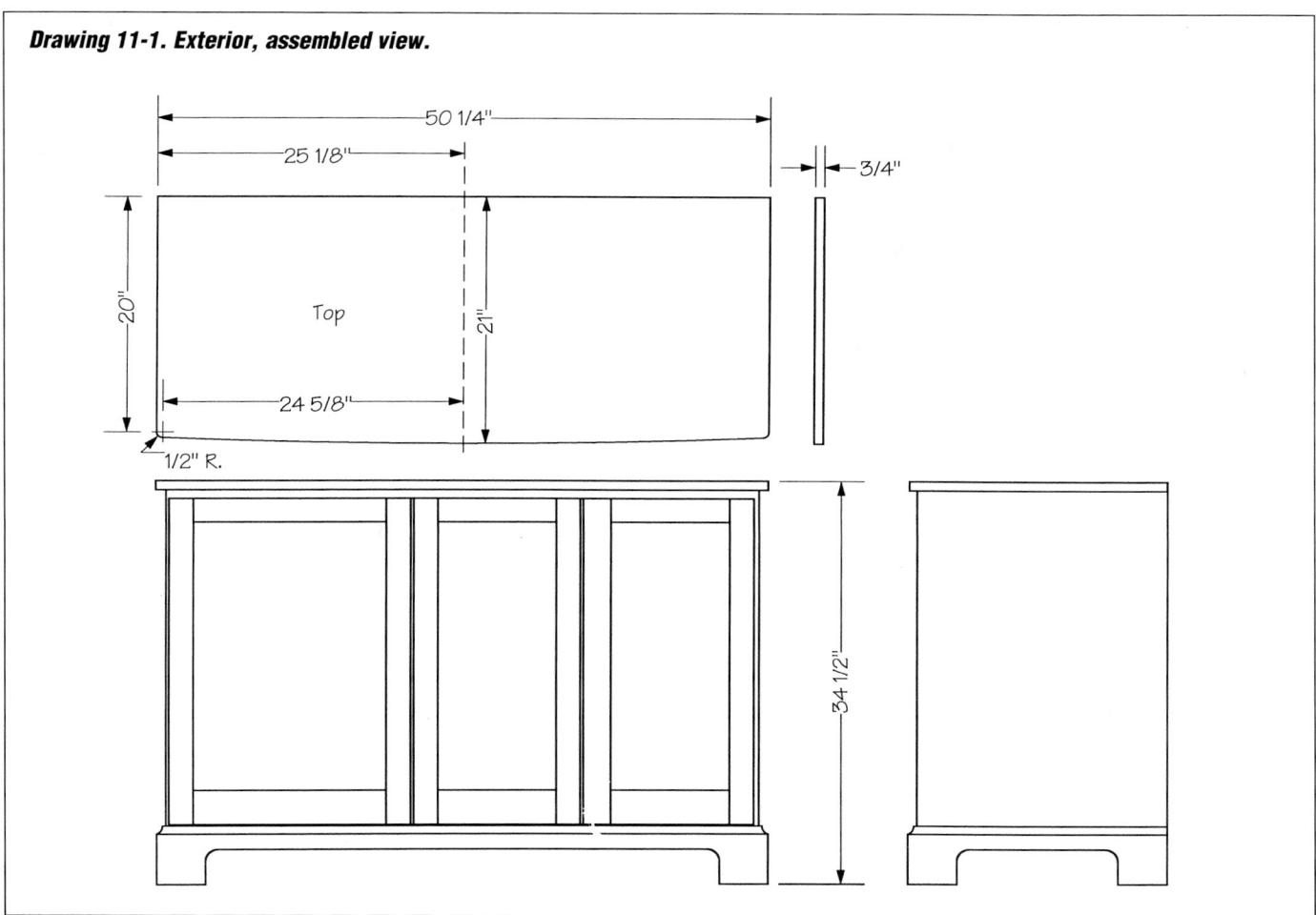

Drawing 11-1. Exterior, assembled view.

tened to the case with clips that allow movement between the two. The top does not present the same problem, since its grain runs parallel to that of the case. However, because of its use, this case has no back, a part usually used to stiffen the case and prevent racking. To compensate for this, the case must be very firmly joined at the top. An overhanging top will not allow a sufficiently strong joint to do this. Thus, we have the top of the case sides held together with rails that are dovetailed into them; the top is then screwed to these rails, making a strong construction.

This piece is really made from a series of panels, and it is best to glue these up first. The top, sides and doors are the parts that will be seen and will determine the looks of the piece. If the panels that make up these parts are made from boards that look as though they belong together, the final piece will have a beauty that only fine wood properly worked can give it. Find boards with distinctive grain patterns for the top and the two sides. The bottom and the middle partition will not be seen and are not so important.

You will need to make six major panels and one minor panel. The finished thickness of the major pan-

els is ¾"; that of the minor is ½". If you're working with S2S material, be careful in the gluing process to get the boards even so you won't lose too much in the smoothing. If, on the other hand, you're able to get rough lumber, then rough the boards out at ¹³⁄₁₆" to allow for smoothing after gluing. The top panel is 21½" x 51"; the two sides and middle divider are 20½" x 30"; the bottom is 20½" x 48½"; and the two fixed shelves are cut from a panel 20" x 49". The minor panel is 20" x 40", and from it you can make the two adjustable shelves for the component section. (If you want more than two of them, make a second panel.) These are all rough sizes. Getting these panels glued up, smoothed to proper thickness, and laid out probably will take a couple of weekends. But don't despair—from then on it will be fun.

The Case

You must begin with the case. The other two units will be built to fit it. Start with the bottom. Cut the panel to proper width and length. Be sure that all four sides are square with each other. (Don't trust your table saw. Put a large carpenter square on the corners

Drawing 11-2. Interior, assembled view.

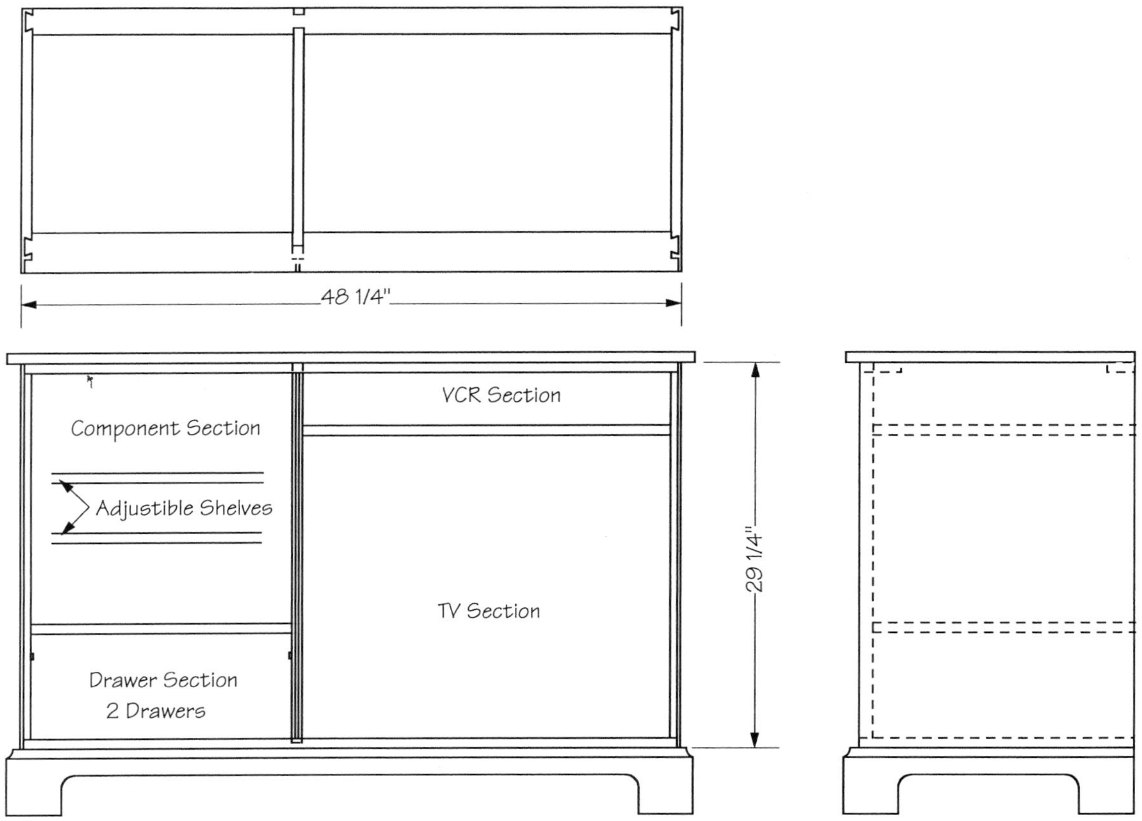

48 1/4"

Component Section

Adjustible Shelves

Drawer Section
2 Drawers

VCR Section

TV Section

29 1/4"

The dovetail joint on the bottom—note position and shape of front pin space.

and check it. If it's out of square at any point, square it up by planing the ends.) Cut the rabbet on the front edge of the top surface. Because of its width, it is best to do this step on a table saw with a high auxiliary fence fastened to your rip fence. Leave about 1/32" for removing the saw marks. This can be done with a shoulder plane or sandpaper. (If you don't have a shoulder plane, it would be worth your while to get one. They do a beautiful job in situations like this, in which you want to take a light cut and do it quickly.)

Next, cut the dado for the middle partition. Use either a router or a dado head on the table saw.

Notice, however, that you're not working with a through dado, so if you do it on the table saw, you will have some finishing to do with a chisel. The position of this dado is important, so check the plans and be careful. Now, you can lay out the dovetails at the ends. Remember, in a dovetail joint, always to cut the tails first, and to mark the pins from the tails. I have shown a suggested dovetail layout on the plans. You don't have to follow it, except for the first cut back from the front edge. It must be 90° to the side and placed at the exact rear of the rabbet. The only other requirement is that the tails be 1/2" deep. Having done this, set the part aside for now.

The front and rear top rails are next. They both finish 3/4" thick; the front is 3" wide, and the rear, 2". The length must be exactly that of the bottom. Don't take the dimension off the drawing; mark it from the bottom you have just finished. The detail drawing shows the dovetails on these parts. The front-rail joint detail is important because it must match the cut on the bottom. Also, the depth of the tails on both ends of both rails must match exactly those on the bottom, so that the distance between the rear of the tails on the bottom and the rails is exactly the same. The notches for

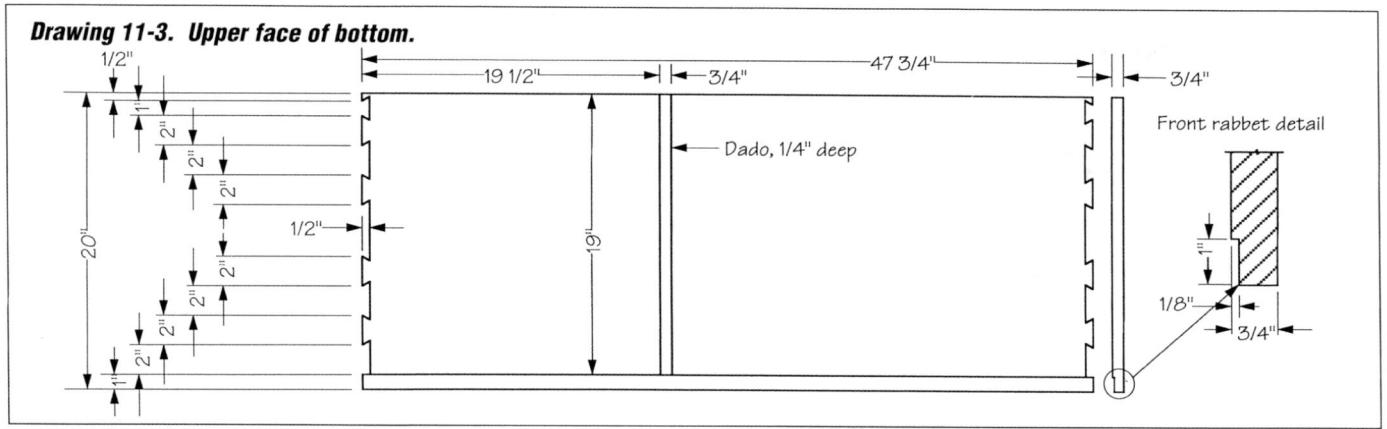

Drawing 11-3. Upper face of bottom.

Dado, 1/4" deep

Front rabbet detail

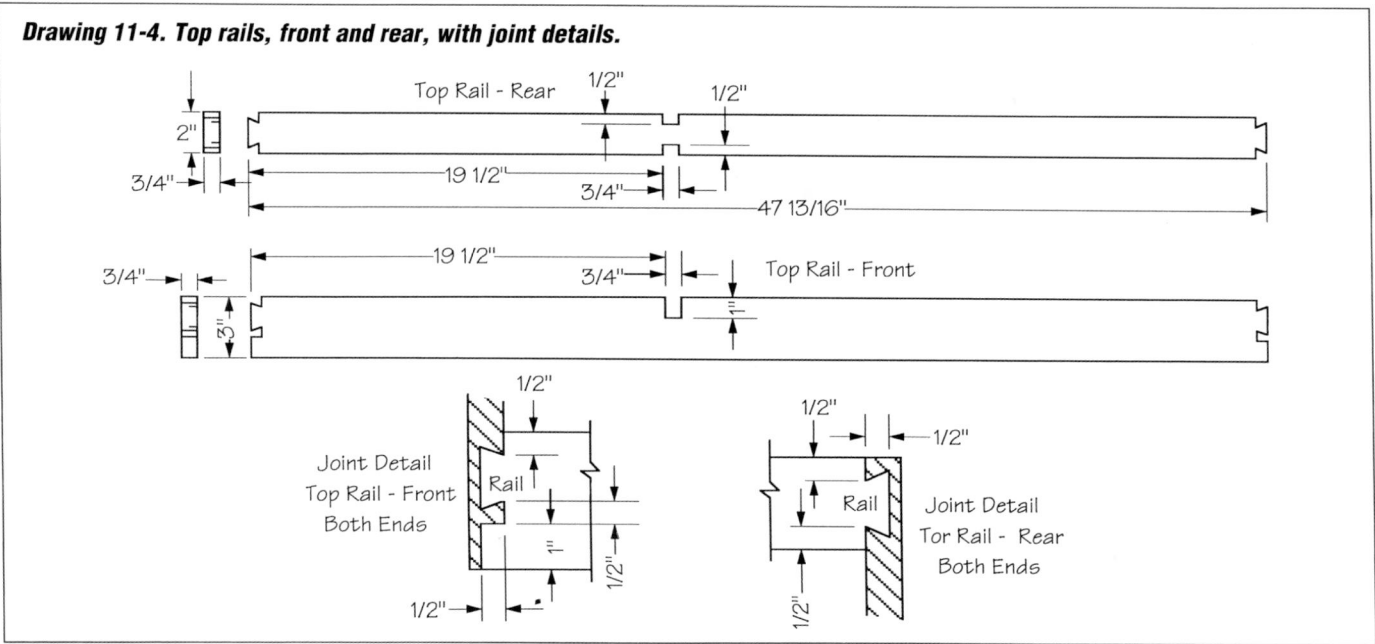

Drawing 11-4. Top rails, front and rear, with joint details.

Top Rail - Rear

Top Rail - Front

Joint Detail
Top Rail - Front
Both Ends

Rail

Rail

Joint Detail
Tor Rail - Rear
Both Ends

the middle partition should also be marked from the bottom so that the divider will be parallel with the sides. The best way to do this is to clamp the rails to the bottom so that the ends of all parts are flush, then mark the dovetail bottoms and the notches with a sharp knife. I must emphasize: If you don't get this right, you won't be able to square the case; and if the case isn't square, the doors won't hang right and the drawers won't fit. A ¹⁄₁₆" off over 29" results in a mess. A little carelessness early on causes many problems at the end.

The sides and middle partition come next. Cut the side panels to size and square them up, then cut the rabbets on the front edges. Because of the depth, it is best to do this step in two cuts on the table saw. Since the depth of the rabbet is ⅔ of the width of the panel edge, you should make the 1"-deep cut first. This will allow the full width of the edge to ride on the table

during the cut. As with the bottom, leave a little stock to take the saw marks out. Now finish the dovetail joints. Start with the bottom. Because this is such a long joint, it is next to impossible to hold these parts in place while marking and have the joint come out accurate. I always clamp both parts over the corner of the workbench and mark the pins with a sharp knife, making as deep a cut as I can so that it will show clearly. Do the same with the top rails. Remember that the rabbets face each other and that they are on the front edge, matching with the rabbet on the bottom. Finish cutting the joints. They should be a tap fit, nice and snug.

Before doing any more work on the sides, do the preliminary work on the middle partition. Cut it to size and square it up. Cut the double rabbet on the front edge and the notches as shown in the drawing. Now, lay the left side and the middle partition on the

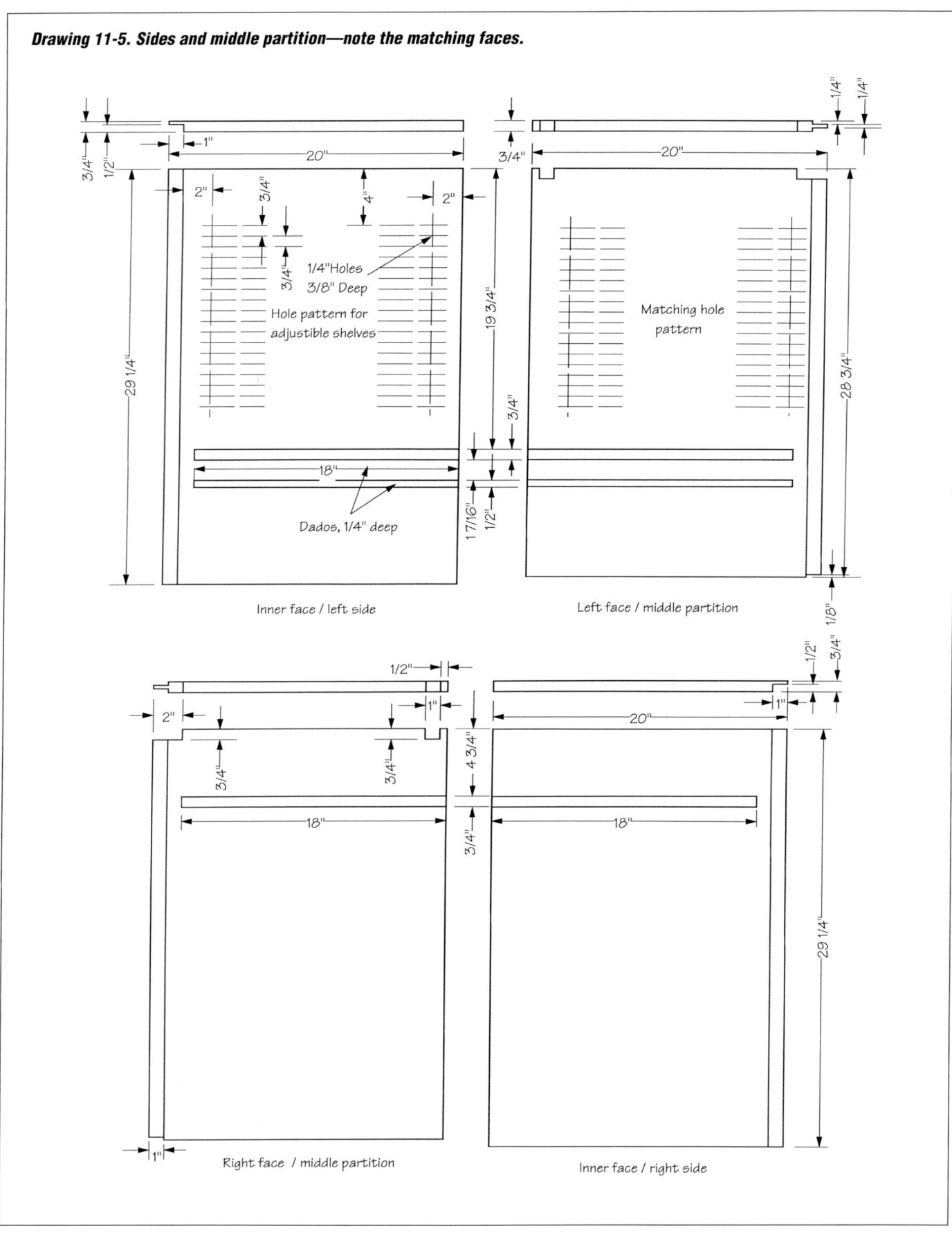

Inner face / left side

Left face / middle partition

Right face / middle partition

Inner face / right side

Setup for marking top rails so they will match the bottom.

bench with the facing surfaces up, the back edges against each other and the top edges flush (see drawing). Clamp them so that they cannot move relative to each other. Lay out the hole patterns for the adjustable shelf supports on both pieces. Mark the position of the two dadoes at the rear edge where they meet. Make this mark heavy and clear so that you won't miscut the dadoes. Turn the middle partition over, and match it with the right side in a similar manner (see drawing). Mark the dadoes for the VCR shelf as you did the previous ones. Now you can drill the holes and cut the dadoes as per the drawing. Be sure the dados are parallel with the top edge of all pieces. The easiest way to accomplish this is to do it on the table saw and use the rip fence as a guide. Finally, cut two strips of wood ⅜" thick to fit the ½" dado on the left side and middle partition, and glue them in place. This should be a rather tight fit. Put glue in only the front 1" of the dado; as with the base sides, the grain lines run at 90° to each other, and gluing the strips their full length will restrict expansion and contraction of the panels.

At this point, assemble the case frame dry. Make sure that everything fits, that it's all square, and that all the dadoes and rabbets are where they should be. If there are any discrepancies, now is the time to correct them (if you can), even if it means making a part over. I can tell you from experience, it's worth the effort. Trying to adjust the rest of your work to one early mistake brings nothing but headaches and poor results. When you take the frame apart for gluing, but before you apply the glue, I suggest that you lay out and cut, on the bottom and the front top rail, the mortices for the hinges. It will be much easier when the parts are separate than when the frame is all assembled. The location is shown in full-size detail in Drawing 11-6. The hinge position relative to the upright members and the back of the bottom rabbet is very important. If you don't get it right, the two outside doors will not open fully and fold back out of the way against the sides. Set the hinge as deep as the thickness of the leaf. If you screw the hinges in place now and then remove them, you will be very happy when you have to reinstall them after the case is glued together. Assuming that everything is, one way or another, the way it should be, glue the parts together, carefully square everything and use clamps if necessary to hold it that way until it dries.

While the frame is drying, cut the two permanent shelves from the panel you glued up for that purpose. Both shelves should be 18½" deep and wide enough to fit easily in the dadoes provided for them. Notch the front corners so that the shelves slide in until their back edge is flush with the back edge of the sides, and round the top and bottom front edges. If they fit too tightly in the dadoes, relieve the top surfaces until they slide into place with gentle pressure. Be sure you relieve the *top*, not bottom, surface. When you have the fit right, put a small amount of glue in the dadoes from the rear to halfway to the front. If you get too

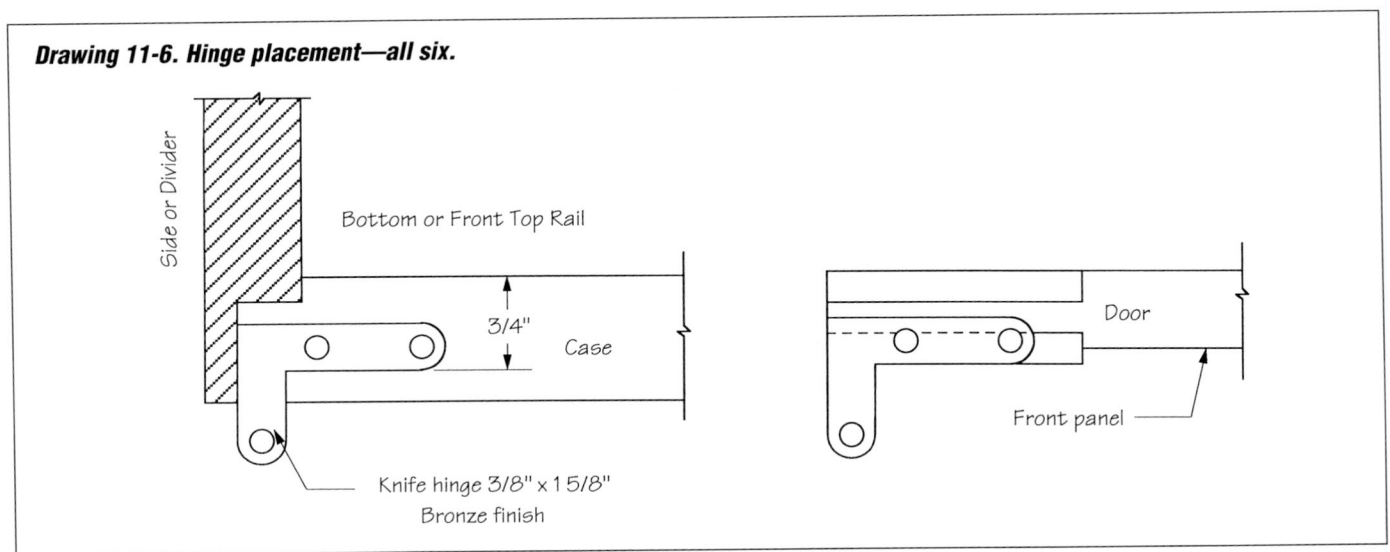

Drawing 11-6. Hinge placement—all six.

Side or Divider

Bottom or Front Top Rail

3/4"

Case

Knife hinge 3/8" x 1 5/8"
Bronze finish

Door

Front panel

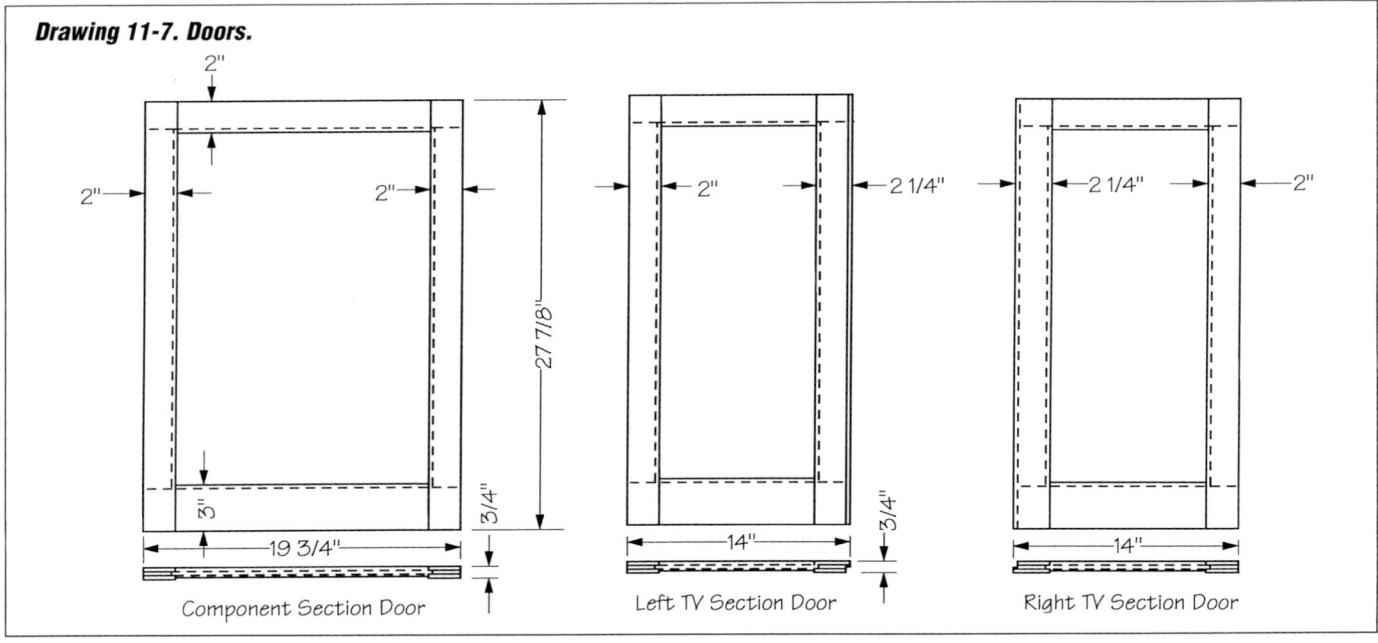

Drawing 11-7. Doors.

Component Section Door

Left TV Section Door

Right TV Section Door

much, when you slide the shelves into place, the excess will be shoved forward and squirt out the front of the joint; then you'll have a mess on your hands. If it happens, don't wipe it up. Let it dry and then remove it with a sharp chisel.

The adjustable shelves are carried by shelf supports described and shown in chapter thirteen. These shelves should be 19" deep, and the width should be slightly less than the width of the section. Round over the top and bottom front edges.

The Doors

Before beginning work on the doors, study Drawings 11-7 and 11-8 carefully. Notice two details in particular: (1) The rails are thinner than the stiles. However, they start out the same and the thickness is not reduced until just before assembly. This makes the cutting of the mortice-and-tenon joints much easier. (2) The meeting stiles of the two TV section doors are 2¼" wide rather than 2" like the others. This is to allow for the ¼" overlap, as shown in the detail drawing.

Cut the stiles and rails to width and thickness according to the drawing, but when it comes to the lengths, take these dimensions from the case rather than the drawing. To get the length for the stiles, measure the space between the leaves of your hinges (usually about ¹⁄₃₂"), double it, and subtract that from the exact height of the door openings. For the component-section door, cut the rail lengths the full width of the door opening. For the TV doors, measure the width of the door opening, divide it by two, and add ¹⁄₈" for the rail length of each door.

Take a slight detour here to prepare and glue up

the door panels; then, while they're drying, you can complete the door frames. From the standpoint of appearance, these panels are, along with the top, the most important parts of the cabinet. They will be noticed more than any other parts, and the way they look can make the difference between an ordinary cabinet and a superior one. The panels will finish approximately ¼" thick. The rough length of all three should be 25". The rough width of the component door panel should be 17½", and that of the two TV doors should be 11" each. Search out three boards, one about 9" wide and two about 6" wide. The two 6" boards should have, as close as possible, the same grain pattern; the 9" one can be different. (Try to find an unusual pattern. To see what the pattern will look like when the finish has been applied, paint it with clear water.) All three boards should be at least ¾" thick. Surface both sides of the boards, then resaw them down the middle. The resulting pieces should be about ⁵⁄₁₆" thick. Open them up like a book, and you have what is called a bookmatched panel. Glue them together, then plane the sawed surface smooth. Plane carefully, because this will be the outer, and thus the visible, surface. If you are diligent in your search, have some luck, and are careful with your resawing and planing, you will have three very striking door panels.

To get back to the door frames, put a high auxiliary fence on your rip fence, put a ¼" dado head in your table saw, set the height at ¼", and set the rip fence so that you will cut a ¼" groove in the exact center of one edge of each frame member. Choose what will be the inside edge of each member, and cut the groove the

Cutting the mortice in the end of a stile.

A hinge properly placed on a door.

full length of the member. Do not change the setting of the rip fence, but raise the head to 1¼". The stiles will have the mortice, and the rails, the tenon. So, the setting you just made will cut the through mortice in the top end of each stile. Raise the head to 2¼", and cut the bottom mortice. It is essential that your dado head be absolutely perpendicular to the table for this cut. (Don't trust the gauge on your saw. Check it with a good, reliable square.) The tenons on both ends of the rails for the component door will be 2" long, and those for the TV doors will be 2" on one end and 2¼" on the other. Cut these tenons according to the directions in chapter eight. If you have been careful with your measurements and used a scale to make them rather than the gauge on your saw, the pieces should fit together nicely. If they're tight, shave the tenon rather than the mortice. This should be a snug fit. If you force an open mortice, you will spread it at the open end and have trouble making the joint come together properly. Fit the frames together, and mark each joint with chalk so that you can identify both pieces that make it up. Also, mark the inside faces of all the rails.

Now is the time to rip the rails to their final thickness. Set the rip fence to ½2" over ⅝", and placing the marked face of the rail against the fence, rip them all.

Finish the sawed face with a very light cut on the jointer. Assemble the frames (no glue). Be sure they're square, and measure the width and length of the panel openings from the bottom of the grooves. Cut the panels to size; the lengths should be ½2" shorter, and the widths, ⅟16" narrower, than the measurements you made.

Disassemble one frame, and try a panel in the groove of one member. It will probably be too thick. Size it on the table saw by raising the blade to ⁵⁄16" and setting the rip fence (with the high auxiliary attachment) to ¼" from the inside of the blade. With the outside face against the fence, run all four edges through. Test it in the groove; it should be an easy, sliding fit. If it's still too tight, move the fence a hair closer to the blade and run the edges through again. Keep this up until you get the right fit; then do all the panels. Assemble all the frames with their panels (dry) to see that everything fits as it should. Put a ⅛" radius curve on the outer inside edges of all frame members. In gluing up the frames, two things are important: (1) Do not put any glue in the panel grooves, because the panels must be able to float freely in those grooves; and (2) Apply glue to the mortices, not the tenons. Put the glue on each face in the top half of the mortice only. Assemble the joint from the top down, not from

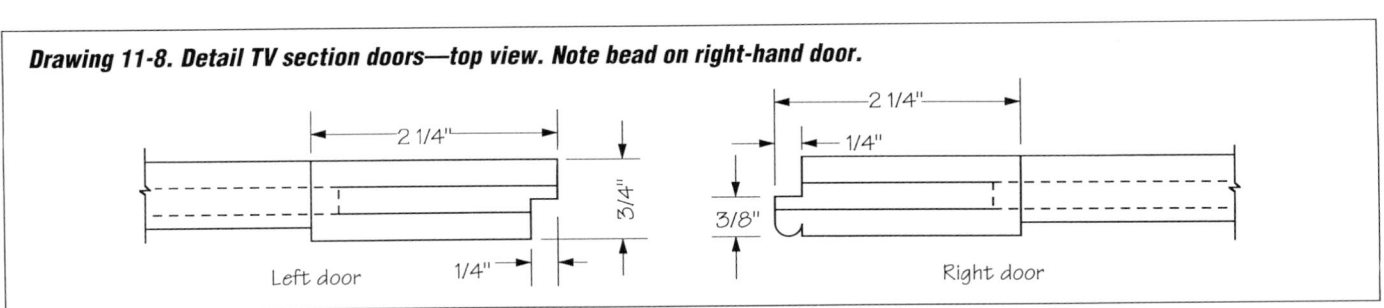

Drawing 11-8. Detail TV section doors—top view. Note bead on right-hand door.

Left door · 2 1/4" · 1/4" · 3/4"

Right door · 2 1/4" · 1/4" · 3/8"

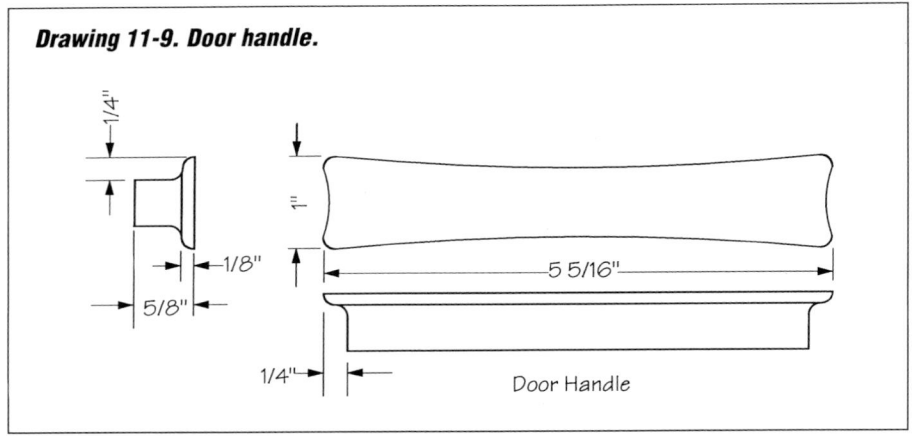

Drawing 11-9. Door handle.

1/4"

1"

1/8"

5/8"

5 5/16"

1/4"

Door Handle

fit the doors in the opening. There should be no gap at the overlap and little or no sideways play in the opening. Mortice the hinges into the doors as shown in Drawing 11-6. Having done this, screw the hinges in place on the doors, then remove them. Now put the lower hinges on the door and the upper hinges on the case. To install the door, tilt the door slightly and place the lower hinge in its mortice on the case; then slide the upper hinge into its mortice on the door. Put one screw in each hinge and tighten it, then try the swing of the door. Make the necessary adjustment to make them close properly and fully and stay closed. Some adjustments are easier made with the door removed. You can easily do this by removing the two screws you just put in and lifting the door out the same way you put it in.

I've always felt that handles are something the builder should decide on. The one shown in Drawing 11-9 is the one I designed and used. Use it, or come up with one of your own design that might please you more. If you use mine, you can see from the picture on page 136 where and how it goes. It is best to attach it from the back through the door with two #6 x 1" brass flat-head wood screws. Counterbore them slightly in the back of the door. My handle was made with a router set up as a shaper using a ¼" quarter round router bit.

the side in, and the tenon will spread the glue over the entire joint as it goes home. When you have glued each door, square it up and make sure it stays that way. Use clamps if necessary.

When the glue has dried, fit the doors to their respective openings. All of them should be about ⅟₁₆" short of the height of the opening. As for the width, the component door should fit with little or no sideways play, and the TV doors should overlap by ¼". Check this by putting the left-hand door in place and marking its inner edge on the bottom. Do the same with the right-hand door. The two marks should be ¼" apart.

Now is the time to cut the overlapping rabbets on the TV doors. As Drawing 11-8 shows, the right-hand door overlaps in front and has a decorative bead cut on the front surface. When you have cut the rabbets, again

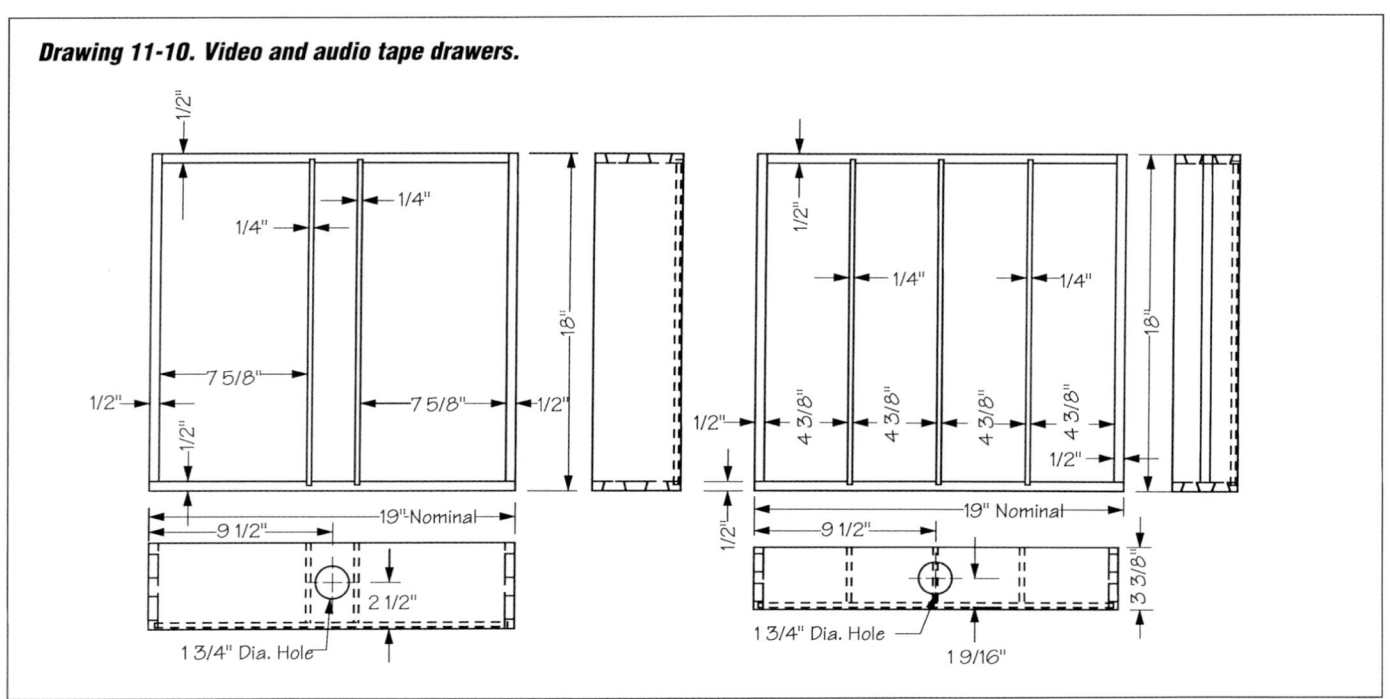

Drawing 11-10. Video and audio tape drawers.

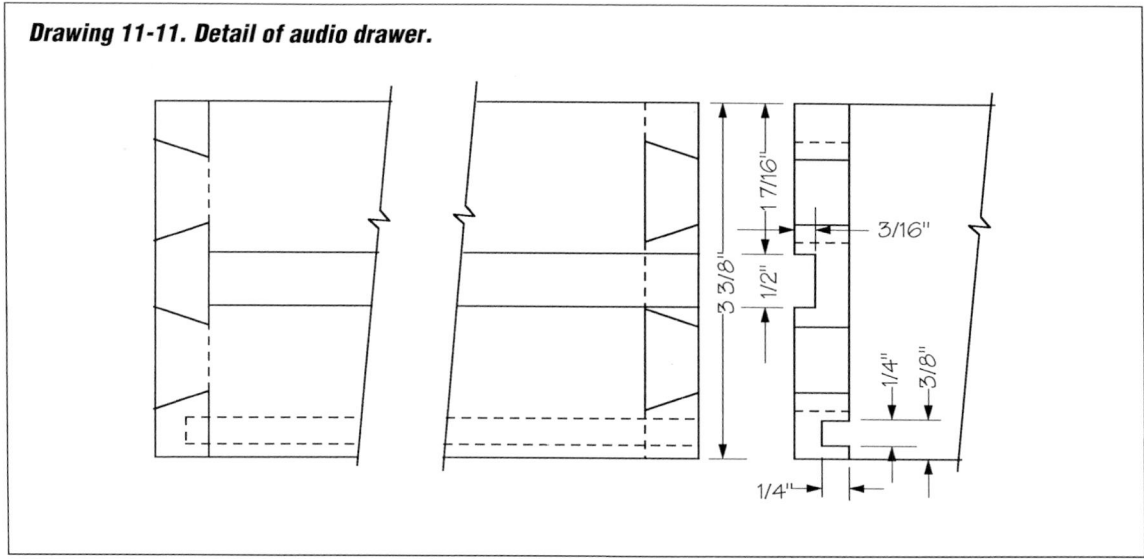

Drawing 11-11. Detail of audio drawer.

1 7/16"

3 3/8"

1/2"

3/16"

1/4"

3/8"

1/4"

Tape drawer handle—roughed out and finished.

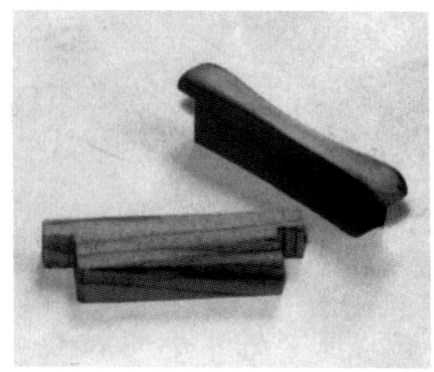

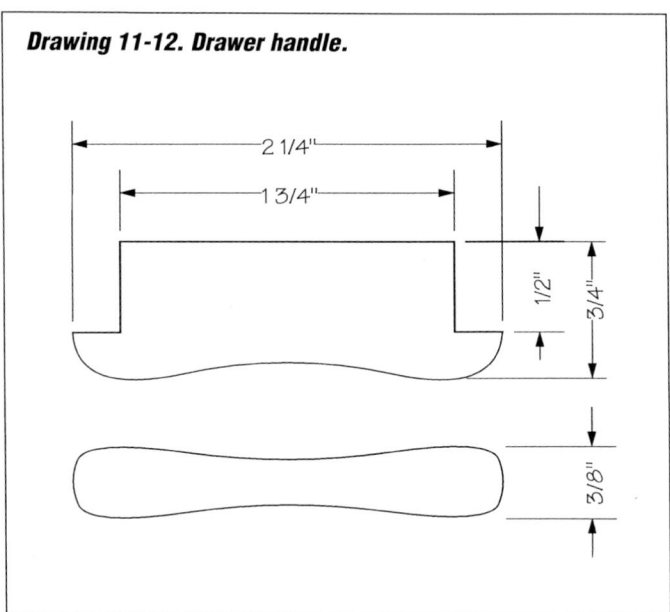

Drawing 11-12. Drawer handle.

2 1/4"

1 3/4"

1/2"

3/4"

3/8"

Handles fitted to the drawers—note that both drawer fronts were cut from a single board.

The Drawers

With the doors in place, the last work on the case is to make drawers for cassette storage. Start by cutting the main pieces and finishing them to ½" thick. The length of the fronts and backs will be determined by the width of the drawer pocket you have created. The length of the sides should be 18". The width of all the audio drawer pieces is 3⅜", and the width of the video drawer pieces is 4⅝" plus or minus, depending on the exact height of the drawer pocket. Cut the sides to size first, and see that they fit together in the drawer opening. You will have to cut the dado in the audio

drawer sides (see Drawing 11-11) so that they will fit over the runners you glued into the sides of the opening. Put one side of each drawer in place and see that they fit and slide easily. If any trimming of the widths is necessary, do it on the video drawer. When you have the fit right, cut all the other drawer parts to these widths.

Note that we are using through dovetails. The tails will go on the sides and the pins on the fronts and backs. In laying out the tails, note that they are not the same front and back. This is important; be sure to do it as shown. Cut the tails first (see chapter eight), and from them mark the pins with a sharp knife. When the joints have been cut and fitted, it's time to cut the groove for the bottom. This is ¼" wide x ¼" deep and

Three-blade molding head suitable for a 10" table saw with ¾" radius quarter-round blades.

Setup to make cove cut on pieces of the base.

Cutting 45° miter on front of base.

is located with its upper edge ⅜" from the bottom edge of the drawer. Note that while on the sides and back the groove goes all the way through, on the front it must be stopped off or it will show on the outside. When the grooves have been cut, rip off the bottom edge of the backs to the top of the groove. This is the time to drill the 1¾" hole in the fronts. (I used a hole saw in the drill press.) Finally, cut the dadoes in the

fronts and backs for the dividers (see drawing on page 145). These pieces of the drawers should now be finish sanded, then dry assembled and tried in the drawer pocket. When you have an easy fit, glue the pieces together. Again, be sure they are square. After assembly, lightly round all exposed edges, including both edges of the holes. In making the bottoms, finish the pieces to ¼" thick. Glue up the necessary panels

Drawing 11-13. Base assembly.

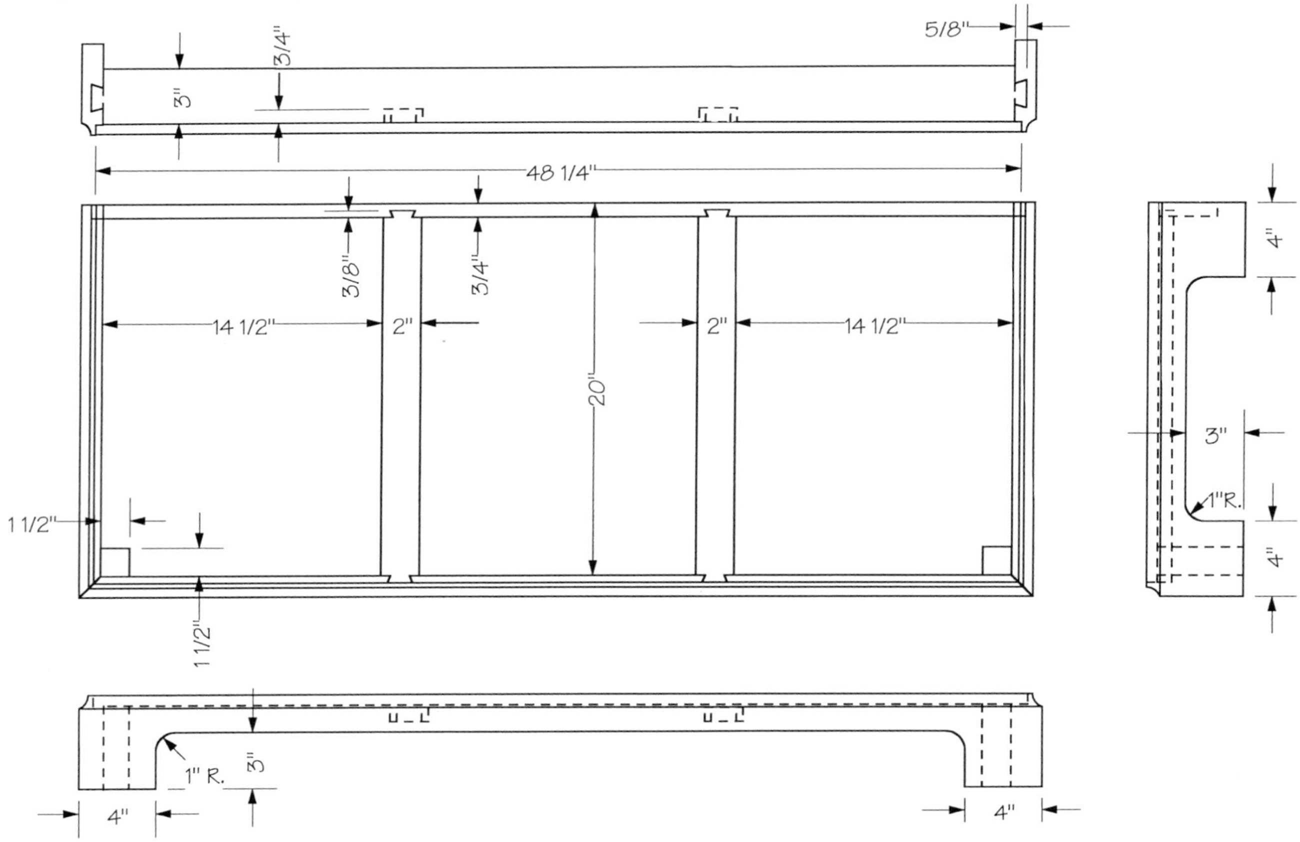

Clamped-up base section set in place on case.

Marking the second side position on front piece for cutting mitered joint.

and size them as before. Rabbet the two side edges and the front edges to fit the grooves. (Use the same method as with the door panels.) Slide the bottoms into place, and fasten them at the center of the back with a #3 x ½" flat-head brass wood screw. Cut the dividers and fit them in place, but do not glue them in. In the upper drawer, the center divider will run right through the hole for the handle and show. To avoid this, cut the divider away for a short distance right behind the hole. Make the drawer handles as shown in Drawing 11-12. Saw out the blanks, and then shape them freehand on a sanding drum. When finished and sanded, glue them in place. They fit in the holes horizontally.

The Base

The base is the difficult part of this project. It has to be made to fit the case, and the mitered corners make this fitting a bit ticklish. The first step is to cut and mold the front and side members. Do this with two boards, one long enough for the front and the other long enough to make both sides. Give each board several inches extra length. Finish the boards to 1⅛" x 5". Then cut the rabbet and the groove as shown on the cross-section drawing. I made the cove cut using ¾" radius quarter-round cutters in a three-blade molding head. The cutters were 1" wide, so I used an auxiliary fence on the rip fence so that I could bury about ³⁄₁₆" of the cutter under the fence in order to get the shape I wanted. When finished, cut the board for the sides into two equal lengths.

The front piece is the key to the entire assembly. Get that right and everything else falls in line. Because this piece is 5" high, the miter can't be cut with the saw blade at 90° using the miter gauge (at least, not on my 10" table saw). Therefore, it has to be

cut flat with the blade set at a 45° angle. Before setting the angle, check that your miter gauge is square with the blade. In setting this angle, do not depend on the gauge on your saw. Get a draftsman's 45° angle and use it. Once you think you have it set, use some scrap and test it. Keep adjusting until you get it exact. Using a miter gauge with a clamping attachment to hold the piece in place, cut one end of the front.

Set the case upside down on something that will bring the height of the bottom to a comfortable working level. (It will be very helpful to have the doors off during this operation.) Cut the miter for the side piece to match the end of the front already cut. Using the

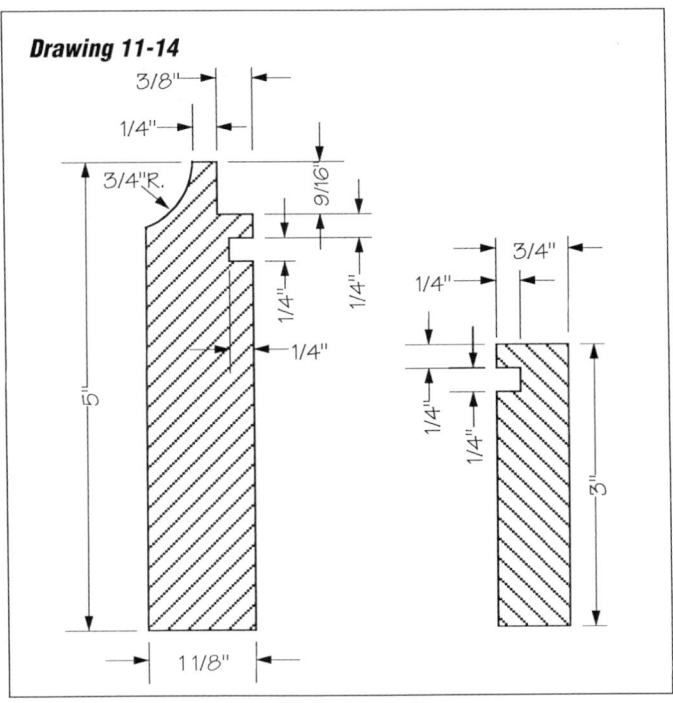

Drawing 11-14

corner block, clamp these pieces together as they will be on the case. Place this clamped-up assembly on the case in its proper position. Now, set the other side piece (before cutting the miter) in position and against the front piece. Being sure that it is at right angles to the bottom of the case, mark the inside edge of the side piece on the front piece. This mark is the inside point of the 45° miter cut on the front piece. Be very careful with this marking because it determines the length of the front piece. If you come up short, the piece is scrap and you will have to start over. Be sure the opposite clamped corner is pressed tightly against the case. Make the cuts on both pieces, and using the other corner block, clamp the second side in position so that both sides and the front are on the case. Mark the length of the side pieces, and measure the distance between them at the rear of the case. This plus 1¼" for the two dovetails is the length of the rear member of the base. Cut it to this length from a piece ¾" x 3", run the groove as shown in Drawing 11-14, then mark and cut the dovetails as shown.

After cutting the sides to length, mark and cut the mating pockets for these joints on the sides. When marking these pockets, be sure that the back is placed so that the groove is on the inside face and at the top. When this is done, fit the sides and the back together, and clamp everything back on the case to see that it fits properly. While you have things in this position, measure the distance from the outside of the back to the inside of the rabbet on the front. This is the length of the two stringers. When you have done this, separate the parts and shape the front and sides. My method for this operation was to produce the curves by cutting 2"-diameter holes with a hole saw and then bandsawing the straight sections. If you're careful with the band saw, you will be able to clean up the straight sections with a spokeshave and finish the entire surface with a file and sandpaper. When you have it the way you want it, put a ⅛" radius curve on the outside edge. Mark on the inside of the front the location of the stringers as shown on the drawing. Mark the edge nearest the side in both cases. Match the back to the front in their relative positions, and transfer the marks just made. Next, cut the braces to length out of ¾" x 2" material, and cut the dovetails on each as shown in Drawing 12-13. Position the braces, and mark and cut the mating pockets.

Now dry assemble all the parts and place the assembly in position on the case. (The corners will be loose, so handle it carefully.) Clamp everything together to be sure it all fits. Take the clamps off, then put glue on two faces of each block and on the mating faces of the miter. Be sparing with the glue—you don't want any to come out of the joint, especially

Finished base held in place by hold-down clips.

between the base and the case. Replace the clamps and let the glue dry. When this setup is dry, remove the base and carefully take the dovetail joints apart, put glue in them, and put them back together. Put the assembly back on the case until the glue is dry. The base is now finished except for sanding surfaces that show. The base is fastened to the case with wooden hold-down clips (see chapter thirteen). The accompanying picture shows how this is done.

The Top

The top is the last—and the easiest— of the three units that make up the entertainment center. You already have the panel from which to make it; just lay out the shape and cut it on the band saw (see Figure 11-1 for layout details). Notice that while the back edge is straight, the sides and front edges have a slight curve to them. This is important: it takes away the sharpness and gives the whole cabinet a softer and more interesting appearance. (Check project two for a way of drawing those curves.) Clean up the curved edges with a spokeshave. Put a ⅛" radius curve on the bottom corner. You can also put one on the top corner, but I think it looks better with a small (say, ⅛") bevel on the top corner. You can do the curves with a router, but it's best to do the bevel with a spokeshave. If you use the bevel, try to keep it sharp. Don't blur the edges. It will stand out better that way. The top is fastened to the case with #8 x 11/4" flat- head wood screws through the top rails. Use four screws per rail. The end ones should be as close to the sides as you can get them and still work the screwdriver. Space the other two evenly between.

As to the finishing, I'll just say what I always say: Don't use stain. If you don't have a finishing schedule of your own, check chapter fourteen for one of mine.

PROJECT CUTTING LISTS

PROJECT 1: A SIMPLE CABINET

Part Name	Rough Sizes	No.	Comments
Case			
Top	1" x 7$^1/4$" x 13"	1	
Bottom	1" x 7$^1/4$" x 13"	1	
Sides	1" x 6$^1/2$" x 30$^1/2$"	2	
Dowels	$^3/8$" dia. x 1$^3/16$"	20	Length is approximate—finalize at assembly.
Door			
Stiles	1" x 1$^1/4$" x 30$^1/2$"	2	
Rails	1" x 1$^1/4$" x 11"	2	
Panel	$^3/8$" x 9$^3/4$" x 29$^1/4$"	1	This is glued up from solid wood.
Hinge Material	See text		
Back Panel			
Stiles	$^3/4$" x 1$^1/4$" x 30$^1/4$"	2	
Rails	$^3/4$" x 1$^1/4$" x 11"	2	
Panel	$^3/8$" x 9$^3/4$" x 29$^3/4$"	1	This is glued up from solid wood.
Screws	#5 x $^3/4$" Brass flt hd wd	10	
Shelves	$^3/8$" x 5$^1/2$" x 10$^1/2$"	?	The number of shelves depends on how many you want.
Shelf Supports	$^3/8$" x $^3/4$" x 10"	?	This piece will make four supports.

PROJECT 2: A LITTLE TABLE

Part Name	Rough Sizes	No.	Comments
Legs	1$^1/2$" x 1$^1/2$" x 23$^3/4$"	4	Joint two adjacent faces of each leg.
Side Rails	1$^3/16$" x 2$^1/4$" x 22$^5/8$"	2	Joint both 1$^3/16$" faces and one 2$^1/4$" face.
End Rails	1$^3/16$" x 2$^1/4$" x 11$^3/4$"	2	Same as side rails.
Top	$^3/4$" x 15" x 27"	1	
Hold-down Clips	$^3/8$" x $^3/4$" x 9$^1/2$"	1	This piece will make eight clips—see text.

PROJECT 4: A HANDSOME CABINET

Part Name	Rough Sizes	No.	Comments
Case			
Sides	1" x 18" x 24"	2	
Top	1" x 18" x 24"	1	
Bottom	1" x 18" x 24"	1	
Doors	1" x 12" x 21"	2	
Drawer Shelf	$1/2$" x 17" x 23"	1	
Drawer Divider	$1/2$" x $4^3/4$" x 17"	1	
Back Panel			
Frame	$5/8$" x $1^1/2$" x 24"	4	
Panel	$3/8$" x 20" x 21"	1	
Base			
Legs	$1^5/8$" sq. x 18"	4	
Front Stretcher	1" x 2" x 23"	1	
Rear Stretcher	1" x 2" x 23"	1	
Side Stretcher	1" x $1^3/4$" x 16"	2	
Drawers			Use a contrasting wood for main drawer parts.
Sides	$1/2$" x $4^1/2$" x 17"	4	
Front and Back	$1/2$" x $4^1/2$" x ?	2 ea.	Length of these parts to be decided by builder.
Bottom	$3/8$" x ? x 17"	2	Width of these parts to be decided by builder.
Shelves	? x 17" x 22"	?	Thickness and number decided by builder.
Hardware			
Hinges-L-shape k one	$3/8$" x 1" x $1^5/8$"	2 pr.	
Friction Catch	$1/4$" dia. barrel	1	These are sometimes called ball catches.

PROJECT 7: TO WRITE A LETTER

Part Name	Finished Sizes	No.	Comments
Legs	Blanks made per text	4	
Top Support	$3/4$" x 3" x 20"	2	
Spreader	$1^1/2$" x 9" x $40^1/2$"	1	This is the size on which to lay out the part.
Top	$3/4$" x 26" x 48"	1	Glue this up from narrower pieces.
Drawer Parts			
Front	$3/4$" x 4" x 20"	1	
Sides	$1/2$" x 4" x $17^3/8$"	2	
Back	$1/2$" x 4" x $17^3/4$"	1	
Bottom	$5/16$" x $17^1/2$" x 17"	1	This is also a glued-up piece—no plywood.
Drawer Hanger	1" x 1" x 18"	2	
Drawer Handle	$1/2$" x 1" x 6"	1	

PROJECT 5: SHOW OFF YOUR TREASURES

Part Name	Finished Sizes	No.	Comments
Case Parts			
Top	$7/8$" x $7^1/4$" x 19"	1	
Bottom	$7/8$" x $6^3/4$" x 18"	1	
Sides	$5/8$" x 6" x 24"	2	
Door Parts			
Top Rail	$5/8$" x $1^1/2$" x 18"	1	
Bottom Rail	$5/8$" x $1^5/8$" x 18"	1	
Outside Stiles	$5/8$" x $1^1/2$" x 24"	2	
Inside Stiles	$5/8$" x 1" x 24"	2	
Glass Molding	$1/8$" x $3/8$" x ?		Cut lengths to fit.
Screws for molding	#1 x $3/8$" Rd. Hd. Brass	24	
Glass Panels	Have cut to fit	2	Thinnest you can get.
Hinges	1" x 1" brass cabinet	2 pr.	
Back Parts			
Back Boards	$3/8$" thick	?	Random width and length to fit.
Splines	$3/32$" x $7/16$" x ?	?	Length to fit.
Screws for back	#4 x $5/8$" flt. hd. brass	?	Use four screws per board.
Shelves	$1/4$" plate glass	2	$1/16$" shorter and narrower than inside of case.
Shelf Supports	$1/4$" x $3/4$" x $1^1/8$"	8	
Cabinet Hangers		2	See picture for these.

PROJECT 8: AN INTERESTING COFFEE TABLE

Part Name	Finished Sizes	No.	Comments
Legs	$1^1/2$" x $1^1/2$" x $15^1/2$"	4	Rough sizes—joint two adjacent sides of each piece.
Stretchers	$5/8$" x 2" x $13^1/2$"	2	
Long Top Supports	$3/4$" x $1^1/2$" x $37^1/2$"	2	
Short Top Supports	$3/4$" x $1^1/2$" x 19"	4	
Top Boards	$7/8$" x 11" x 46"	2	

PROJECT 9: ABOUT A DINING TABLE

Part Name	Sizes	No.	Comments
Legs	$1^3/4$" x $1^3/4$" x 27"	4	Rough sizes—joint two adjacent sides.
Stretchers	$3/4$" x 3" x 23"	4	Finished sizes
Top Supports	$3/4$" x $1^1/2$" x $30^3/4$"	4	Finished sizes
Top Panel	$13/16$" x $42^1/2$" sq.	1	Rough sizes
Brace Blocks	$1^1/2$" x $2^1/2$" x 13"	2	Rough sizes

PROJECT 11: THAT'S ENTERTAINMENT

Name	Rough Sizes	No.	Comments
Top	1" x 21^1/2" x 51"	1	
Case			
Bottom	1" x 20^1/2" x 48^1/2"	1	
Sides and Mid Partition	1" x 20^1/2" x 30"	3	
Fixed Shelves	1" x 20" x 49"	1	Cut two shelves from one panel.
Adjustable Shelves	^{5}/8" x 20" x 40"	1	Cut two shelves from one panel.
Front Top Rail	1" x 3^1/4" x 49"	1	
Rear Top Rail	1" x 2^1/4" x 49"	1	
Base			
Front	1^3/8" x 5^1/4" x 52"	1	
Sides	1^3/8" x 5^1/4" x 44"	1	Cut two sides from one piece.
Back	1" x 3^1/4" x 50"	1	
Stringers	1" x 2^1/4" x 21"	2	
Corner Blocks	1^3/4" sq. x 10"	1	Cut two blocks from one piece.
Drawers			
Top Drawer			
Front and Rear	^{5}/8" x 3^5/8" x 19^1/2"	1 ea.	
Sides	^{5}/8" x 3^5/8" x 18^1/2"	2	
Separators	^{3}/8" x 3" x 18"	3	
Bottom Drawer			
Front and Rear	^{5}/8" x 4^7/8" x 19^1/2"	1 ea.	
Sides	^{5}/8" x 4^7/8" x 18^1/2"	2	
Separators	^{3}/8" x 3^7/8" x 18"	2	
Bottom Both Drawers	^{3}/8" x 19" x 18"	1 ea.	
Doors			
Component Section			
Stiles	1" x 2^1/4" x 28^1/4"	2	
Top Rail	1" x 2^1/4" x 20"	1	
Bottom Rail	1" x 3^1/4" x 20"	1	
Panel	^{3}/8" x 17" x 25"	1	
TV Section (two doors)			
Outside Stiles	1" x 2^1/2" x 28^1/2"	2	
Inside Stiles	1" x 2^1/2" x 28^1/2"	2	
Top Rails	1" x 2^1/4" x 14^1/2"	2	
Bottom Rails	1" x 3^1/4" x 14^1/2"	2	
Panels	^{3}/8" x 11" x 25"	2	

Index